IDEAS AND INVESTIGATIONS IN SCIENCE **LIFE SCIENCE**

IDEAS AND INVESTIGATIONS IN SCIENCE

LIFE

Harry K. Wong
Las Lomitas School District
Menlo Park, California

SCIENCE

Leonard Bernstein
Louis T. Wright Junior High School
New York, New York

Edward Shevick
Portola Junior High School
Tarzana, California

Prentice-Hall, Inc., Englewood Cliffs, New Jersey

IDEAS AND INVESTIGATIONS IN SCIENCE

LIFE SCIENCE
Part One: Ideas 1-7
Part Two: Ideas 8-12
Clothbound: Ideas 1-12
Laboratory Data Book
Teachers Manual
Laboratory Equipment
Laboratory Data File

IDEAS AND INVESTIGATIONS IN SCIENCE-LIFE SCIENCE
Harry K. Wong, Leonard Bernstein, and Edward Shevick

© 1973 by Prentice-Hall, Inc.
Englewood Cliffs, New Jersey 07632.
All rights reserved.
No part of this book may be
reproduced in any form or by
any means without permission
in writing from the publisher.
Printed in the United States of America.

ISBN 0-13-449744-9   10 9 8 7 6 5 4 3 2

Prentice-Hall International, Inc., **London**
Prentice-Hall of Australia, Pty. Ltd., **Sydney**
Prentice-Hall of Canada, Ltd., **Toronto**
Prentice-Hall of India Private Ltd., **New Delhi**
Prentice-Hall of Japan, Inc., **Tokyo**

Title page illustrations adapted from photos by United Press
International and Photo Researchers, Inc.

Design and graphics by Lee Ames.

To The Student

Welcome to a new world of learning—a new way of learning. Welcome to IIS. IIS is a science program made for *you*. You like to do things with your hands. Everyone does! You want to know more about plants and animals. It's natural. Do you like to laugh? Do you like to have fun? Are you with it? If so, you'll like IIS.

How do we know you'll like it? You told us what you wanted. Pictures, cartoons, the whole scene. And we used it to write this book. Thanks for giving us your ideas.

We think you'll like your new cartoon classmates—Peter, Paul, Maria, David, and Phideau. And we believe you'll learn a lot with their help.

Good luck this year! We hope you have as much fun learning as we had writing IIS.

Contents

Idea 1

INVESTIGATION **1** Try It; You'll Like It   1
2 Love, A Little More of It This Year   6
3 Keep the Faith, Baby   15
4 The Dawning of the Age of Asparagus   22
5 I Know I Put It Somewhere   31
6 What's Your Game Plan   36

Idea 2

INVESTIGATION **1** Are You in Shape?   43
2 Growing for a Change   50
3 Do You Hear Those New Sensations?   54
4 Don't Let Me Dry Out   60
5 Take a Deep Breath   66
6 Where's the Menu?   71

Idea 3

INVESTIGATION **1** To See or Not to See…That Is the Mystery   76
2 The Beast from the Barrel   84
3 They Come in Many Shapes and Sizes   93
4 This Is Where It's At   101
5 The Wonderful World of the Cell   109
6 You Can't Blow Your Nose with This Tissue   117

Idea 4

INVESTIGATION **1** The Root of the Problem   125
2 Look Ma, No Teeth   131
3 The Wildest Recipe of All   138
4 Green Power   144
5 Let's Throw Some Light on the Subject   150
6 The Bush that Made It   157

Idea 5

INVESTIGATION **1** I Tried It and I Nearly Died   164
2 It's a Real Gasser   169
3 Sounds Fishy to Me   173
4 You'll Get a Rise Out of This   179
5 Let's Break It Apart   183
6 The Little Old Heatmaker, Me   188

Idea 6

INVESTIGATION **1** You'll Wind Up Broke, Every Time   194
2 Getting It Through to You   200
3 It Gets It All Around   206
4 Smoke and Make the Doctors Rich   211
5 The Ameba and the Osmond Brothers   217
6 The Debbil Made Me Do It   221
7 Get Really Stoned   226

Idea 7

INVESTIGATION   **1**   Come Look at My Goose Tree   231
  2   This Will Break You Up   236
  3   Let's Get Together   240
  4   You Can't Buy Parts For It   244
  5   The World's Full Court Press   248

Idea 8

INVESTIGATION   **1**   The Drip of Life   254
  2   When You're Hot, You're Hot   260
  3   You've Got to See the Light   265
  4   Soul Food Special   270
  5   Change Is the Name of the Game   276
  6   Where on Earth Is Life?   280

Idea 9

INVESTIGATION   **1**   An Ocean of Life   287
  2   Don't Bug Me   291
  3   It Pays to Have a Backbone   298
  4   Stick with Me   304
  5   Two Can Live Better than One   310
  6   It's Not Hard to Find   314

Idea 10

INVESTIGATION   **1**   Things Change   320
  2   Stay Cool, Brother   326
  3   Seeing Is Believing   331
  4   It Came from Outer the Sink   338
  5   Make It or Forget It   346

Idea 11

INVESTIGATION   **1**   Stop Hassling Me   351
  2   Life in the Yellow Pages   355
  3   Hawks Don't Eat Zucchinis   364
  4   It's Finger-Lickin' Good   364
  5   Spin, Spin Your Tangled Web   370
  6   This Is My World   375

Idea 12

INVESTIGATION   **1**   We Have to Be Together   379
  2   The Greatest Invention Since the Wheel   383
  3   We're Still Going Around and Around   389
  4   Don't Get All Tapped Out   393
  5   Live Dangerously—Take a Deep Breath   397
  6   All It Needs Is a Little Love   401

Idea 1
Investigation 1

TRY IT; YOU'LL LIKE IT

A. PLEASE DON'T SHAKE ME

A carpenter may build a home. To do this, he must have certain skills.

Rogers/Monkmeyer

Ballard/DPI

A secretary works in an office. She may use different machines. She must have certain skills.

A scientist solves problems. To solve problems, you need certain skills too. You will practice one of these skills in this Investigation.

Seaver/March of Dimes

You will do many things in this class. To help you keep track, blanks have been left after the Step numbers in your data book. Check off each Step as you do it.

1. Your teacher will give you a bottle of liquid. Do not remove the stopper.

Do not remove the stopper

2. Look at the liquid.

•3. Describe what you see. (Write your answer in the space provided on your data sheet.)

•4. Check with your classmates. What do they see?

> You've just discovered something. Everyone may not see the same thing. This can cause trouble if you're trying to solve a problem.
>
> A scientist must *observe* carefully. Observation takes practice. Observation takes patience.

•5. What is one important skill of a scientist?

B. THE JOKER'S ON YOU

Many people look, but do not see. This is because observation takes practice and patience. In this next part, you will need patience.

6. Your teacher will give you a deck of cards.

7. Remove the Jacks, Queens, and Kings from the deck. These are the only cards you will use.

•8. Look at the 4 Kings. Find at least three differences. List them on your data sheet.

•9. Look at the 4 Queens. Find at least two differences.

• 10. Look at the 4 Jacks. Find at least two differences.

• 11. Look at all 12 cards. Find at least two differences.

• 12. Check with your classmates. What did they observe in question 11?

You've just observed something again. Everyone does not see the same thing.

• 13. What must scientists do to solve problems?

C. THIS IS A REAL CUT-UP

You're going to play a game. If you've played it before, don't give away the secret. If you don't know the secret, this will test your powers of observation. Everyone will play. Try it! You'll like it!

The game is called "Crossed or Uncrossed." Here are the rules:

(a) Sit in a circle.

(b) The teacher will point to one student to start. This student will pass a pair of scissors to the person on his left. The scissors will continue around the circle in a clockwise direction.

(c) Each person must explain how the pair of scissors was received and how it is passed. Each person must say, "I received the scissors (*crossed* or *uncrossed*) and I pass the scissors (*crossed* or *uncrossed*)."

(d) If you say the wrong thing, take the seat to the right of the student who started.

(e) After an error, start again with the first student.

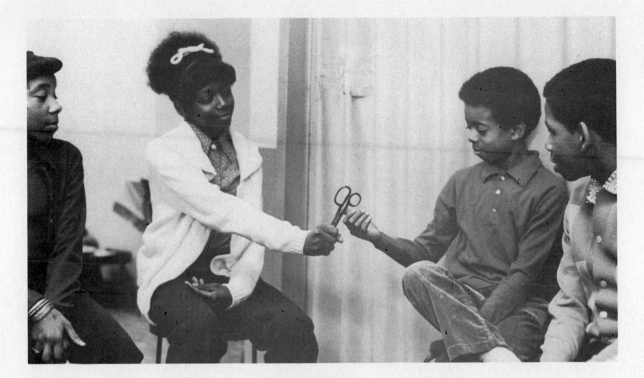

•14. Your problem is to find the secret of the game. What did you observe?

•15. What must you do to solve a problem?

D. LET'S PUT OUR MINDS TOGETHER

You have seen three problems. You saw a liquid that changes colors. You looked at 12 playing cards. And, you played a game with a secret.

•16. To solve each of the problems, what did you have to do?

•17. What must a scientist do to solve a problem?

•18. What is one important skill of a scientist?

You will discover one concept in each Investigation. A concept is an idea. In other words, what did you learn in this Investigation?

Re-read your answers to questions 16, 17, and 18. Then write your concept on your data sheet.

THE CONCEPT.

LOVE, A LITTLE MORE OF IT THIS YEAR

A. ARE YOU ALL THUMBS?

You will make a ruler just like Peter's ruler. Remember to check off each Step on your data sheet, as you do it.

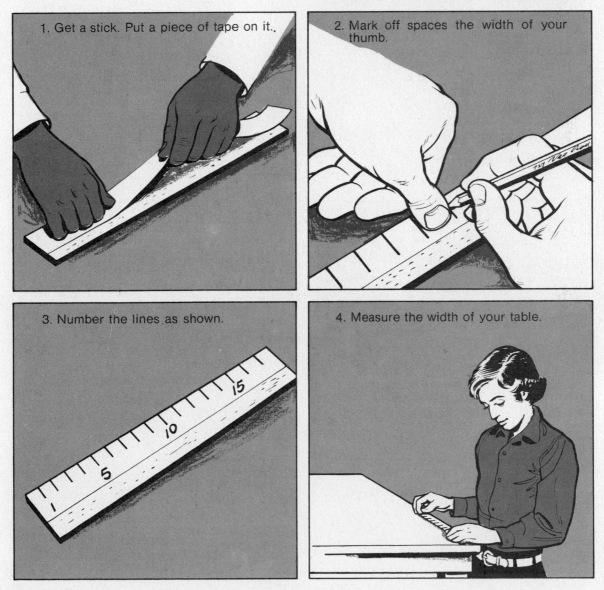

1. Get a stick. Put a piece of tape on it.

2. Mark off spaces the width of your thumb.

3. Number the lines as shown.

4. Measure the width of your table.

• 5. How many thumbs wide is your table?

All the tables in your classroom are probably the same size.

•6. Check with some of your classmates. How wide did their tables measure?

•7. You have a problem. The tables *seem* to be different sizes. Why?

•8. What are some problems with using the thumb as a unit of measurement?

In the last Investigation, you learned that a scientist must observe accurately.

•9. What other skill must a scientist have?

B. THIS IS A NEW ONE ON ME

The metric ruler is the most popular ruler in the world.
It's very easy to use. There are no fractions. All you
have to do is count by 1's and 10's.

This is an enlarged drawing of a section of a metric ruler. Each unit or line is a *millimeter*, or *mm* for short.

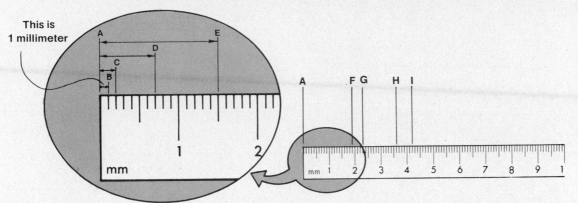

This is 1 millimeter

There is 1 millimeter between **A** and **B**.

There are 2 millimeters between **A** and **C**.

There are 7 millimeters between **A** and **D**.

There are 15 millimeters between **A** and **E**.

To make it easier to read, every 5th and 10th line is longer.

• 10. How many millimeters are between **A** and **F**?

• 11. How many millimeters are between **A** and **G**?

• 12. How many millimeters are between **A** and **H**?

• 13. How many millimeters are between **A** and **I**?

14. Get a metric ruler. Study it carefully.

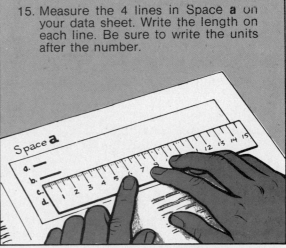

15. Measure the 4 lines in Space **a** on your data sheet. Write the length on each line. Be sure to write the units after the number.

Good question, Paul. There are numbers on your ruler. On the metric ruler, 10 millimeters equals 1 *centimeter*.

There are 10 millimeters or 1 centimeter between **A** and **B**.

There are 2 centimeters between **A** and **C**.

There are 5 centimeters between **A** and **D**.

If the line is between two numbers, write down the smaller number. Here, it is 8. Then put a decimal point after the 8. Count the lines after the 8. Then write that number after the decimal point. Phideau's ear is 8.7 centimeters long.

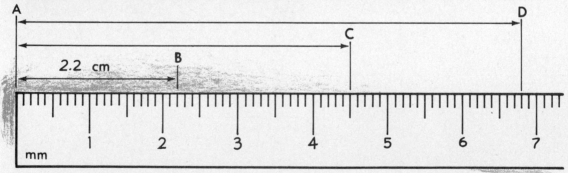

There are 22 millimeters or 2.2 centimeters between **A** and **B**.

There are 4.5 centimeters between **A** and **C**.

There are 6.8 centimeters between **A** and **D**.

16. In Space **b** on your data sheet, measure the 4 lines in millimeters and in centimeters. Write the length on each line. Be sure to write the units after the numbers. You can use **cm** for centimeter.

• 17. What system of measurement have you been using?

• 18. What must a scientist be able to do accurately?

C. I'LL RACE YOU

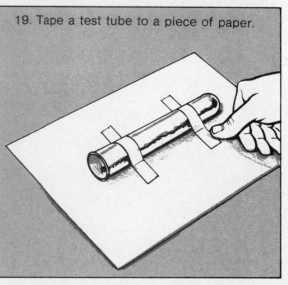

19. Tape a test tube to a piece of paper.

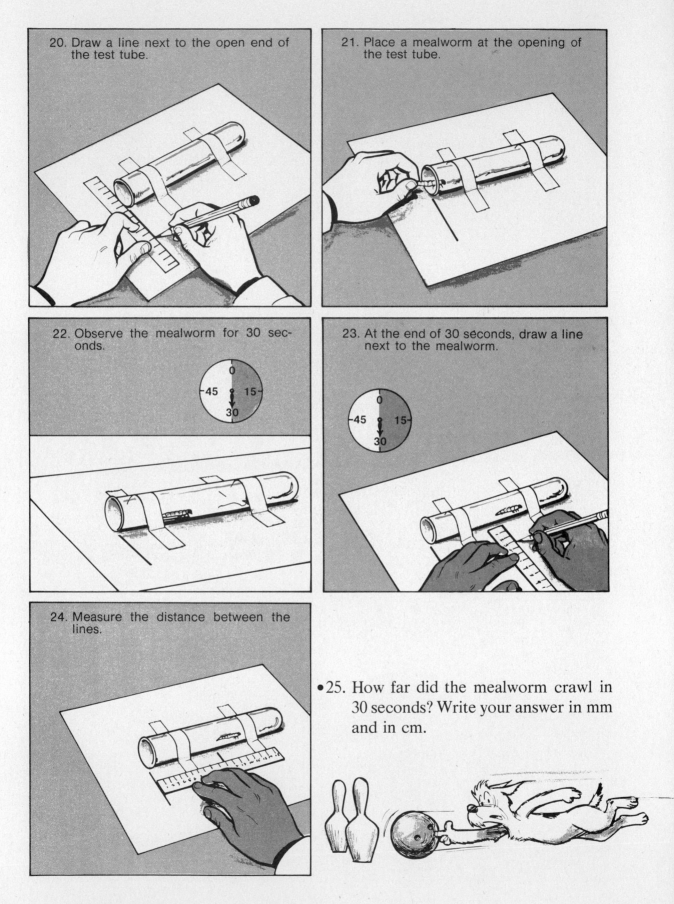

20. Draw a line next to the open end of the test tube.

21. Place a mealworm at the opening of the test tube.

22. Observe the mealworm for 30 seconds.

23. At the end of 30 seconds, draw a line next to the mealworm.

24. Measure the distance between the lines.

•25. How far did the mealworm crawl in 30 seconds? Write your answer in mm and in cm.

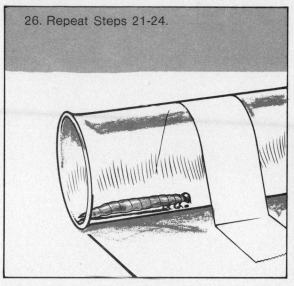
26. Repeat Steps 21-24.

•27. How far did the mealworm crawl in 30 seconds? Write your answer in mm and in cm.

28. Find 2 classmates willing to race their mealworms against yours. Give the mealworms names.

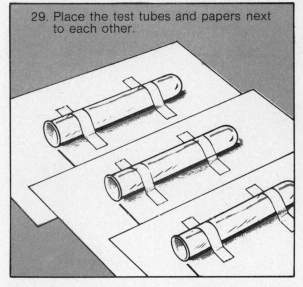
29. Place the test tubes and papers next to each other.

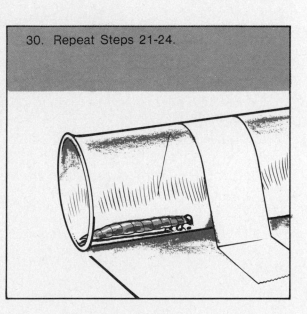
30. Repeat Steps 21-24.

•31. How far did each mealworm crawl in 30 seconds?

•32. What must a scientist be able to do accurately?

D. A LITTLE MORE OF IT

In the last Investigation, you learned one scientific skill, observation.

•33. In this Investigation, you have learned another scientific skill. What is it?

Re-read your answers to questions 18, 32, and 33. Then write the concept.

THE CONCEPT.

Investigation 3

KEEP THE FAITH, BABY

You have done very well! You have learned two concepts:

(a) One scientific skill is making careful observations.
(b) Another scientific skill is making accurate measurements.

You will learn about another scientific skill in this Investigation.

A. ARE YOU WELL BALANCED?

It is very easy to weigh things in the metric system. You only have to know one word, *gram*. The gram is the unit of weight in the metric system.

You will be using a *balance* to weigh things. The balance is like a see-saw. If two boys of the same weight are on a see-saw, it will balance.

A laboratory balance works the same way. You put an object on one pan. Then you add known weights to the other pan until it balances.

Many schools have a balance with only one pan. The known weights are on the other side of the pan. You move the weights along the bars until the pan and weights are in balance.

Ohaus Scale Corp.

Ohaus Scale Corp.

1. Get a balance. Carry it with both hands.

CAUTION

THE BALANCE IS A DELICATE INSTRUMENT, USE IT WITH CARE!

You must zero the balance before you use it. The pointer can be at zero.

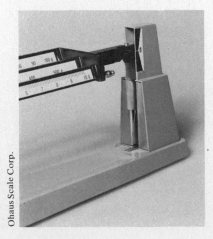

Ohaus Scale Corp.

Or, the pointer can swing the same number of lines on each side of zero.

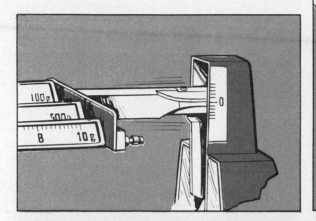

2. Lightly tap the pan to get the balance swinging.

3. Find the knob used to zero the balance. Ask your teacher for help if you need it.

4. Keep the balance swinging lightly. Adjust the knob until the balance is zeroed.

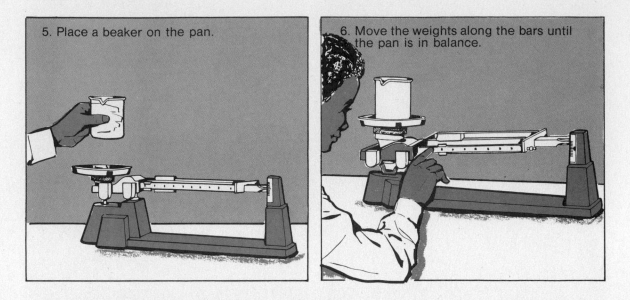

5. Place a beaker on the pan.

6. Move the weights along the bars until the pan is in balance.

• 7. What is the weight of the beaker? Use the correct unit after the number.

• 8. Your teacher will give you some more objects to weigh. Write their names on your data sheet. Then weigh each one.

B. SCIENTISTS HAVE FAITH

You've learned to use the balance well. Now you will use the scale to learn about another scientific skill.

WHY IS THIS CALLED A SCALE AND NOT A BALANCE?

SCALES HAVE SPRINGS IN THEM! BALANCES DON'T!

HELP! I'VE JUST PUT ON 15,000 POUNDS!

COOL IT! THAT'S A METRIC SCALE! IT WEIGHS IN GRAMS, NOT POUNDS!

Some scales are metric, as Phideau just discovered. Others read in pounds.

• 9. What do you weigh?

• 10. What do you think a bath scale will read if you stand on it?

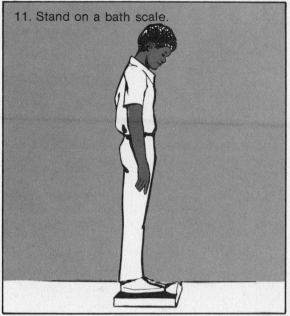

11. Stand on a bath scale.

• 12. What does the bath scale read?

• 13. Why were you able to guess your weight?

Scientists make guesses. They make guesses all the time. And, they are often right. This is because many things in nature happen over and over the same way.

A *prediction* is an educated guess. Predicting helps a scientist solve problems. If you have a problem and don't know the answer, a prediction will help. The prediction helps you to see where you are going.

•14. Suppose you were to stand on the scale again. What do you predict it would read?

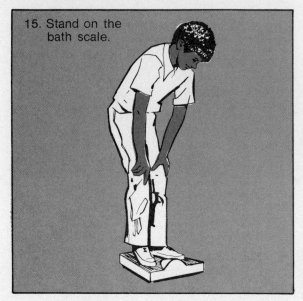
15. Stand on the bath scale.

•16. What does it read?

•17. Did you predict correctly? Why were you able to predict correctly?

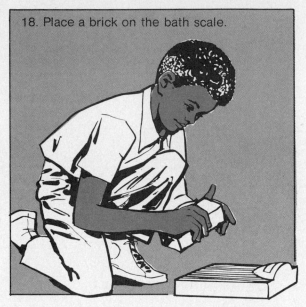
18. Place a brick on the bath scale.

•19. How much does the brick weigh?

•20. What do you predict you would weigh if you held the brick?

•21. What is your reason for your prediction?

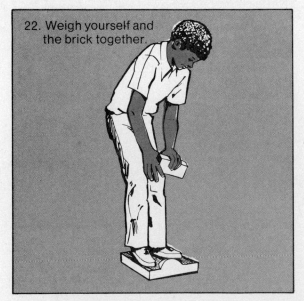
22. Weigh yourself and the brick together.

•23. How much do you and the brick weigh together?

•24. Did you predict correctly? Why were you able to predict correctly?

You have done a lot of weighing in this Investigation. But this Investigation is really about a different scientific skill.

• 25. What is another skill scientists should have? (*Hint:* Look at questions 17 and 24.)

C. YOU DON'T HAVE TO GUESS AT THIS ONE

• 26. What can scientists do to help them solve problems?

• 27. What is another skill used by scientists?

Re-read questions 25, 26, and 27.

THE CONCEPT.

THE DAWNING OF THE AGE OF ASPARAGUS

There are many ways to describe what scientists do. Basically, they try to learn what happens in nature. Scientists also want to know *why* things happen. To reach this goal, they observe, measure, and predict.

A. POUR IT ON ME

You have learned how to measure length in the metric system. You have also learned how to measure weight in the metric system.

You are about to learn another scientific skill. But first you need to learn how to measure volume.

You will use a *graduated cylinder* to measure volume. The graduated cylinder is a scientific measuring cup. There are lines on the cylinder. The lines show how much is in the cylinder. Your graduated cylinder measures in *milliliters,* or *ml* for short. This is the metric unit of volume.

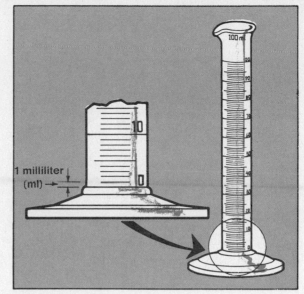

Look at the picture of the 100 ml graduated cylinder. There are 10 spaces between 0 and 10. Therefore each line stands for 1 milliliter.

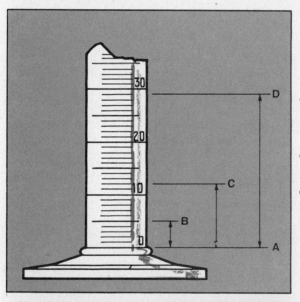

• 1. What is the volume between **A** and **B**? Be sure to use the correct unit.

• 2. What is the volume between **A** and **C**?

• 3. What is the volume between **A** and **D**?

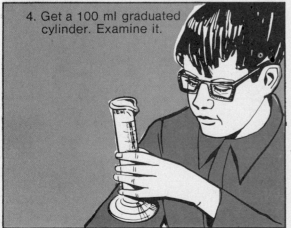

4. Get a 100 ml graduated cylinder. Examine it.

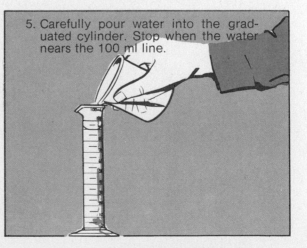

5. Carefully pour water into the graduated cylinder. Stop when the water nears the 100 ml line.

6. Note the surface of the water. It is curved. Measure at the **bottom** of the curve.

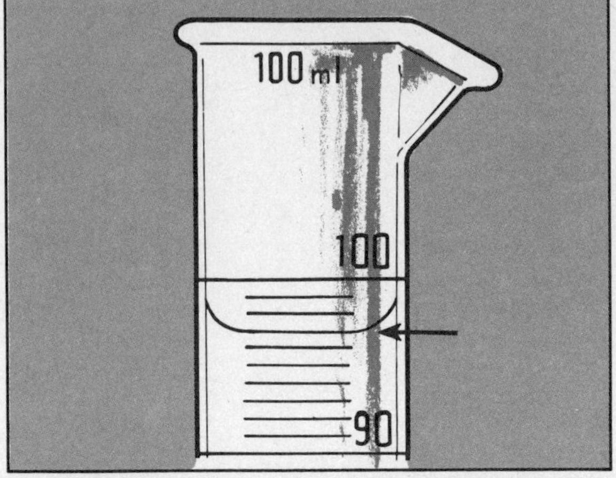

100 ml

100

90

7. To measure 100 ml of water, finish adding the water from a dropper.

100 ml

100

90

8. Get a cut-off milk carton from your teacher.

MILK

9. Pour the 100 ml of water into the carton. Write "100 ml" in Space **a** on your data sheet.

100 ml

MILK

10. Measure another 100 ml of water. Pour it into the carton. Record this in Space **a.**

← Measure 100 ml

MILK

11. Continue to measure and add water to the carton. Stop when the carton is full. Record each amount of water in Space **a.**

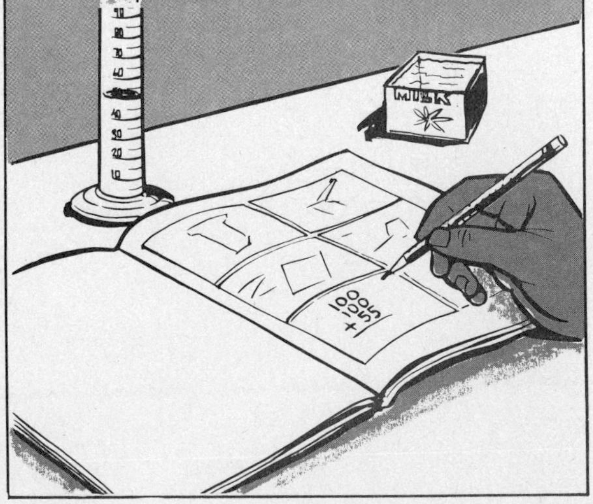

MILK

12. In Space **a**, add up the volume of water you added to the carton.

$$\begin{array}{r} 100 \\ 100 \\ +\ 55 \\ \hline 5 \end{array}$$

•13. How much water does the carton hold?

•14. Your teacher will give you some more containers. Write their names on your data sheet. Then find the volume of each.

B. WHAT EVERY GOOD EXPERIMENT SHOULD HAVE

WHAT'S AN EXPERIMENT?

THAT'S WHAT YOU DO TO TEST A PREDICTION!

A PREDICTION IS JUST A GUESS! IT'S A POSSIBLE ANSWER TO A PROBLEM. THE PREDICTION HAS TO BE TESTED!

AND THAT'S CALLED THE EXPERIMENT!

RICE ON!

You will use a common aquarium plant for this next part. The plant is called Elodea.

ELODEA? HOW ABOUT USING MY ASPARAGUS?

I HAVE OTHER PLANS FOR YOUR ASPARAGUS!

Carolina Biological Supply Co.

Elodea

Here's the problem.

•15. What do you predict will happen to the Elodea if it is put in salt water?

•16. What do you call testing a prediction?

•21. What should be in another test tube with a piece of Elodea?

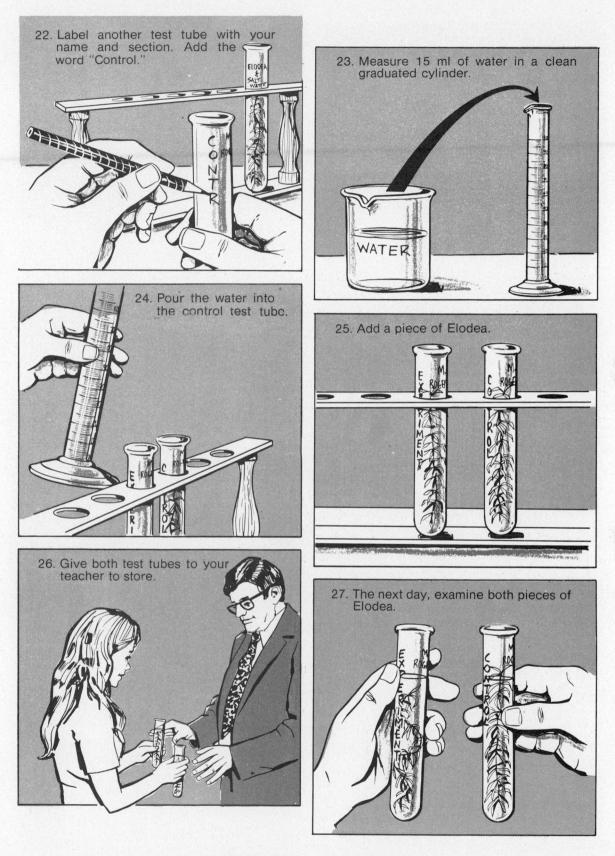

22. Label another test tube with your name and section. Add the word "Control."

23. Measure 15 ml of water in a clean graduated cylinder.

24. Pour the water into the control test tube.

25. Add a piece of Elodea.

26. Give both test tubes to your teacher to store.

27. The next day, examine both pieces of Elodea.

•28. Describe what you see.

When you do an experiment, everything must be the same except for the one thing being tested.

- •29. Name everything that is the same in both tubes.

- •30. What is the only difference in the test tubes?

- •31. What caused the Elodea to wilt in one of the tubes?

- •32. Every experiment must have a comparison. What was the comparison in this experiment?

- •33. What do you call the comparison?

- •34. What must every experiment have?

C. DOES YOUR PLANT HAVE A STOMACH ACHE?

- •35. What do you predict will happen to Elodea in water with Alka-Seltzer?

- •36. What do you call testing a prediction?

37. Get 2 test tubes.

38. Label both tubes with your name and section. Label one tube "Experiment" and the other "Control."

• 39. How much water are you going to put in each test tube?

40. Go ahead and add the water.

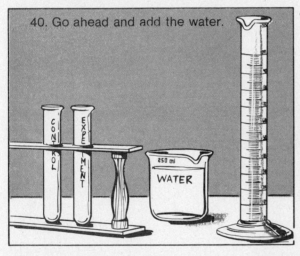

• 41. Where are you going to put the Alka-Seltzer?

42. Go ahead and fizz it.

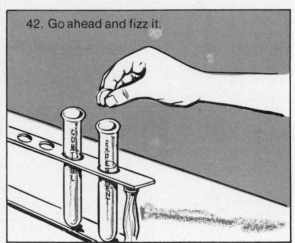

• 43. Where are you going to put the Elodea?

44. Go ahead and plant it.

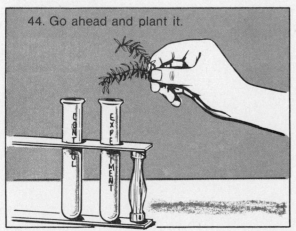

• 45. What is in the experiment tube?

• 46. What is in the control tube?

47. Give the tubes to your teacher to store overnight.

48. The next day, look at your Elodea.

• 49. What happened to it?

• 50. Name everything that is the same in both tubes.

• 51. What is the only difference in the test tubes?

• 52. If anything happened to the Elodea, what was the cause?

• 53. Every experiment must have a comparison. What was the comparison in this experiment?

• 54. What do you call the comparison?

• 55. What must every experiment have?

D. YOU ARE NOW IN CONTROL

You've done very well. Let's put it all together.

• 56. What do you call testing a prediction?

• 57. What must every experiment have?

Re-read your answers to questions 56 and 57. Then write the concept.

THE CONCEPT.

I KNOW I PUT IT SOMEWHERE

Here are the four concepts you've learned so far:

(a) Careful observations help solve problems.

(b) Accurate measurements help solve problems.

(c) A prediction is a possible answer to a problem.

(d) A controlled experiment tests a prediction.

A. LET'S CLEAN UP THIS MESS

Go back to the last Investigation and answer these three questions.

• 1. What happened to the Elodea left overnight in water?

• 2. What happened to the Elodea left overnight in salt water?

• 3. What happened to the Elodea left overnight in Alka-Seltzer?

Notice that you had to turn the pages back and forth. You had to spend time looking for the answer. Wouldn't it be easier to have everything in one place?

The results of an experiment are called *data*. Data are usually organized in a *table*. During an experiment, data can be recorded quickly and accurately in a table. Then when the experiment is finished, the data can be examined easily.

Look at Table 1 on your data sheet. It is a simple table you can use to organize your data from questions 1-3.

All tables have columns running up and down. They also have rows running across. There is always a label at the beginning of each column and each row. The first column in Table 1 tells you where the Elodea was placed. The second column is labeled "Observation." This is where you write down what happened to the Elodea.

4. Refer back to question 1. This is what happened to the Elodea in water. Write this observation in space (a) of Table 1. You do not have to write a full sentence. Just use a few key words.

5. Refer back to question 2. This is what happened to the Elodea in salt water. Write this observation in space (b) of Table 1.

6. Refer back to question 3. This is what happened to the Elodea in Alka-Seltzer. Write this observation in space (c) of Table 1.

•7. Where should data be recorded?

•8. What is the purpose of a data table?

•9. Why do scientists use data tables?

B. AND THIS LITTLE FINGER CRIED OUCH

We'll come back later and see who won. In the meantime, let's see how strong your finger is.

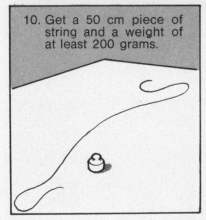
10. Get a 50 cm piece of string and a weight of at least 200 grams.

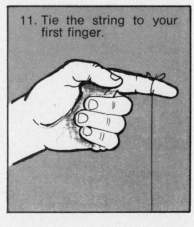
11. Tie the string to your first finger.

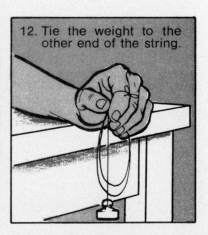
12. Tie the weight to the other end of the string.

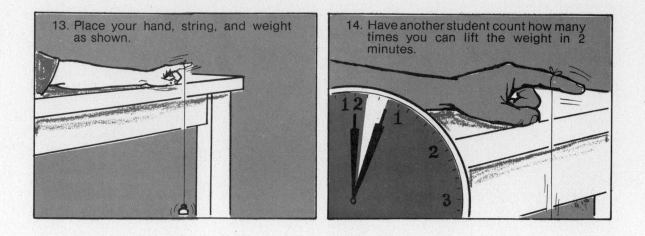

13. Place your hand, string, and weight as shown.

14. Have another student count how many times you can lift the weight in 2 minutes.

Table 2 on your data sheet looks something like the table in Part A. It has two columns. The first column tells you how many times you tried the finger lifting. The second column tells you how many times you lifted the weight in each trial.

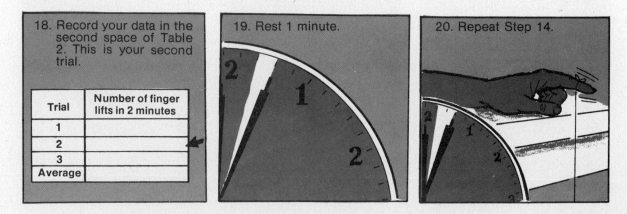

15. In the first space of Table 2, write down how many times you lifted the weight.

Trial	Number of finger lifts in 2 minutes
1	
2	
3	
Average	

16. Rest 1 minute.

17. Repeat Step 14.

18. Record your data in the second space of Table 2. This is your second trial.

Trial	Number of finger lifts in 2 minutes
1	
2	
3	
Average	

19. Rest 1 minute.

20. Repeat Step 14.

21. Record your data for the third trial in Table 2.		22. Calculate the average of your 3 trials. First, add the 3 numbers.	23. Then, divide by 3. Record the average in the last space of Table 2.	

21. Record your data for the third trial in Table 2.

Trial	Number of finger lifts in 2 minutes
1	
2	
3	
Average	

22. Calculate the average of your 3 trials. First, add the 3 numbers.

23. Then, divide by 3. Record the average in the last space of Table 2.

Trial	Number of finger lifts in 2 minutes
1	
2	
3	
Average	

•24. Were you able to lift the weights the same number of times in each trial?

•25. Did you do better or worse with each trial?

Notice how easy it was for you to answer questions 24 and 25. All you had to do was look at the table. Tables are useful because they organize data. They also help you compare data.

C. YOU CAN REST THE FINGER NOW

•26. What do you call the results of an experiment?

Let's see what you've learned.

•27. Where should data be recorded?

•28. What is the purpose of a table?

•29. Why do scientists use data tables?

THE CONCEPT.

WHAT'S YOUR GAME PLAN?

We all need a game plan, whether it's for football, science, or our lives.

Science has to do with the mind. The scientist uses his mind to find answers to problems. You can solve problems, too. All you need is a game plan.

You have already learned the game plan of science. It includes the five concepts you have learned so far. They are:
- (a) Observe carefully.
- (b) Measure accurately.
- (c) Make predictions.
- (d) Use controlled experiments.
- (e) Organize data in tables.

A. COOL IT, MAN

The time has come for you to put the game plan of science into use. You're going to solve a problem on your own.

To solve this problem, you need to learn how to use a *thermometer*. A thermometer measures temperature.

1. Get a thermometer from your teacher.

2. Look for the colored liquid inside the thermometer.

The colored liquid moves up or down depending on the temperature.

Find the letter "C" on your thermometer. This shows that your thermometer measures in degrees *Celsius*. There are 100 spaces between 0 and 100. The freezing point of water is 0°C. The boiling point of water is 100°C.

• 3. Look at two numbers next to each other.   How many spaces are between them?

• 4. How many degrees does each space represent?

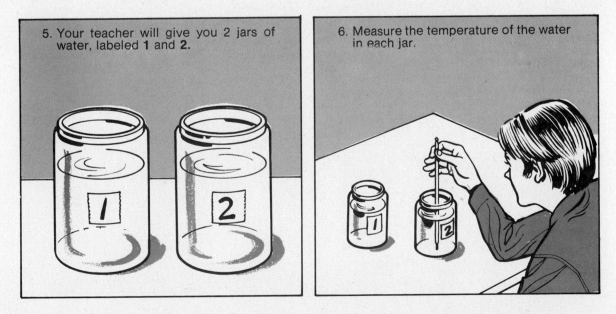

5. Your teacher will give you 2 jars of water, labeled **1** and **2**.

6. Measure the temperature of the water in each jar.

• 7. What is the temperature of the water in jar **1**?

• 8. What is the temperature of the water in jar **2**?

9. Show your answers to questions 7 and 8 to your teacher before going on.

B. LET'S TAKE A THINKING BREAK

Some schools give their students a break in the morning. It may be called "nutrition" or "recess." Adults call it a "coffee break."

There's your problem. Which way will cool a cup of hot chocolate faster? Should you add milk or blow on it?

• 10. What do you predict the answer will be?

• 11. How can you test your prediction? On your data sheet, write out your game plan.

Here is one way to test your prediction. Does it look like your game plan?

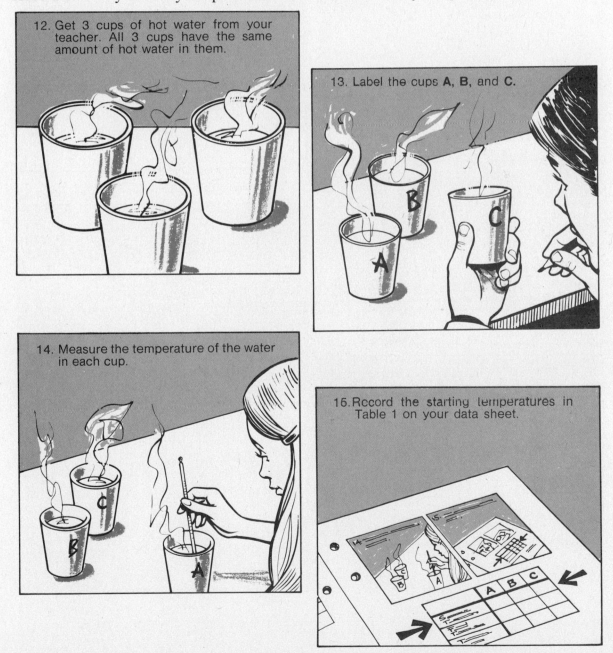

12. Get 3 cups of hot water from your teacher. All 3 cups have the same amount of hot water in them.

13. Label the cups **A**, **B**, and **C**.

14. Measure the temperature of the water in each cup.

15. Record the starting temperatures in Table 1 on your data sheet.

16. Measure out 25 ml of cold water in your graduated cylinder.

• 17. What time is it now?

18. Add the cold water to cup **A**.

25 ml water

19. Blow on cup **B** for 2 minutes. Take turns with your partner.

20. Do not disturb cup **C**.

21. After 2 minutes, measure the temperature in each cup.

22. Record the final temperatures in Table 1.

	A	B	C
	90	90	90

• 23. Which cup was the control?

24. Go back to Table 1. For each cup, subtract the final temperature from the starting temperature. Write your answers in the last row.

•25. Which cup cooled the most?

•26. What would happen if you added more cold water to cup **A**?

•27. What would happen if you blew faster on cup **B**?

•28. To cool hot chocolate quickly, what should you do?

Merrim/Monkmeyer

C. ANOTHER PROBLEM SOLVED

Congratulations! You've used your science skills to solve a practical problem. You can solve many other problems, too. All you need to do is plan your thinking with a game plan. For science is a way of solving problems. All you have to do is:

Observe.

Measure.

Predict.

Experiment.

Organize your data.

•29. What do scientists try to solve?

•30. How do the skills you've learned help a scientist?

•31. What is science?

Re-read questions 29, 30, and 31.

THE CONCEPT.

THE PLAN WORKED

You have just finished your first Idea. Congratulations! You did very well. This Idea was about how to solve problems.

To find out how to solve problems, you did six Investigations. You learned the following concepts:

    (a) Careful observations help solve problems.
    (b) Accurate measurements help solve problems.
    (c) Predictions are possible answers to problems.
    (d) Controlled experiments test predictions.
    (e) Data tables organize results from experiments.
    (f) Science is a way of solving problems.

You will use your science skills over and over again this year.

• 32. What will these skills help you do?

• 33. What do scientists try to do?

• 34. What is science about?

Each Idea will be like this one. You will learn one concept at a time. Then you will put all the concepts together to form a bigger Idea.

Re-read the six concepts and questions 32, 33, and 34. Then write in your data book what this entire Idea has been about.

THE IDEA.

Idea 2 Investigation 1

ARE YOU IN SHAPE?

You should be very proud of yourself! You've just finished the first Idea! It had to do with science. Science is a way of thinking. Everyone likes to think. Everyone likes to ask questions. Everyone likes to solve problems. This is why you may like science. It is a method used to discover more about the world.

Everyone wants to find out more about the world, especially about himself. And this is what this course is all about. It is about living things, especially you.

A. HAVE YOU EVER SEEN A SQUARE PEA?

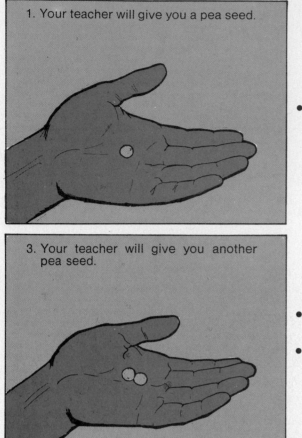

1. Your teacher will give you a pea seed.

• 2. In one word, describe its shape.

3. Your teacher will give you another pea seed.

• 4. In one word, describe its shape.

• 5. How do the shapes of your 2 peas compare?

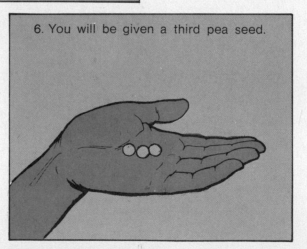

6. You will be given a third pea seed.

• 7. In one word, describe its shape.

• 8. How do the shapes of your 3 peas compare?

• 9. When someone says, "peas," what shape do you think of?

• 10. In other words, describe the shape of peas.

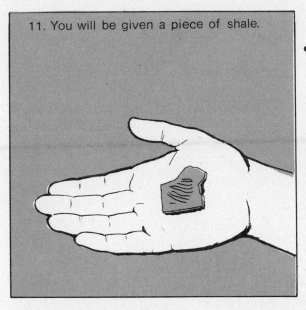

11. You will be given a piece of shale.

•12. In one word, describe its shape.

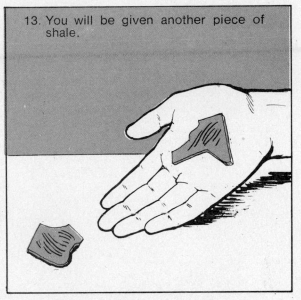

13. You will be given another piece of shale.

•14. In one word, describe its shape.

•15. How do the shapes of your 2 pieces of shale compare?

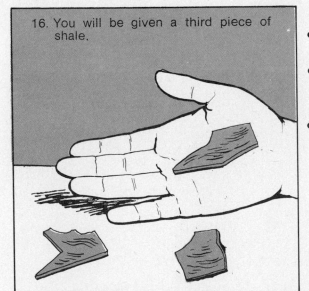

16. You will be given a third piece of shale.

•17. In one word, describe its shape.

•18. How do the shapes of your 3 pieces of shale compare?

•19. In other words, shale does not have a definite ___?___

20. You will be given 3 living things of the same kind. For example, you may be given 3 leaves or 3 starfish.

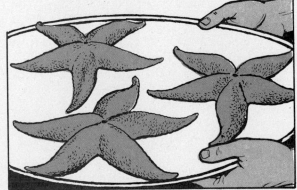

•21. Describe the 3 living things.

22. You will be given 3 non-living things of the same kind. For example, you may be given 3 pieces of copper or 3 pieces of glass.

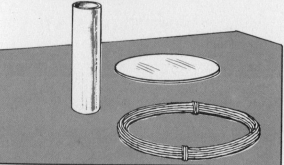

•23. Describe the 3 non-living things.

•24. You know a tree when you see one. Most trees have a certain __?__

•25. You know a dog when you see one. Most dogs have a certain __?__

•26. Each kind of living thing has a certain __?__

•27. Each kind of non-living thing does not have a certain __?__

B. HAVE YOU EVER SEEN A SIX-FOOT MAPLE LEAF?

UPI

28. You will be given a leaf.

•29. Your teacher will tell you what kind of leaf it is. Write the name on your data sheet.

•30. What is the size of this leaf? It may help to compare it to the size of your hand.

31. You will be given a second leaf. Notice that it is the same kind you already have.

•32. What is the size of this leaf?

•33. What can you say about the sizes of these 2 leaves?

34. You will be given a third leaf of the same kind.

•35. What is the size of this third leaf?

•36. What can you say about the sizes of these 3 leaves?

Compare results with your classmates. Some of them may have different kinds of leaves.

•37. What other kinds of leaves did your classmates look at? Write the names on your data sheet.

•38. What did your classmates discover about the sizes of their 3 leaves?

•39. In other words, each kind of leaf has a certain ?

40. You will be given a rock.

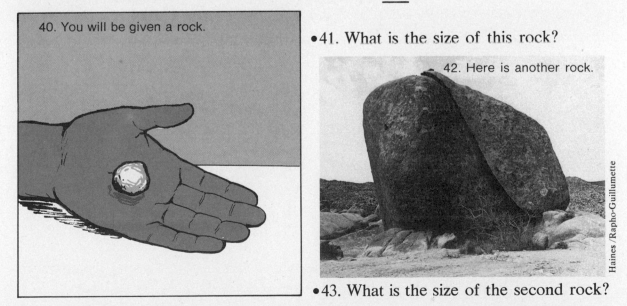

•41. What is the size of this rock?

42. Here is another rock.

Haines/Rapho-Guillumette

•43. What is the size of the second rock?

44. Here is another rock. It is called the Rock of Gibraltar.

•45. What is the size of this rock?

•46. How do the sizes of the 3 rocks compare?

RCA

What is the size of this rock?

•47. In other words, rocks do not have a definite ___?___

48. You will be given 3 living things. For example, you may be given 3 worms or shown 3 students.

•49. What are the sizes of the 3 living things?

50. You will be given 3 non-living things. For example, you may be given 3 glasses or 3 papers.

•51. What are the sizes of the 3 non-living things?

•52. When you see an elephant, you know it's an elephant. Elephants have a certain ?

•53. When you see a bird, you know it's a bird. Birds have a certain ?

•54. Each kind of living thing has a certain ?

•55. Each kind of non-living thing does not have a certain ?

C. LET'S GET TOGETHER FOR A NEW VIBRATION

Let's put the pieces together to see what we get.

•56. What can we say about the shape of each kind of living thing?

•57. What can we say about the size of each kind of living thing?

•58. What are 2 ways that living things differ from non-living things?

THE CONCEPT.

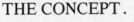

Idea 2 Investigation 2

GROWING FOR A CHANGE

Living things differ in many ways from non-living things. You have just learned one way:

Each kind of living thing has a certain size and shape.

How else do living and non-living things differ?

A. DO YOUR CLOTHES STILL FIT?

Babies are very much alive. They have a certain size and shape. You were once the size of this baby. Most babies weigh about 7 pounds at birth. They are about 20 inches long.

• 1. How much do you weigh?

• 2. How much more do you weigh than a newborn baby? (*Hint:* Subtract the baby weight above from your weight.)

Very simply put, you have grown.

• 3. What is your height in inches?

• 4. How much taller are you than the newborn baby?

• 5. What have you been doing since birth?

• 6. Look at your fingernails. What do they do every day?

• 7. What does your hair do every day?

• 8. What do living things do that non-living things cannot do?

B. CARS DO NOT GROW ON TREES

Cars do not grow. But trees grow. Every tree keeps a record of its growth. Each year a tree adds a new ring. The rings are like a data table. By counting the number of rings, you can tell how old a tree is. A thick ring means the tree grew a lot in one year. A thin ring means the tree did not grow much.

9. Your teacher will give you a magnifying glass and part of a branch.

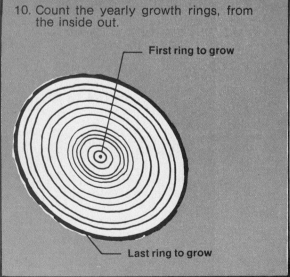

10. Count the yearly growth rings, from the inside out.

First ring to grow

Last ring to grow

•11. How many rings did you count?

•12. How old is the branch?

•13. In what year did the branch grow the most?

•14. In what year did the branch grow the least?

•15. What do the rings show us the branch is doing?

•16. What is one difference between a living and a non-living thing?

C. MY, HOW YOU'VE CHANGED

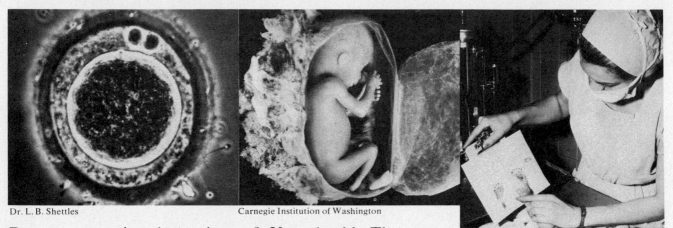

Dr. L. B. Shettles   Carnegie Institution of Washington   Mt. Sinai Hospital

Do you recognize these pictures? You should. They are pictures of you. The left picture is a human egg. The next picture shows it five months later. And, the last picture is the newborn baby.

In Parts A and B, you learned that living things *grow*. As living things grow, they may also do something else.

•17. Look at the 3 pictures again. Besides growing, what else happened to the egg?

Here are three more pictures. The left picture is a caterpillar. The next is the cocoon the caterpillar spins. And the last is the butterfly that comes out of the cocoon. All three are the same animal.

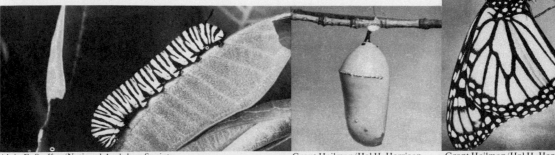

Alvin E. Staffan/National Audubon Society   Grant Heilman/Hal H. Harrison   Grant Heilman/Hal H. Harrison

•18. Besides growing, what else happened to the caterpillar?

•19. Besides growing, what else do living things do?

20. Here's a pea seed from the last Investigation. Make a drawing of this pea seed in Space **a** on your data sheet.

21. You will be given a soaked pea seed that is 3 days old. Make a drawing of this pea seed in Space **b** on your data sheet.

22. You will be given a pea plant that is 7-10 days old. Make a drawing of this pea plant in Space **c** on your data sheet.

•23. Look at your 3 drawings. What 2 things happened to the pea seed?

D. SUMMING IT UP

•24. Would a small rock become a big boulder? Why?

•25. Would a Chevrolet become a Cadillac? Why?

•26. Would a pea seed become a pea plant? Why?

•27. What two things are living things able to do?

THE CONCEPT.

Idea 2 Investigation 3

DO YOU HEAR THOSE NEW SENSATIONS?

You have been investigating differences between living and non-living things. So far you have learned that:

(a) Each kind of living thing has a certain size and shape.
(b) Living things grow and change.

Let's look at another difference.

A. I DIG THOSE NEW VIBES

How do you react to a new sound? Do the new vibrations give you a new sensation? What do we mean by "react," "vibrations," and "sensation"?

Chuck Pulin

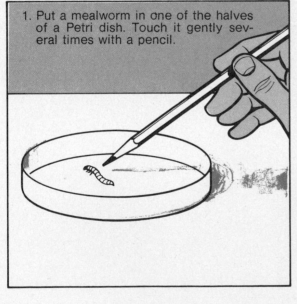

1. Put a mealworm in one of the halves of a Petri dish. Touch it gently several times with a pencil.

• 2. What did the mealworm do?

3. Put a piece of rock in the other half of the Petri dish. Touch it gently with a pencil.

•4. What did the rock do?

•5. How did the mealworm react differently than the rock?

You probably said that one moved and the other did not move. Why did the mealworm move? Let's add two new words to your vocabulary. A change in the world around a living thing is called a *stimulus*. When a living thing feels a stimulus, a reaction takes place. A reaction to a stimulus is called a *response*.

STIMULUS RESPONSE

6. Cover half of an open Petri dish with aluminum foil.

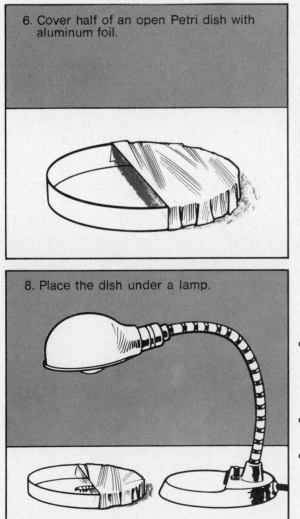

7. Place the mealworm in the middle of the dish.

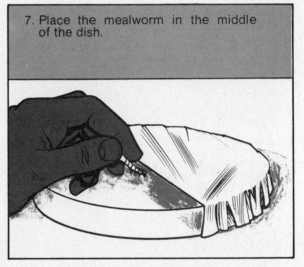

8. Place the dish under a lamp.

• 9. Did the mealworm go to the light side or the dark side? (Repeat the experiment a few times before answering.)

•10. What was the stimulus?

•11. What was the response?

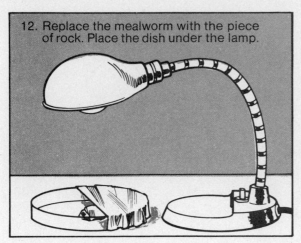

12. Replace the mealworm with the piece of rock. Place the dish under the lamp.

• 13. How does the rock respond?

• 14. How did the mealworm respond differently than the rock?

• 15. Use the words *stimulus* and *response* (or *respond*) in your next sentence. What can living things do that non-living things cannot do?

B. ADAPT OR THE WORLD PASSES YOU BY

You have probably been told never to look at the sun. It can blind you.

SUNLIGHT MUST BE A STRONG STIMULUS!

CLOSING OR COVERING YOUR EYES WOULD BE A GOOD RESPONSE!

BUT WHAT WOULD HAPPEN IF YOU CAN'T RESPOND?

Good question, Peter. Response has to do with staying alive. Living things that can respond have a better chance of staying alive. Your eyes show a good example of how you respond.

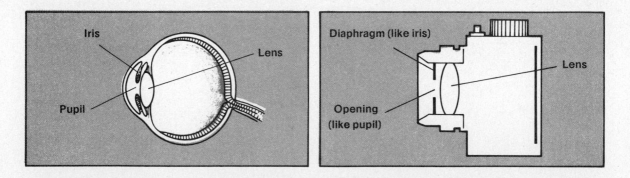

Iris
Lens
Pupil

Diaphragm (like iris)
Lens
Opening (like pupil)

Your eye is like a camera. Light enters the hole in the center. This hole is called the *pupil.* The picture falls on the back of the eye. The *iris* of the eye controls the amount of light coming in. Let's see this happen.

16. Stand in front of your partner's chair.

17. Ask your partner to close or cover his eyes for 1 minute.

18. Remove the hands or open the eyes. Observe the pupils in the center of the eyes.

• 19. What happened to the size of the pupils as the eyes opened?

20. Shine a light into your partner's eyes.

• 21. What happened to the size of the pupils?

• 22. What was the stimulus?

• 23. What was the response?

• 24. Bright lights can be harmful to the eyes. If the iris did not respond, what might happen to the eyes?

This boy is being checked for marijuana. If he is on pot, his eyes will not respond. Smoking pot slows your ability to respond in many ways.

- 25. What might happen to a person who can't respond to a stimulus?

- 26. What must living things do to stay alive?

C. WE ALL DO IT

Maybe plants don't like rock music. But do they respond to other kinds of stimulus?

27. Observe the large box your teacher has. There is a plant inside the box. The plant has been there for a few days.

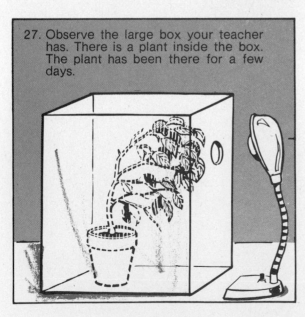

- 28. What do you see on one side of the box?

- 29. What is reaching the plant through this opening?

- 30. How do you predict the plant will respond to this stimulus?

Your teacher will remove the box. Observe the plant and check your prediction.

• 31. How did the plant respond to the stimulus?

• 32. What must living things do to stay alive?

D. PUTTING IT ALL TOGETHER

Let's review what you have learned.

• 33. Dust gets in your nose and you sneeze. What is the stimulus and what is your response?

• 34. What stimulus caused David to wake up?

• 35. Would you expect David's bed to react to the alarm clock? Why?

• 36. What can living things do that non-living things cannot?

• 37. What must living things do to stay alive?

THE CONCEPT.

Idea 2 Investigation 4

DON'T LET ME DRY OUT

There's more, Phideau. There is much more to being alive. Living things have certain needs. Let's study one of these needs.

A. IT'S A WET WORLD

Your teacher will give you 2 beakers, 10 seeds, and 10 pebbles.

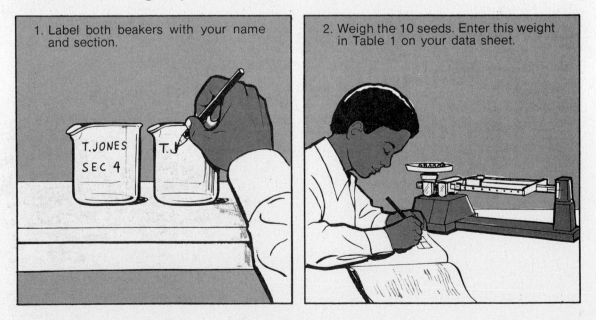

1. Label both beakers with your name and section.

2. Weigh the 10 seeds. Enter this weight in Table 1 on your data sheet.

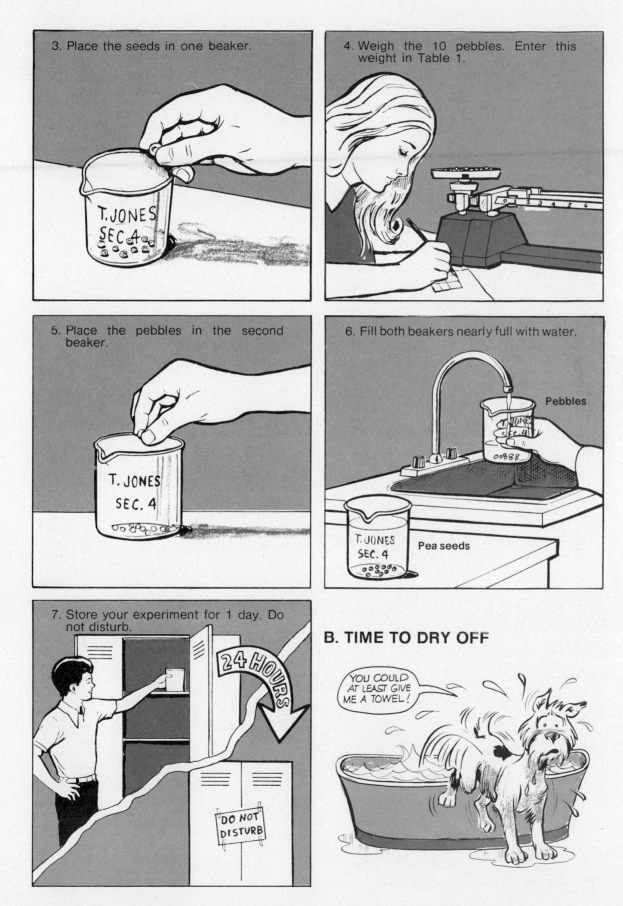

3. Place the seeds in one beaker.

4. Weigh the 10 pebbles. Enter this weight in Table 1.

5. Place the pebbles in the second beaker.

6. Fill both beakers nearly full with water.

Pebbles

Pea seeds

7. Store your experiment for 1 day. Do not disturb.

24 HOURS

DO NOT DISTURB

B. TIME TO DRY OFF

YOU COULD AT LEAST GIVE ME A TOWEL!

8. After 1 day, remove the seeds from the beaker.

9. Carefully dry the seeds with paper towels.

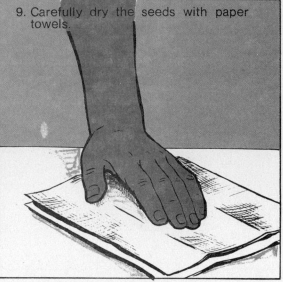

10. Weigh the seeds. Enter this weight in Table 1.

- 11. What was the weight of the seeds at the start of the experiment?

- 12. What is the weight of the seeds now?

- 13. What happened to the weight of the seeds?

- 14. What do you think caused this change?

- 15. What were the seeds placed in?

- 16. What do you think got into the seeds?

17. Remove the pebbles from the beaker.

18. Dry the pebbles with paper towels.

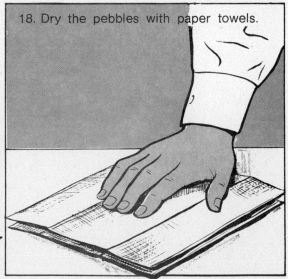

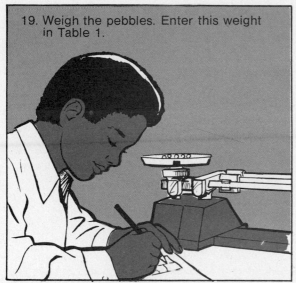
19. Weigh the pebbles. Enter this weight in Table 1.

•20. What was the weight of the pebbles at the start of the experiment?

•21. What is the weight of the pebbles now?

•22. What happened to the weight of the pebbles?

•23. What did the seeds do that the pebbles did not?

•24. What did the seeds take in?

•25. Seeds are living things. What do living things take in that non-living things do not?

C. I'M GLAD YOU ASKED THAT

Your teacher will give you a covered jar. It contains some strips of test paper.

WHAT'S SO SPECIAL ABOUT WATER?

I GUESS ALL LIVING THINGS NEED IT!

HOW DO YOU KNOW WHEN IT'S PRESENT?

MAYBE YOU CAN TEST FOR IT?

HOW DO YOU DO THAT?

26. Use your forceps. Remove one of the paper strips from the jar.

•27. What color is the dry test paper?

28. Wet one end of the paper.

•29. What color is the wet test paper?

•30. What caused the paper to change color?

> This paper is used to test for water. If water is present, the paper will always turn pink. If there is no water, the paper remains blue.

D. THE BREATH OF LIFE

 You have learned that living things take in water. You have also learned how to test for the presence of water. Let's see if you can use this test to learn more about living things.

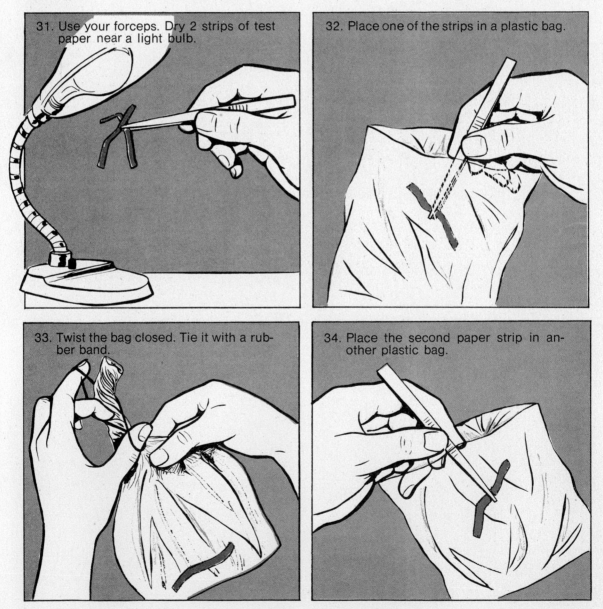

31. Use your forceps. Dry 2 strips of test paper near a light bulb.

32. Place one of the strips in a plastic bag.

33. Twist the bag closed. Tie it with a rubber band.

34. Place the second paper strip in another plastic bag.

35. Hold the bag to your mouth. Blow into it several times.

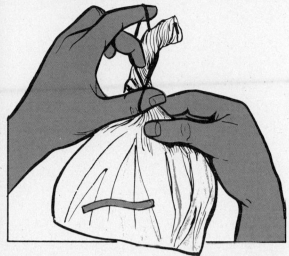

36. Twist the bag closed. Tie it with a rubber band.

• 37. Which bag is your control?

• 38. Which bag is your experiment?

• 39. Look at the paper in the control bag. What color is it?

• 40. What does this show?

• 41. Look at the paper in the experiment bag. What color is it?

• 42. What does this show?

• 43. How is the air in the two bags different?

• 44. How can you tell?

• 45. Which bag contains water?

• 46. How do you think it got there?

• 47. What is in the air you breathe out?

• 48. What might be in the air other animals breathe out?

E. THE DRIP OF LIFE

The world wouldn't be much fun without water. But living things need water for more than fun.

• 49. What do living things take in?

• 50. What do living things give off?

THE CONCEPT.

Launois/Black Star

Idea
2
Investigation 5

TAKE A DEEP BREATH

> In the last Investigation, you learned that:
>
> Living things take in and give off water.

Living things need water. Without water there would be no life on earth. Living things have other needs as well. Does this picture give you a clue to what else living things might need?

© 1970 Buffalo Courier Express photo by Ron Mascati

A. BAD BREATH IS BETTER THAN NO BREATH

You breathe. Cats, dogs, and birds also breathe. So do fishes, insects, and plants. All living things breathe. They don't all breathe the same way, but they breathe.

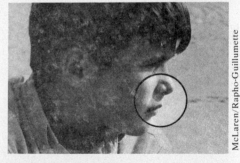

McLaren/Rapho-Guillumette

A person breathes through his nose and mouth.

Walter Chandoha   Browning/DPI   Wilson/Black Star

Cats, dogs, and birds breathe the same way.

A fish breathes through the mouth and gills.

Walter Chandoha

Insects breathe through tiny slits on the sides of their bodies.

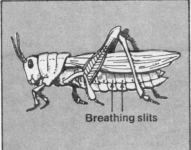

Breathing slits

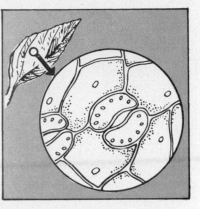

Plants also breathe. They breathe through tiny holes in their leaves.

B. I'LL HUFF AND I'LL PUFF

1. Sit quietly and relax.

2. Count the number of times you breathe in 1 minute. Count in and out as 1 breath.

•3. How many times did you breathe in 1 minute?

The number of times you breathe in one minute is called your *breathing rate*.

- 4. What do you think you are breathing?

- 5. Compare your breathing rate with those of your classmates. How does your breathing rate compare with theirs?

- 6. What do you think your classmates are breathing?

7. Stand up and run in place near your desk for 1 minute.

8. Sit down. Count the number of times you breathe in 1 minute.

- 9. How many times did you breathe in 1 minute after exercising?

- 10. Why do you think your breathing rate changed? That is, what did you need?

This runner has just finished a mile.

- 11. What is the runner breathing in and out fast?

- 12. What do you think living things take in and give off?

- 13. What do you think living things need to stay alive?

C. BUBBLES IN MY BREAD

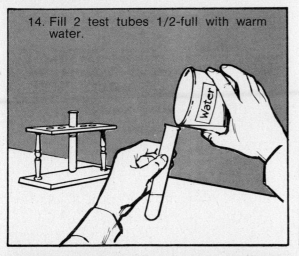

14. Fill 2 test tubes 1/2-full with warm water.

15. Add a yeast mixture to one test tube. The mixture contains living yeast plants plus something to help them grow.

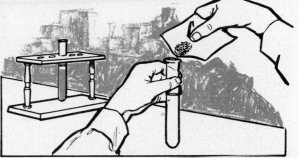

16. Add a few pebbles to the other tube.

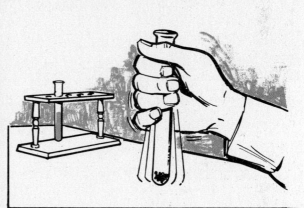

17. Shake both tubes gently.

18. Wait a few minutes.

• 19. Which of the 2 tubes contains something living?

• 20. What do you observe in the yeast tube?

• 21. What do you observe in the pebble tube?

• 22. What do living yeast plants give off that pebbles do not?

• 23. What do living things give off that non-living things do not?

D. THE LAST BREATH

Leon Deller/Monkmeyer

Whales live in water, but they are not fishes. They have lungs.

• 24. Why must whales keep coming up to the surface?

NASA

• 25. What do you think this astronaut is breathing in?

• 26. Why must astronauts carry their own air to the moon?

Bahamas Tourist News Bureau

• 27. What do you think this scuba diver is breathing in?

• 28. Notice the bubbles. What does this tell you the diver is giving off?

• 29. What do living yeast plants give off that pebbles do not?

• 30. Would you expect a desk to take in and give off air?

  Why?

• 31. Would you expect an insect to take in and give off air?

  Why?

• 32. What do living things take in?

• 33. What do living things give off?

THE CONCEPT.

Idea 2 Investigation 6

WHERE'S THE MENU?

You are really making progress! Here's what you learned in the last two Investigations.

  (a) Living things take in and give off water.
  (b) Living things take in and give off air.

Is there anything else living things must take in?

A. A FEAST FOR YEAST

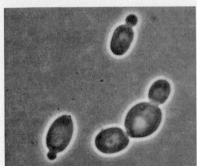

Standard Oil of Indiana

The yeast plants you worked with look like this. You saw them giving off bubbles as they grew.

Yeast plants can help us discover something else living things must take in.

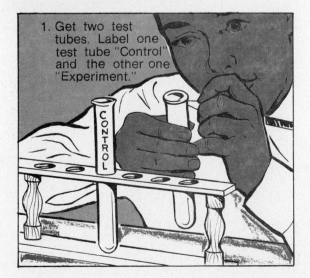

1. Get two test tubes. Label one test tube "Control" and the other one "Experiment."

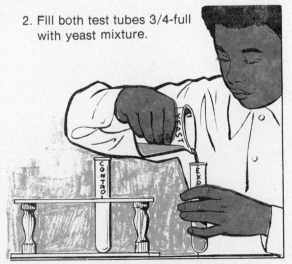

2. Fill both test tubes 3/4-full with yeast mixture.

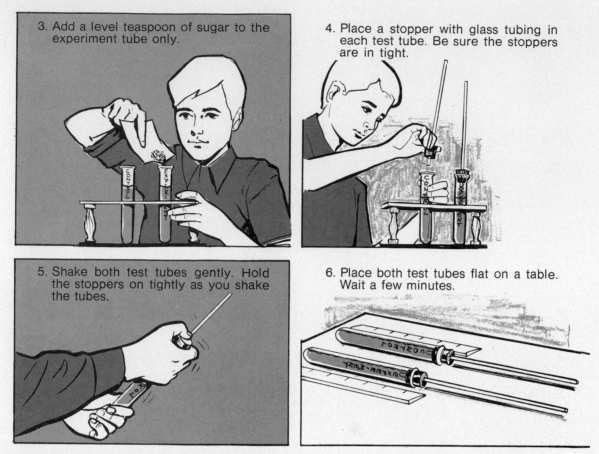

3. Add a level teaspoon of sugar to the experiment tube only.

4. Place a stopper with glass tubing in each test tube. Be sure the stoppers are in tight.

5. Shake both test tubes gently. Hold the stoppers on tightly as you shake the tubes.

6. Place both test tubes flat on a table. Wait a few minutes.

- 7. What is the only difference between the 2 test tubes?

- 8. What do you observe in the tube without sugar?

- 9. What do you observe in the tube with sugar?

- 10. Which yeast plants are growing better?

- 11. In order to grow, what must yeast plants take in?

Sugar is only one kind of food. The yeast plants could have grown with molasses or many other sugary foods.

Robert C. Hermes/National Audubon Society

- 12. Besides air and water, what must you take in to stay alive?

- 13. What food is this praying mantis taking in?

- 14. What do you think all living things must take in?

B. I'LL HAVE MINE WITH ONIONS

THERE ARE LOTS OF DIFFERENCES BETWEEN LIVING AND NON-LIVING THINGS!

I THINK DAVID HAS DISCOVERED ONE OF THEM!

You've learned that living things must take in food. What kinds of food have you been taking in?

• 15. What foods did you eat for breakfast?

• 16. What foods did you eat for your last lunch?

• 17. What foods did you eat for your last dinner?

• 18. What snacks have you eaten between meals in the last 24 hours?

A Guide to Good Eating

Use Daily:

Milk Group

3 or more glasses milk — Children smaller glasses for some children under 9

4 or more glasses — Teen-agers

2 or more glasses — Adults

Cheese, ice cream and other milk-made foods can supply part of the milk

Meat Group

2 or more servings

Meats, fish, poultry, eggs, or cheese—with dry beans, peas, nuts as alternates

Vegetables and Fruits

4 or more servings

Include dark green or yellow vegetables; citrus fruit or tomatoes

Breads and Cereals

4 or more servings

Enriched or whole grain Added milk improves nutritional values

This is the foundation for a good diet. Use more of these and other foods as needed for growth, for activity, and for desirable weight.

National Dairy Council

This chart shows the types of food you should be eating every day. By eating some of each group, you get a *balanced diet*. A balanced diet helps you grow and stay healthy.

Review the foods you ate in the last 24 hours.

• 19. What milk foods have you eaten?

• 20. Meats and eggs can help you grow. What meats and eggs have you eaten?

• 21. Vegetables and fruits contain vitamins to keep you healthy. What vegetables and fruits have you eaten?

•22. Bread and cereals contain energy foods. What bread and cereals have you eaten?

•23. What four food groups do you need for a balanced diet?

San Diego Zoo Photo

•24. Why must these animals be fed?

•25. What must all living things take in?

C. WHAT'S FOR DESSERT?

•26. What's wrong with this cartoon?

•27. What kind of food did the yeast plants take in?

•28. What must living things take in?

THE CONCEPT.

WINDING IT UP

Mazeltov! You've just come to the end of another Idea. This Idea has been about life. How can we tell if something is alive?

You have been studying differences between living and non-living things. You now know that living things are alive because they have the same characteristics. These characteristics are listed as your six concepts. Review them.

Leonard Kamsler

Tennis players don't doubt that Chris Evert is alive. Let's use her to review this Idea.

Does she have a definite size and shape?

Has she grown and changed?

If a player served to her, would she respond?

Does she need to take in and give off air and water?

Does she take in food?

• 29. How do we know that Chris Evert is alive?

• 30. How can you tell if something is alive?

• 31. What do all living things have?

Re-read questions 30 and 31. Summarize the entire Idea.

THE IDEA.

TO SEE OR NOT TO SEE... THAT IS THE MYSTERY

Did you know that your finger-print is like your name? It belongs only to you. No two fingerprints are the same. They may look alike, but they are different.

A. THE CASE OF THE WIGGLY LINE

1. Put a glass plate on top of a piece of black paper.

VERY INTERESTING!

2. Press your thumb down on the center of the glass plate.

3. Sprinkle some powder on the glass where you pressed your thumb.

4. Gently brush away the powder.

5. Look carefully at your fingerprint. Compare your print with the prints of other students.

• 6. What differences can you see?

You may need some help. Let's try Step 5 again, this time using a *magnifying glass*.

Scientists call this kind of curved glass a *lens*.

- 7. Use the lens to look at the fingerprints. What can you see?

- 8. How are the lines different?

- 9. What did the lens do?

- 10. How did the lens help you tell the fingerprints apart?

- 11. Why do you think lenses would be important tools for scientists?

B. THEY MAKE SUCH A NICE PAIR

Many things that scientists study are so small that lenses are needed to see them.

Microscopes use lenses to *magnify* or make objects look larger. A simple microscope uses only a single lens. It can magnify only 5 or 10 times. You have already used a simple microscope in the first part of this Investigation. It wasn't hard, was it?

Let's take a look at another microscope.

This is a *compound microscope*. It uses a pair of lenses to magnify objects. Some compound microscopes can magnify almost 1,000 times.

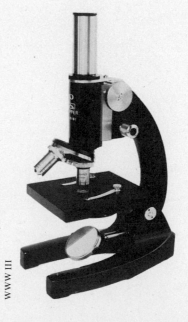

WWW III

Let's get ourselves together.

• 12. What is a simple microscope?

• 13. What is a compound microscope?

• 14. How are they the same?

• 15. How are they different?

• 16. Why do scientists use microscopes?

C. FIND THE MISSING LETTER

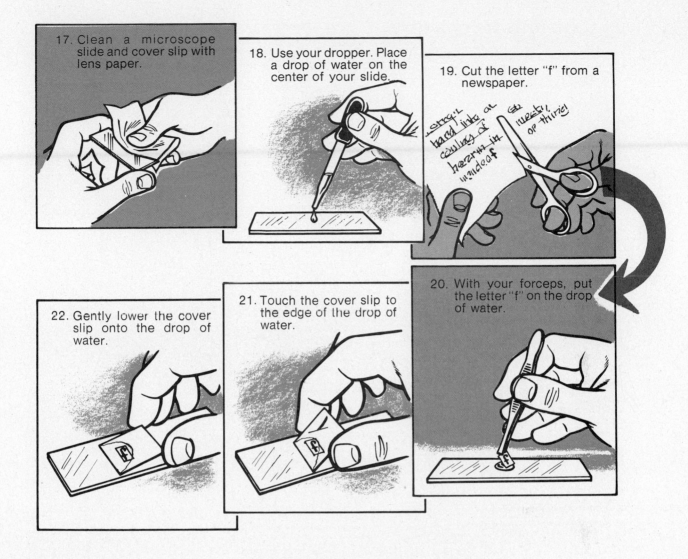

• 23. Why is it important to clean the slide and cover slip?

D. LOOK INTO MY EYEPIECE

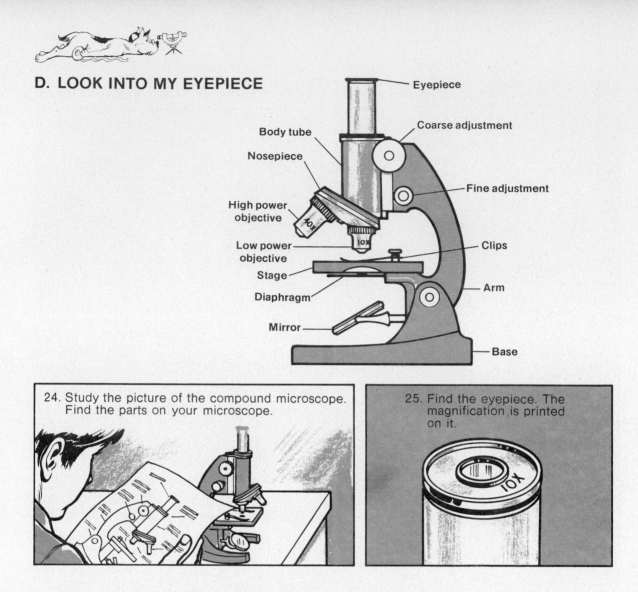

Eyepiece

Coarse adjustment

Body tube

Nosepiece

Fine adjustment

High power
objective

Low power
objective

Clips

Stage

Arm

Diaphragm

Mirror

Base

24. Study the picture of the compound microscope. Find the parts on your microscope.

25. Find the eyepiece. The magnification is printed on it.

• 26. What is the magnification of the eyepiece?

27. Find the low power objective. The magnification is printed on this too.

• 28. What is the magnification of the low power objective?

• 29. What is the magnification of the high power objective?

• 30. How can you tell the two objectives apart?

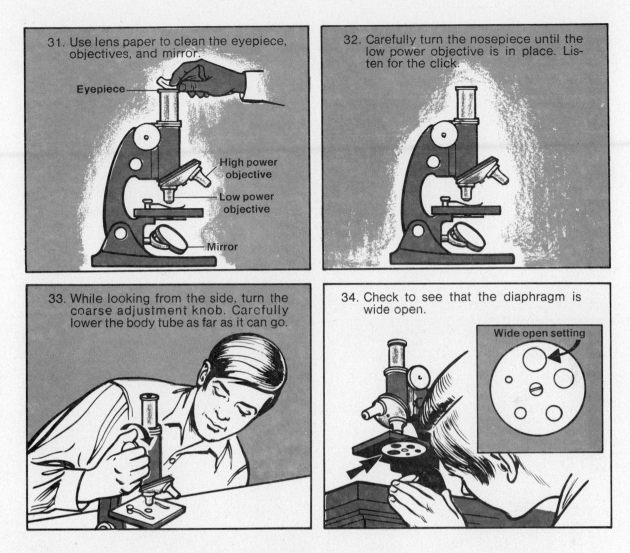

31. Use lens paper to clean the eyepiece, objectives, and mirror.

Eyepiece

High power objective

Low power objective

Mirror

32. Carefully turn the nosepiece until the low power objective is in place. Listen for the click.

33. While looking from the side, turn the coarse adjustment knob. Carefully lower the body tube as far as it can go.

34. Check to see that the diaphragm is wide open.

Wide open setting

• 35. What do you think is the job of the diaphragm?

36. Look into the eyepiece. Tilt the mirror until you see a bright circle of light.

• 37. What does the mirror do?

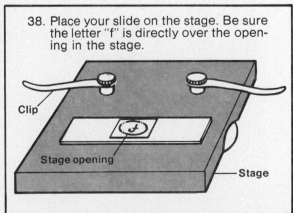

38. Place your slide on the stage. Be sure the letter "f" is directly over the opening in the stage.

Clip

Stage opening

Stage

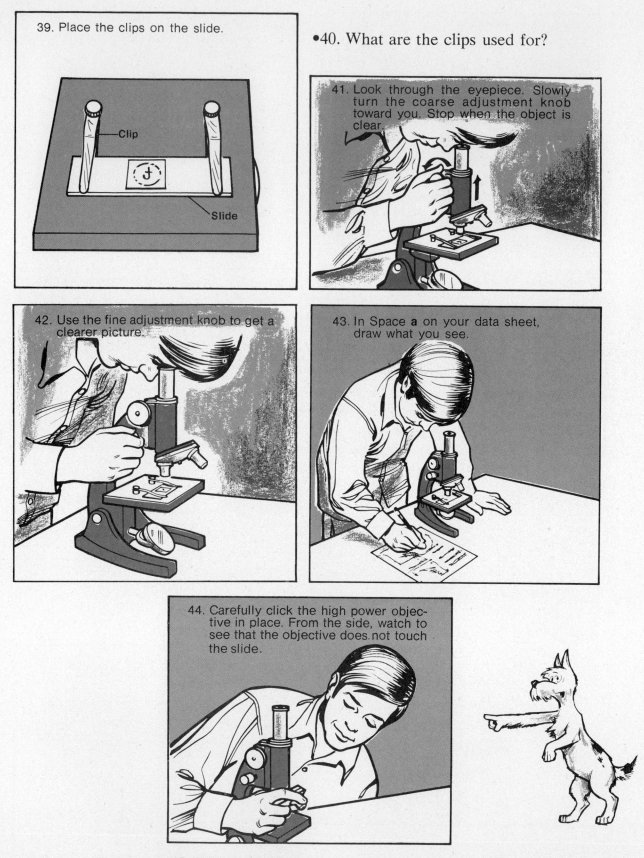

39. Place the clips on the slide.

•40. What are the clips used for?

41. Look through the eyepiece. Slowly turn the coarse adjustment knob toward you. Stop when the object is clear.

42. Use the fine adjustment knob to get a clearer picture.

43. In Space **a** on your data sheet, draw what you see.

44. Carefully click the high power objective in place. From the side, watch to see that the objective does not touch the slide.

•45. Why is it important to watch as the objectives are changed?

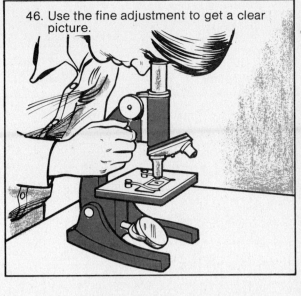

46. Use the fine adjustment to get a clear picture.

•47. Explain why *only* the fine adjustment is used with the high power objective.

48. In Space **b** on your data sheet, draw what you see.

•49. What does the compound microscope help you do?

•50. Why do you think scientists need such a tool?

•51. Re-read questions 13 and 49. What kind of thing is studied with the compound microscope?

THE CONCEPT.

Idea 3 Investigation 2

THE BEAST FROM THE BARREL

In the last Investigation you learned that:

The microscope is a tool used to magnify small objects.

The microscope has been used to study living things for over 300 years. Many things have been learned about plants and animals. One of the most important things learned was an answer to the question, "What are living things made of?"

HMMM! EVERYONE KNOWS THAT LIVING THINGS ARE MADE OF BONES, MUSCLES, AND SKIN. — OR *ARE* THEY?

A. THAT LITTLE OLD LENSMAKER, ME

One of the first men to study living things under the microscope was a Dutchman, Antony van Leeuwenhoek. Do you have a hobby? Leeuwenhoek's hobby was grinding glass into small lenses. Using these lenses, Leeuwenhoek built a simple microscope.

© Rijksmuseum Amsterdam

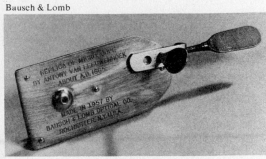

This is what Leeuwenhoek's microscope looked like.

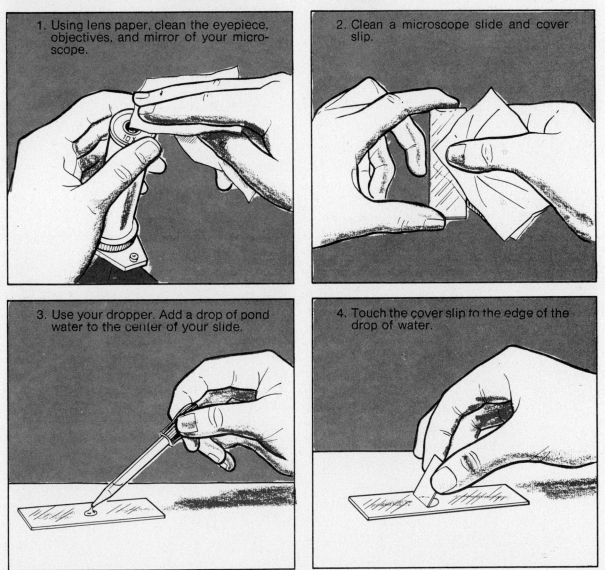

1. Using lens paper, clean the eyepiece, objectives, and mirror of your microscope.

2. Clean a microscope slide and cover slip.

3. Use your dropper. Add a drop of pond water to the center of your slide.

4. Touch the cover slip to the edge of the drop of water.

Idea 3/Investigation 2

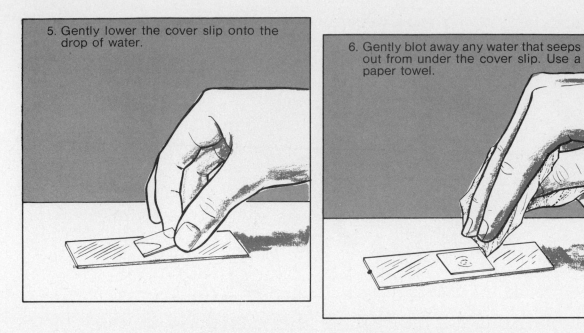

5. Gently lower the cover slip onto the drop of water.

6. Gently blot away any water that seeps out from under the cover slip. Use a paper towel.

- 7. Which objective will you use? (*Hint:* See page 83.)

- 8. How will you know it is in place?

- 9. What has to be done to the diaphragm?

- 10. What has to be done to the mirror?

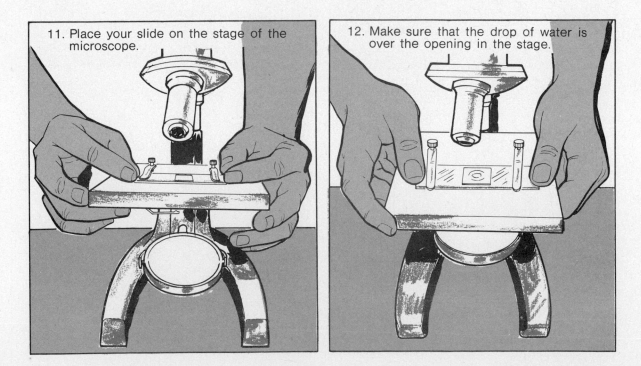

11. Place your slide on the stage of the microscope.

12. Make sure that the drop of water is over the opening in the stage.

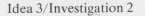

13. While looking from the side, turn the coarse adjustment knob. Carefully lower the body tube as far as it will go.

14. Focus on the slide.

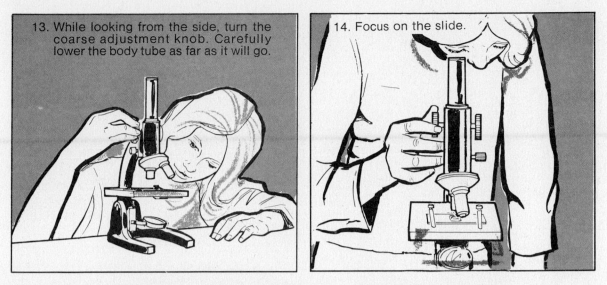

If you don't see anything, ask your teacher for help. You may also want to make another slide. Don't give up; Leeuwenhoek didn't.

15. In Space **a** on your data sheet, draw what you see.

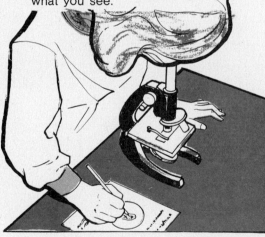

• 16. Describe what you saw.

• 17. How could you tell if anything was alive?

• 18. How many living things did you see?

• 19. How were they different?

Did you see any of these?

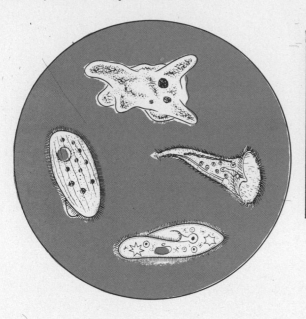

20. Remove your slide and clean up.

B. DON'T POP YOUR CORK

While Leeuwenhoek was studying animals, Robert Hooke, an Englishman, was studying plants. He built his own compound microscope. It looked very different from the one you are using.

Historical Pictures Service, Chicago

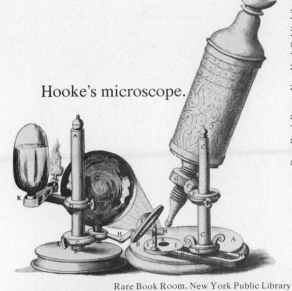

Hooke's microscope.

Here is one of Hooke's drawings.

Hooke wrote about the tiny boxes. They reminded him of the honeycomb of a bee. Hooke called these tiny boxes *"cells."*

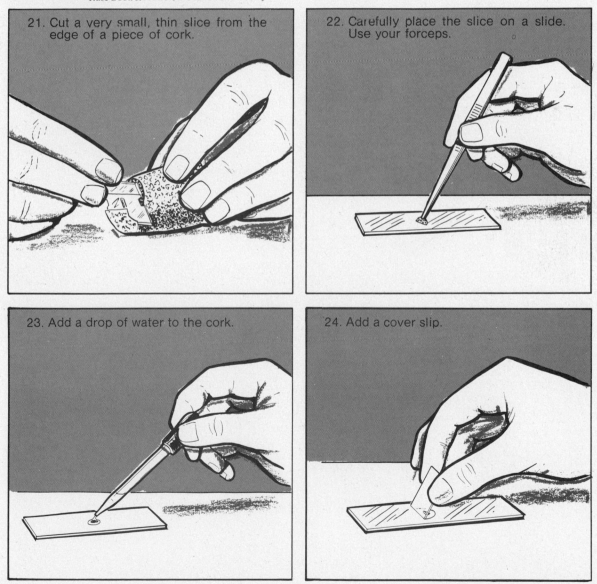

21. Cut a very small, thin slice from the edge of a piece of cork.

22. Carefully place the slice on a slide. Use your forceps.

23. Add a drop of water to the cork.

24. Add a cover slip.

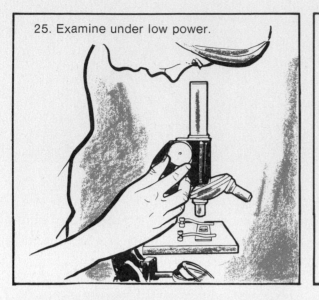

25. Examine under low power.

26. Examine under high power.

27. In Space **b** on your data sheet, draw what you see.

• 28. What does the cork look like?

• 29. What did Hooke call the tiny boxes of cork?

• 30. What did Leeuwenhoek call the little animals he found?

• 31. Why was the work of Leeuwenhoek important?

• 32. Why was the work of Robert Hooke important?

C. WE STILL DO IT

Scientists today still use the word first used by Robert Hooke. They now know that all living things are made of *cells*.

• 33. Who was one of the first men to look at animal cells?

• 34. What tool did he need to look at cells?

• 35. Who was one of the first men to look at plant cells?

• 36. What tool did he need to look at cells?

THE CONCEPT.

THEY COME IN MANY SHAPES AND SIZES

The work of Leeuwenhoek and Hooke was only the beginning of cell study. Newer and better microscopes were built. Scientists were able to learn more about living things.

SCIENTISTS LEARNED THAT SOME LIVING THINGS ARE MADE OF ONLY ONE CELL!

SOME ARE MADE OF MILLIONS OF CELLS!

THAT'S RIGHT! ALL LIVING THINGS ARE MADE OF CELLS!

The "beasties" studied by Leeuwenhoek were one-celled animals. You studied some of these animals in the last Investigation. Do you remember what they looked like?

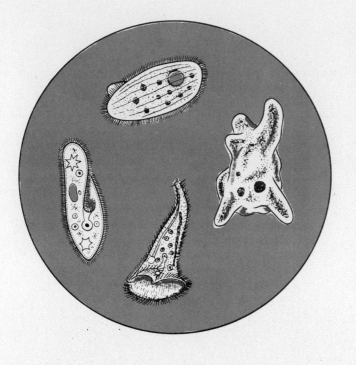

1. How are these animals different? List some of the differences you can see.

In Idea 2, you learned that living things have a certain size and shape. Do cells have a certain size and shape?

2. How are the animals in the picture different in size?

3. How are their shapes different?

A. CAN YOU FIGURE IT OUT?

Here is a picture of different plant and animal cells.

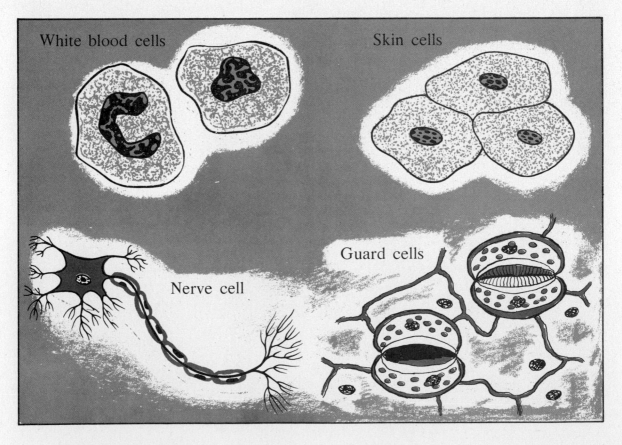

White blood cells

Skin cells

Nerve cell

Guard cells

• 4. What do you notice about their size?

• 5. What do you notice about their shape?

• 6. How are their sizes and shapes the same?

• 7. How are their sizes and shapes different?

• 8. Re-read questions 6 and 7. What can you say about the size and shape of cells?

B. IF YOU HAVE THE SHAPE, YOU HAVE THE JOB

Hundreds of years ago, knights wore suits of metal armor to protect them. Plants and animals also need protection. The armor of plants and animals is not metal. This special armor is made of covering cells. Let's look at some of these cells.

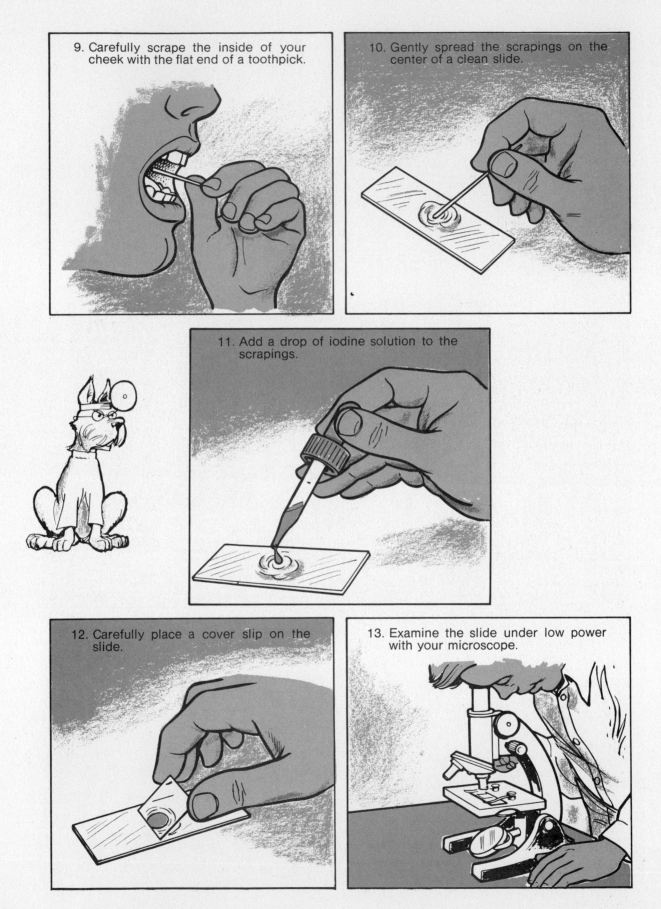

9. Carefully scrape the inside of your cheek with the flat end of a toothpick.

10. Gently spread the scrapings on the center of a clean slide.

11. Add a drop of iodine solution to the scrapings.

12. Carefully place a cover slip on the slide.

13. Examine the slide under low power with your microscope.

14. Examine the cells under high power.

15. In Space **a** on your data sheet, draw what you see.

• 16. What is the shape of the cells?

• 17. How large is the space between the cells?

• 18. Re-read questions 16 and 17. Why are the shapes of the cells good for protection?

C. IS THIS SCIENCE OR COOKING?

You're doing great. Let's look at some onion cells. Let's see how these compare with the protecting cells from inside your cheek.

• 19. Can you predict how these cells might look?

• 20. Why did you make this prediction?

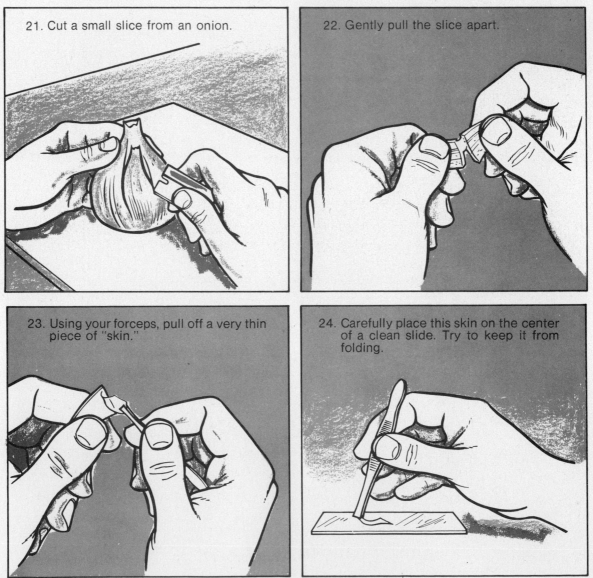

21. Cut a small slice from an onion.

22. Gently pull the slice apart.

23. Using your forceps, pull off a very thin piece of "skin."

24. Carefully place this skin on the center of a clean slide. Try to keep it from folding.

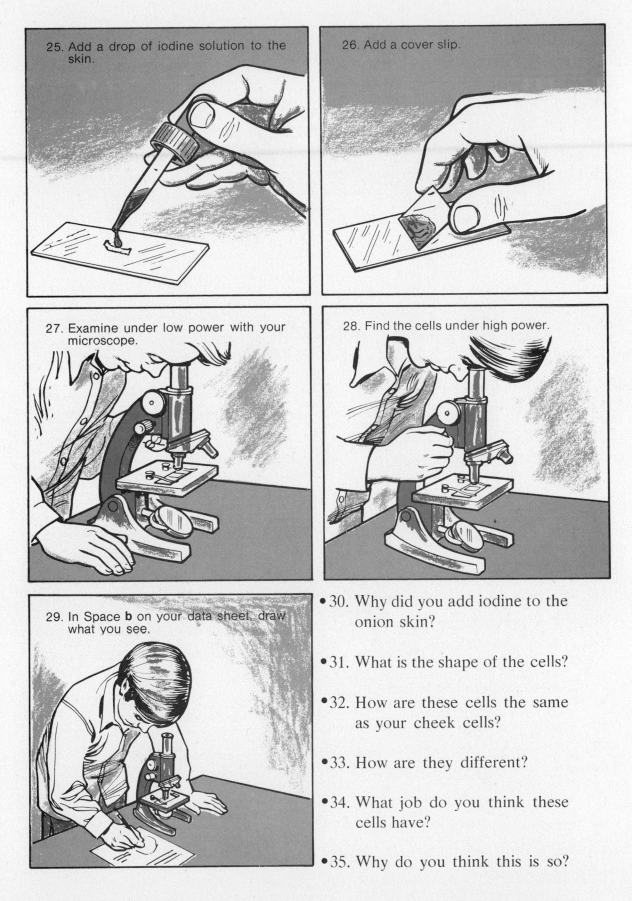

25. Add a drop of iodine solution to the skin.

26. Add a cover slip.

27. Examine under low power with your microscope.

28. Find the cells under high power.

29. In Space **b** on your data sheet, draw what you see.

• 30. Why did you add iodine to the onion skin?

• 31. What is the shape of the cells?

• 32. How are these cells the same as your cheek cells?

• 33. How are they different?

• 34. What job do you think these cells have?

• 35. Why do you think this is so?

D. DO YOU GET THE MESSAGE?

You have seen that plant and animal cells have different shapes. Why is this so? To find the answer, let's put together what we've learned.

Telephone wires carry messages. These messages can travel from your home to your friends' homes. Other wires can carry messages from city to city or state to state.

• 36. What is the shape of the wire?

• 37. Why do you think the wires are made this way?

This is a picture of two nerve cells. Nerve cells are like telephone wires. They carry messages from one part of the body to another.

• 38. What shape does the nerve cell have?

• 39. Why do you think this is a good shape?

• 40. Your skin is made of the same kind of cells as the inside of your cheek. Why is this important?

• 41. Re-read your last three answers. What does the shape of a cell have to do with its job?

THE CONCEPT.

Idea 3 Investigation 4

THIS IS WHERE IT'S AT

In the last Investigation you learned that:
    The shape of a cell is related to its job.

So far we have learned two important things about cells.
    (a) Cells have special shapes.
    (b) Cells have special jobs.

What about these jobs we've been talking about? We know that cells are living things. Do they eat, drink, and breathe? If so, how do cells do these things? Where is it all at?

A. NOT ONIONS AGAIN

1. Make a slide of onion cells. You did this in the last Investigation.

HERE WE GO AGAIN!

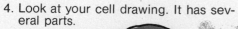

2. Examine the cells carefully.

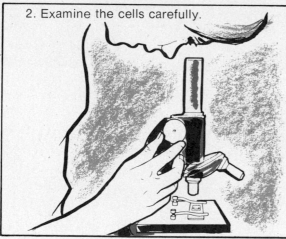

3. In Space **a** on your data sheet, draw one of the cells.

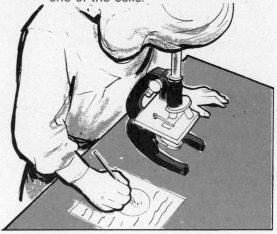

4. Look at your cell drawing. It has several parts.

The outside covering is called the *cell wall.* Only plant cells have cell walls. They protect the cells and help them keep their shape.

5. Label the cell wall on your drawing.

• 6. Where is the cell wall found?

• 7. What is the job of the cell wall?

• 8. Why is the job of the cell wall important?

Inside the cell wall is a thin covering called the *cell membrane*. The job of the cell membrane is to allow food and oxygen to come into the cell. It also allows waste materials to leave the cell.

9. Label the cell membrane on your drawing.

The dark, round part inside the cell is called the *nucleus*. The nucleus controls everything that goes on inside the cell.

Scientists have learned that if the cell nucleus is removed, the cell soon dies.

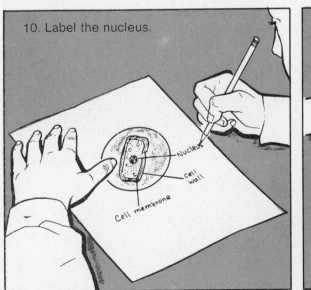

10. Label the nucleus.

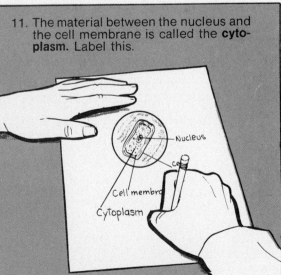

11. The material between the nucleus and the cell membrane is called the **cytoplasm.** Label this.

The "happenings" of the cell take place in the cytoplasm. By "happenings" we mean everything that keeps the cell alive.

• 12. List the parts of the cell just studied. See if you can list their jobs also.

B. WHAT'S IN THE FISH TANK?

Do you have a fish tank at home? Do you have any water plants growing in it? Elodea is a common water plant. You used it in Idea 1. What else can you learn from this plant?

Chuck Druss/Crystal Aquarium

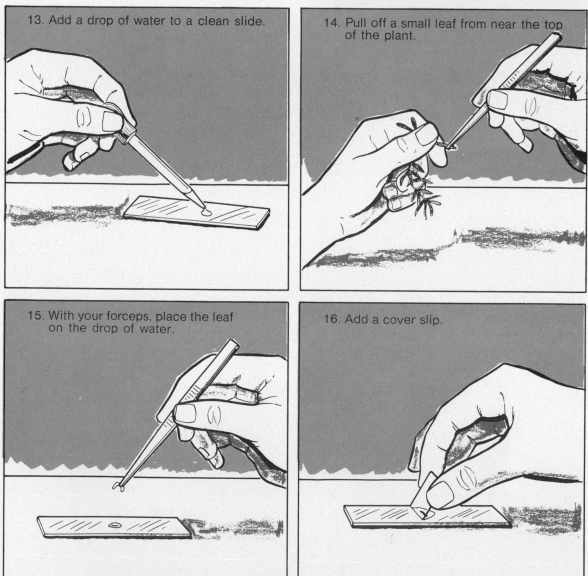

13. Add a drop of water to a clean slide.

14. Pull off a small leaf from near the top of the plant.

15. With your forceps, place the leaf on the drop of water.

16. Add a cover slip.

17. Examine the cells under low power.

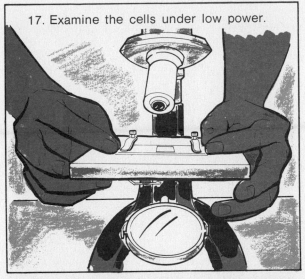

18. In Space **b** on your data sheet, draw one of the cells.

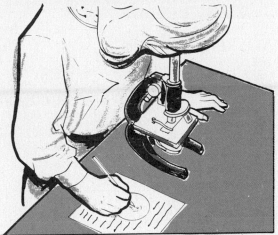

19. Label the nucleus and cytoplasm. Also label the cell wall and cell membrane.

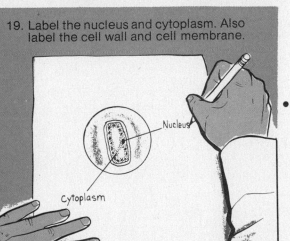

Nucleus

Cytoplasm

• 20. What parts of this cell can you name?

The small green dots are called *chloroplasts*. These are small sacs that contain *chlorophyll*.

WHAT'S CHLOROPHYLL?

DOESN'T IT MAKE YOUR BREATH SMELL NICE?

PLANTS DON'T USE IT THAT WAY!

THAT'S RIGHT! PLANTS USE IT TO MAKE FOOD!

HOW ABOUT THAT!

21. Label the chloroplasts on your drawing.

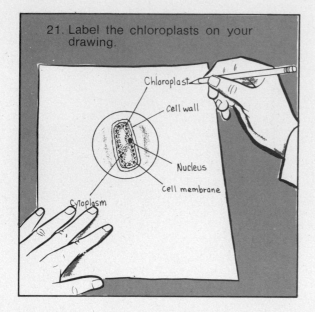

22. Try to find a **vacuole.** These are small, clear spaces in the cytoplasm. They are used for storage.

• 23. How is this cell like the onion cell?

• 24. How is this cell different from the onion cell?

C. NO MORE NAMES, I HOPE

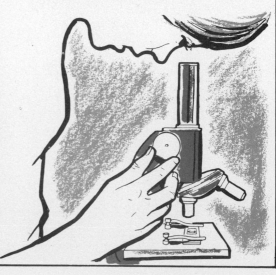

25. Make a fresh slide of Elodea.

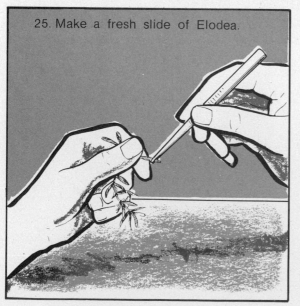

26. Examine under low power.

27. Add a drop of salt water to one edge of the cover slip.

28. Touch the opposite edge of the cover slip with a piece of paper towel.

29. Look carefully at the cell wall and cell membrane.

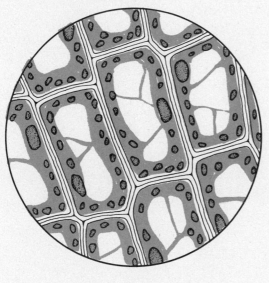

30. Turn to page 102 and read about the cell wall.

• 31. What happened to the cell when you added salt water?

• 32. How do you think this happened?

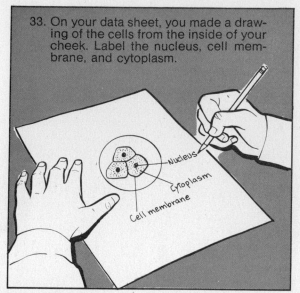

33. On your data sheet, you made a drawing of the cells from the inside of your cheek. Label the nucleus, cell membrane, and cytoplasm.

Look at your drawing of the Elodea cell.

• 34. How are the Elodea cells and the cheek cells the same?

• 35. How are they different? List as many differences as you can.

D. IT ALL HAPPENS HERE

You have seen that plant and animal cells have three important parts.

• 36. What is the job of the nucleus?

• 37. What happens in the cytoplasm?

• 38. What is the job of the cell membrane?

• 39. Where do the cell activities take place?

THE CONCEPT.

THE WONDERFUL WORLD OF THE CELL

You have studied cells just as scientists do. You have looked at plant and animal cells. You have learned that these cells are alike in some ways and different in others.

In the last Investigation, you learned that the cell membrane allows food, water, and oxygen to get into the cell. This is so important that the life of the cell depends upon it. Materials are always moving into and out of the cell.

Don't take our word for it; try it yourself.

A. PASS THE SALT

Your teacher will give you two labeled test tubes. Tube **A** contains Elodea and pond water. Tube **B** contains Elodea and salt water.

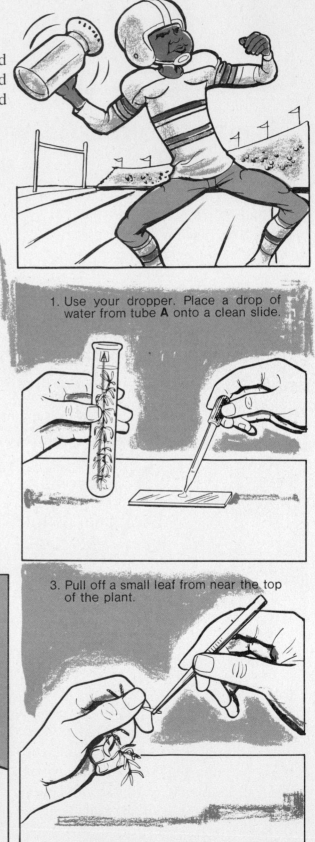

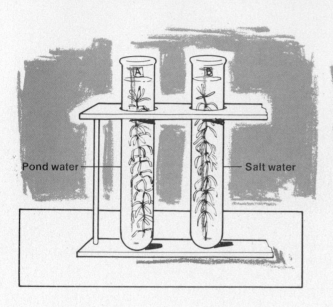

Pond water — Salt water

1. Use your dropper. Place a drop of water from tube **A** onto a clean slide.

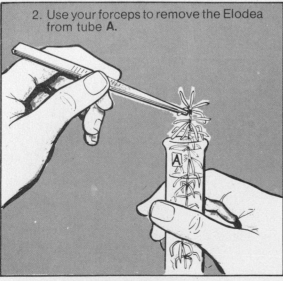

2. Use your forceps to remove the Elodea from tube **A**.

3. Pull off a small leaf from near the top of the plant.

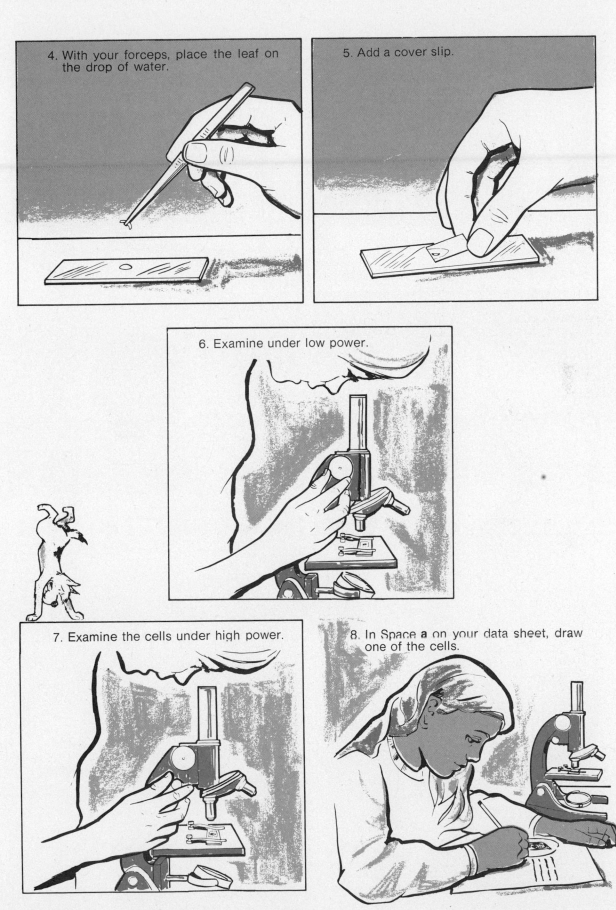

4. With your forceps, place the leaf on the drop of water.

5. Add a cover slip.

6. Examine under low power.

7. Examine the cells under high power.

8. In Space **a** on your data sheet, draw one of the cells.

9. Label the nucleus.

10. Label the cell membrane.

11. Label the vacuole.

12. Study your drawing carefully.

•13. Describe the shape of the cell.

•14. What does the vacuole look like?

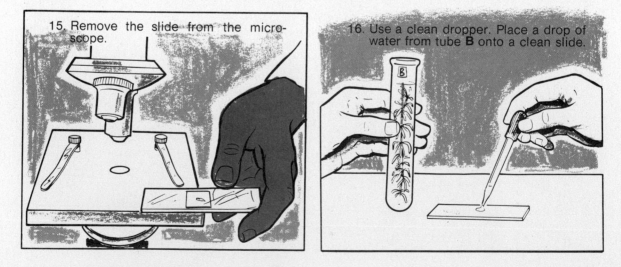

15. Remove the slide from the micro-scope.

16. Use a clean dropper. Place a drop of water from tube **B** onto a clean slide.

17. Remove the Elodea from tube **B**.

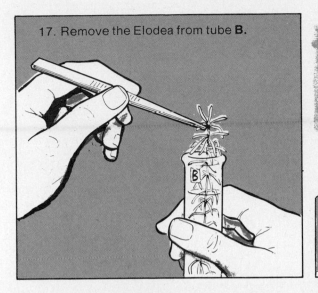

18. Pull off a small leaf from near the top of the plant.

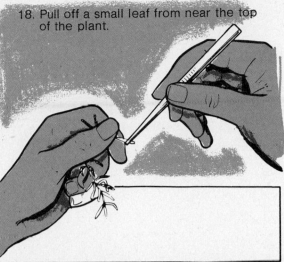

19. Place the leaf on the drop of water.

20. Add a cover slip.

21. Examine the cells under low power.

22. Examine the cells under high power.

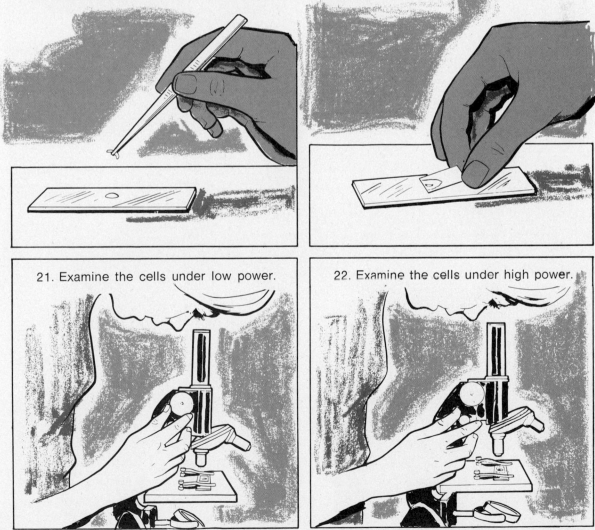

23. In Space **b** on your data sheet, draw one of the cells.

• 24. Describe the shape of the cell.

• 25. What does the vacuole look like?

• 26. How are these cells different from those from tube **A**?

• 27. What do you think caused this change?

• 28. How do you know that something moved through the cell membrane?

• 29. Materials can move through the cell membrane. Why is this important?

FAT CELLS! THIN CELLS! HOW DOES IT ALL HAPPEN?

IF THERE'S A WAY IN, THERE'S A WAY OUT!

That's right, Phideau. There are other ways to get in and out of cells.

B. GOING INTO A CELL

When salt dissolves in water, the salt particles become very tiny. These particles are called *molecules.* You can taste the salt, but you cannot see it. Many substances that dissolve in water can move into and out of cells. In this way, cells are able to take in what they need. These materials are changed and used by the cell.

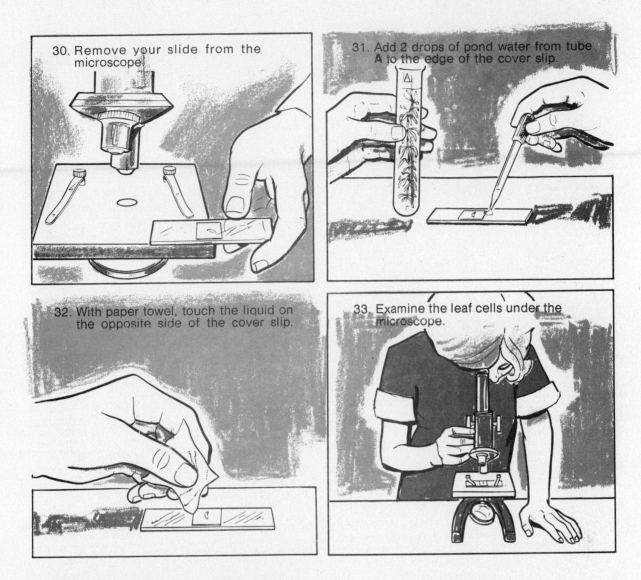

30. Remove your slide from the microscope.

31. Add 2 drops of pond water from tube **A** to the edge of the cover slip.

32. With paper towel, touch the liquid on the opposite side of the cover slip.

33. Examine the leaf cells under the microscope.

•34. Describe the shape of the cells.

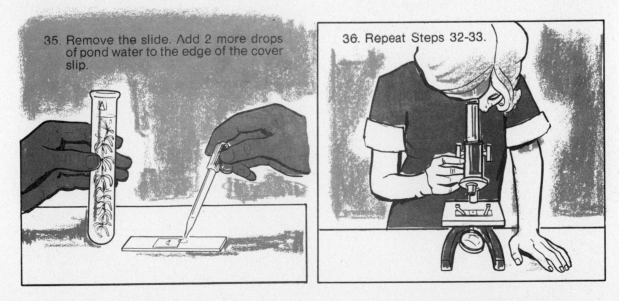

35. Remove the slide. Add 2 more drops of pond water to the edge of the cover slip.

36. Repeat Steps 32-33.

• 37. What has happened to the cell?

• 38. What do you think caused this change?

C. THE KEY TO IT ALL

• 39. How do materials enter the cell?

• 40. Why must materials dissolve before they can enter the cell?

• 41. Why must materials be able to pass into and out of the cell?

• 42. Why is this important?

• 43. What does the life of a cell depend upon?

Re-read your answers to questions 41 and 43. Write the concept.

THE CONCEPT.

Idea 3 Investigation 6

YOU CAN'T BLOW YOUR NOSE WITH THIS TISSUE

In the last two Investigations you learned that:
(a) Cells have special parts.
(b) Each cell part has a special job.
(c) Dissolved materials can enter and leave the cell.

Using dissolved materials, all of the cell parts work together to help keep the cell alive. In many-celled animals, groups of cells work together to do a job.

A. PUTTING CELLS TOGETHER

Have you ever done a jigsaw puzzle? If you have, you know that many of the pieces look alike. We can use a jigsaw puzzle to help us learn about cells and groups of cells that look alike.

Your teacher will give you a sheet of paper containing puzzle pieces.

1. Carefully cut out the puzzle pieces.

2. In your data book, put the puzzle pieces inside the outline.

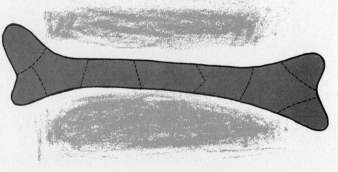

3. When you finish your puzzle, study it.

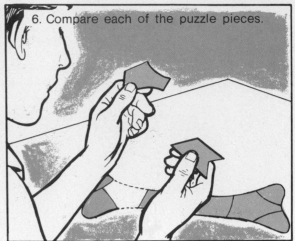

6. Compare each of the puzzle pieces.

• 4. What does your puzzle look like?

• 5. What do each of the puzzle pieces look like?

• 7. What do you notice?

• 8. What is the bone made of?

Besides working to stay alive, bone cells also have special jobs. Bone cells work together to protect soft parts of the body. They also work together with muscles to help you move. Groups of cells that look alike and work together to do a special job are called *tissues*.

Skin tissue, nerve tissue, muscle tissue, and blood are examples of body tissues. Each of these tissues has a special job. Look at the pictures.

Nerve Tissue

Carolina Biological Supply Co.

Skin Tissue

Muscle Tissue

Blood Tissue

• 9. What are each of the tissues made of?

•10. What do you notice about the cells in any one of the tissues?

•11. In your own words, explain what a tissue is.

B. THIS ORGAN DOESN'T PLAY MUSIC

Groups of different tissues work together to form *organs.* Examples of organs in plants are roots, stems, and leaves. Wings, fins, heart, and stomach are examples of animal organs.

The organs of your body have special jobs. The arms and legs are organs used for movement, protection, and getting food.

•12. Can you predict which tissues you might find in the arm?

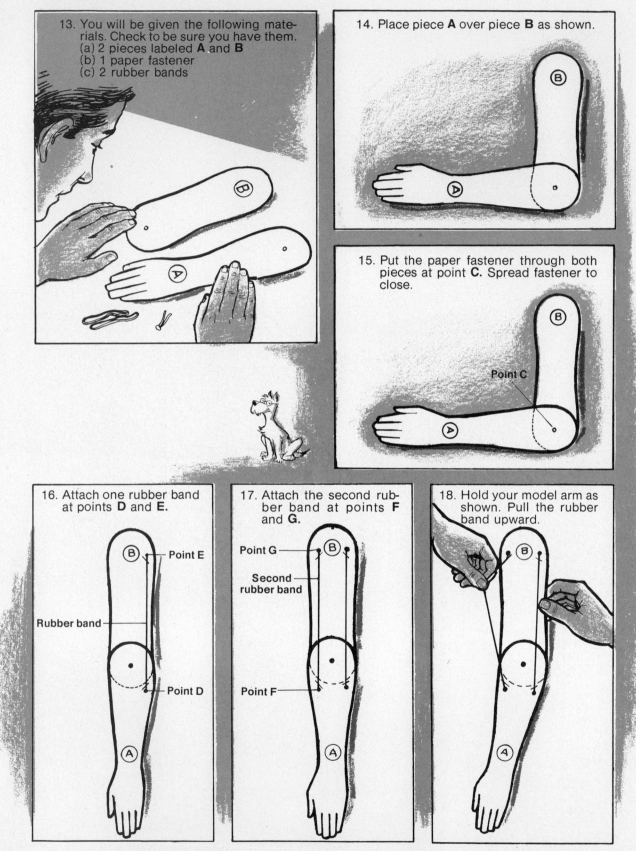

13. You will be given the following materials. Check to be sure you have them.
    (a) 2 pieces labeled **A** and **B**
    (b) 1 paper fastener
    (c) 2 rubber bands

14. Place piece **A** over piece **B** as shown.

15. Put the paper fastener through both pieces at point **C**. Spread fastener to close.

Point C

16. Attach one rubber band at points **D** and **E**.

Point E

Rubber band

Point D

17. Attach the second rubber band at points **F** and **G**.

Point G

Second rubber band

Point F

18. Hold your model arm as shown. Pull the rubber band upward.

Congratulations! You've made a working model of the arm.

•19. When you pull the rubber band, what happens?

•20. Which tissue causes movement?

•21. Which tissue does the rubber band represent?

•22. To which tissue is the rubber band attached?

•23. Which two tissues does your model contain?

•24. Look at the tissues on page 118. Which of these tissues are also found in the arm?

•25. How do the tissues of your arm work together?

•26. What do we call groups of tissues that work together to do a job?

•27. What is an organ?

C. ALL SYSTEMS GO!

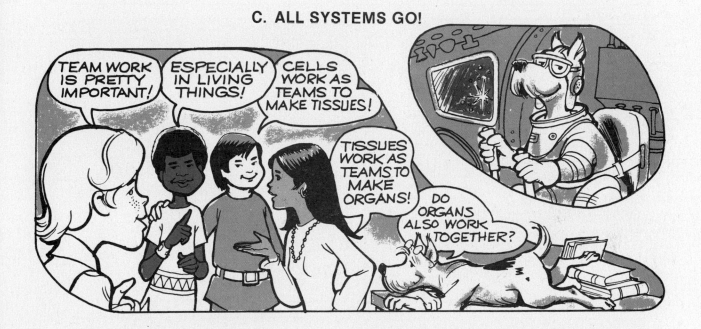

They sure do, Phideau! Groups of organs work together to form *organ systems*. Each system has a special job. Working together, the organ systems of living things keep them alive.

We can make a word puzzle to put together what we've learned.

Your teacher will give you an envelope containing cards with words and arrows on them.

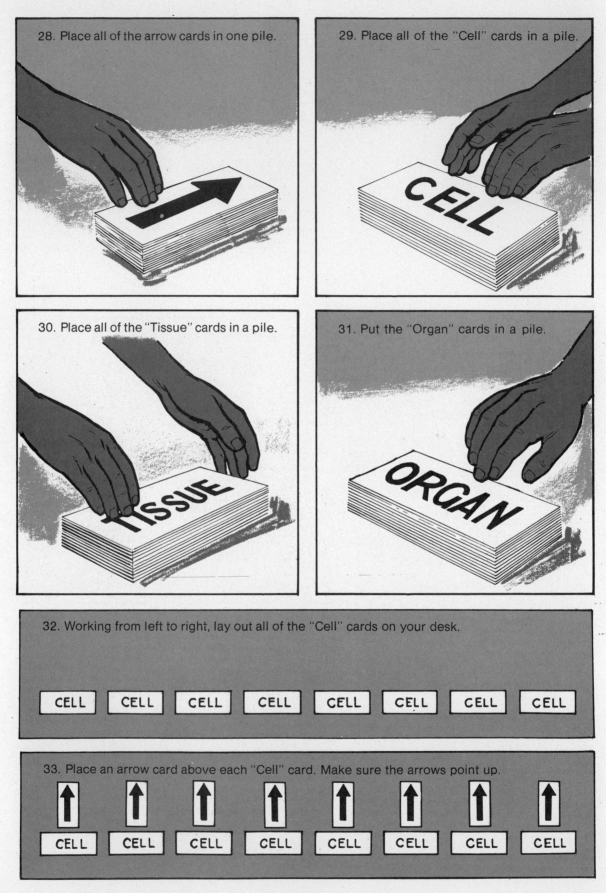

28. Place all of the arrow cards in one pile.

29. Place all of the "Cell" cards in a pile.

30. Place all of the "Tissue" cards in a pile.

31. Put the "Organ" cards in a pile.

32. Working from left to right, lay out all of the "Cell" cards on your desk.

CELL CELL CELL CELL CELL CELL CELL CELL

33. Place an arrow card above each "Cell" card. Make sure the arrows point up.

CELL CELL CELL CELL CELL CELL CELL CELL

34. Place a "Tissue" card above each arrow card.

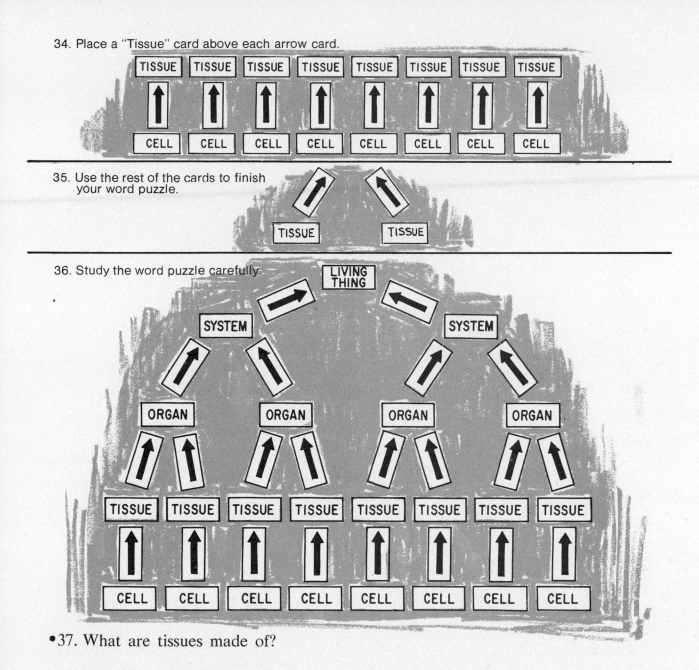

35. Use the rest of the cards to finish your word puzzle.

36. Study the word puzzle carefully.

•37. What are tissues made of?

•38. What do we call groups of cells that work together to do a job?

•39. What are organs made of?

•40. What do we call groups of tissues that work together to do a job?

•41. What are systems made of?

•42. What do we call groups of organs that work together to do a job?

Re-read your answers to questions 37-42. Look at the word puzzle again.

THE CONCEPT.

WE ALL SHARE IT

Right on! Another Idea completed. This Idea was about what living things are made of. What are living things made of?

To find out what living things are made of, you did six Investigations. You learned that:

(a) The microscope is a tool used to magnify small objects.
(b) The microscope is a tool used to study cells.
(c) The shape of a cell is related to its job.
(d) The life activities of a cell take place within the cytoplasm.
(e) The life of a cell depends upon the ability of dissolved materials to enter and leave the cell.
(f) Cells are organized into tissues, tissues into organs, and organs into systems.

Robert Hooke was one of the first men to study plants under the microscope. You studied cork under the microscope.

•43. What did Robert Hooke call the tiny boxes in cork?

We still use this name today. For over 300 years, scientists have used the microscope to study cells.

•44. What have scientists learned that plants are made of?

Leeuwenhoek was one of the first men to study tiny animals under the microscope.

•45. What are animals made of?

Re-read questions 44 and 45.

•46. What are all living things made of?

Write the Idea Summary.

THE IDEA.

Idea 4 Investigation 1

THE ROOT OF THE PROBLEM

In Idea 2 you learned that living things need water. Animals get water when they drink. They also get water in the foods they eat. Plants are living things. How do they get water?

A. ROOTS DON'T BLUSH

Your teacher will give you some seedlings. The roots of these seedlings have been placed in water containing a red dye.

1. Examine the root with a magnifying glass.

• 2. What do you notice about the root?

• 3. How do you think the root became colored?

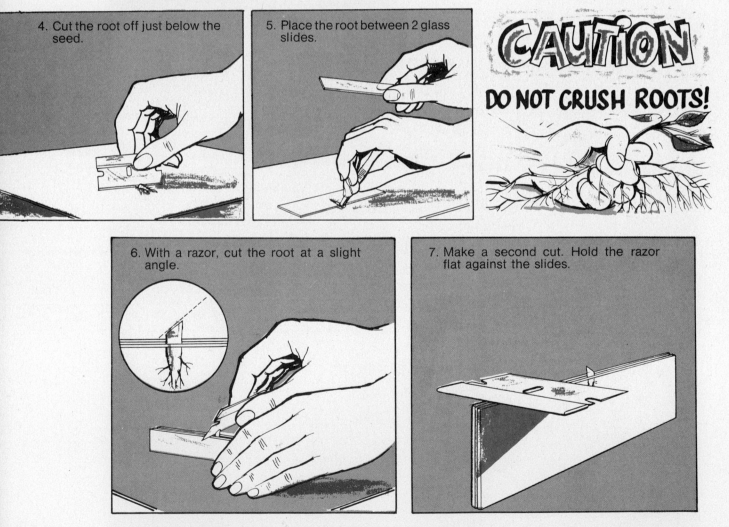

4. Cut the root off just below the seed.

5. Place the root between 2 glass slides.

CAUTION

DO NOT CRUSH ROOTS!

6. With a razor, cut the root at a slight angle.

7. Make a second cut. Hold the razor flat against the slides.

You may have to practice Steps 6 and 7 several times. You need a slice thin enough to examine under the microscope.

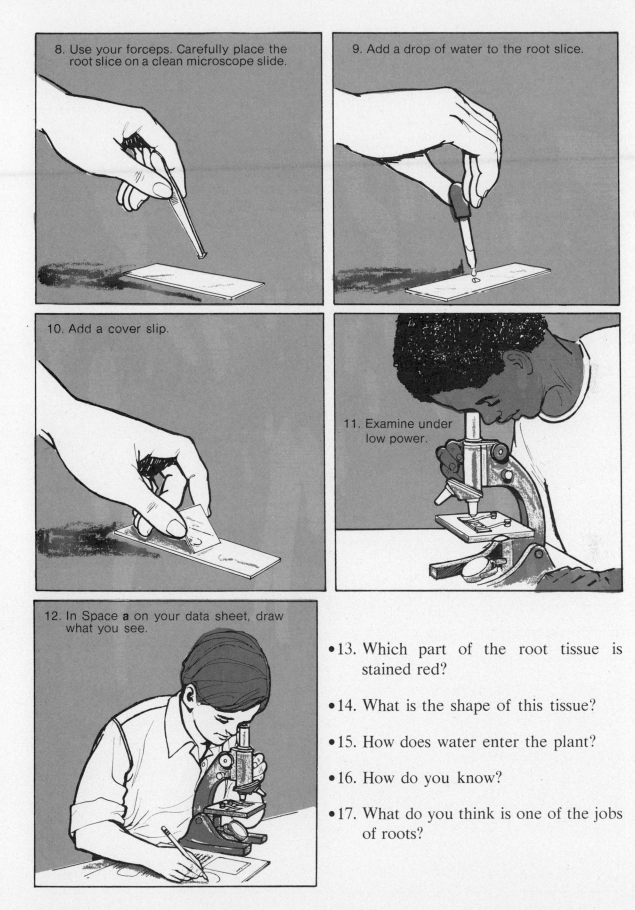

8. Use your forceps. Carefully place the root slice on a clean microscope slide.

9. Add a drop of water to the root slice.

10. Add a cover slip.

11. Examine under low power.

12. In Space **a** on your data sheet, draw what you see.

• 13. Which part of the root tissue is stained red?

• 14. What is the shape of this tissue?

• 15. How does water enter the plant?

• 16. How do you know?

• 17. What do you think is one of the jobs of roots?

B. IS IT MEASLES?

You don't have to be a doctor to know that celery can't get measles. But how can you explain red spots on celery?

MAYBE IT'S FRECKLES!

ARE YOU FOR REAL?

WHAT CAN THE RED SPOTS BE?

DIDN'T THE SAME THING HAPPEN TO THE ROOT?

18. Stand a celery stem in a beaker of water containing red dye.

19. After several minutes, remove the celery from the beaker.

20. Cut the celery about 1 cm from the bottom.

21. Examine the parts of the stem which are colored red.

22. In Space **b** on your data sheet, draw what you see

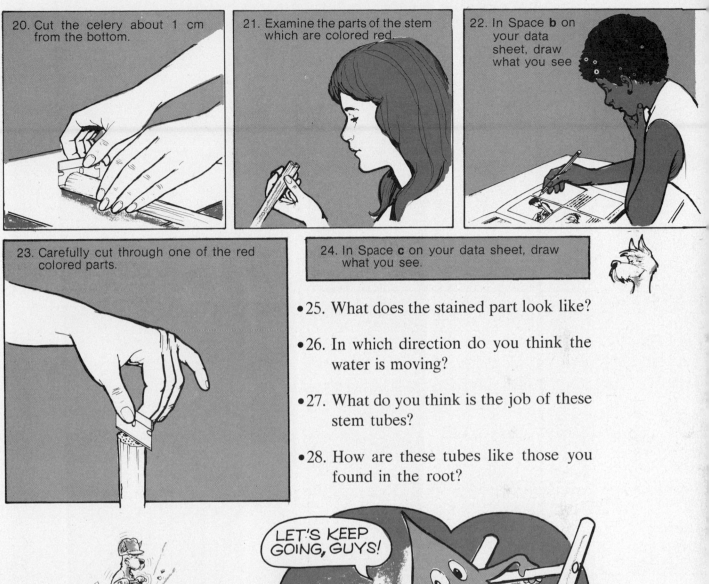

23. Carefully cut through one of the red colored parts.

24. In Space **c** on your data sheet, draw what you see.

- 25. What does the stained part look like?

- 26. In which direction do you think the water is moving?

- 27. What do you think is the job of these stem tubes?

- 28. How are these tubes like those you found in the root?

C. STILL GOING STRONG

LET'S KEEP GOING, GUYS!

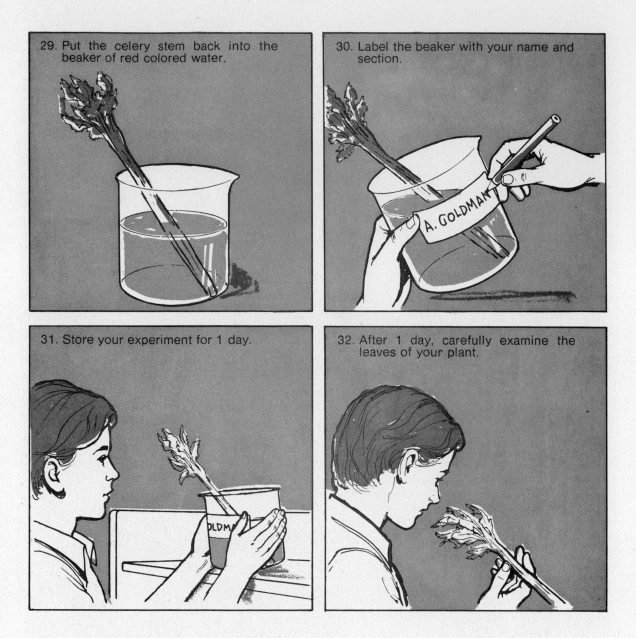

29. Put the celery stem back into the beaker of red colored water.

30. Label the beaker with your name and section.

31. Store your experiment for 1 day.

32. After 1 day, carefully examine the leaves of your plant.

• 33. What happened to the leaves?

• 34. Where did the water come from?

• 35. How does water reach the stems and leaves of plants?

• 36. What part of the plant takes in water?

Re-read your answers to questions 35 and 36. Write the concept.

THE CONCEPT.

Idea 4 Investigation 2

LOOK MA, NO TEETH

You have learned that plants need water. In the last Investigation, you learned that plants take in water through their roots. Water is very important to plants, but plants also need other materials.

Our friends are asking some good questions. In this Investigation, you will try to find the answers to these questions.

A. COLOR ME YELLOW

Bromthymol blue is used to test for carbon dioxide. If this gas is present, the liquid changes from blue to yellow. The new liquid is called *bromthymol yellow*. Bromthymol yellow changes back to blue when carbon dioxide is removed.

1. Get 2 test tubes. Label them with your name and section.

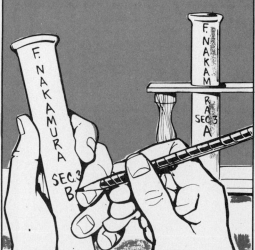

2. Label one test tube **A**. Label the other test tube **B**.

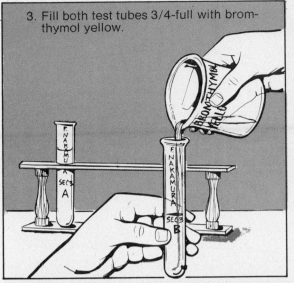

3. Fill both test tubes 3/4-full with brom-thymol yellow.

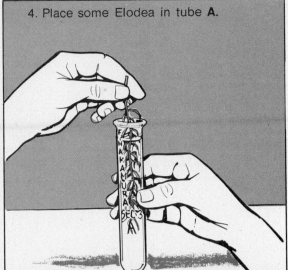

4. Place some Elodea in tube **A**.

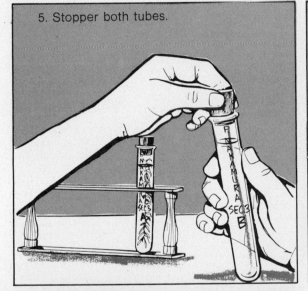

5. Stopper both tubes.

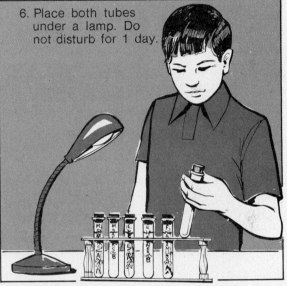

6. Place both tubes under a lamp. Do not disturb for 1 day.

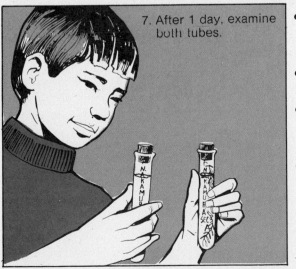

7. After 1 day, examine both tubes.

• 8. What color change took place in the tube marked **A**?

• 9. What does this show?

• 10. What do you think caused this change?

• 11. What happened in tube **B**?

• 12. What does this show?

• 13. How can you explain this?

• 14. What does bromthymol yellow contain? (*Hint:* Look at the last cartoon.)

• 15. What did the plant remove from tube **A**?

B. NO TEETH, NO CAVITIES

Your teacher will give you a plant leaf.

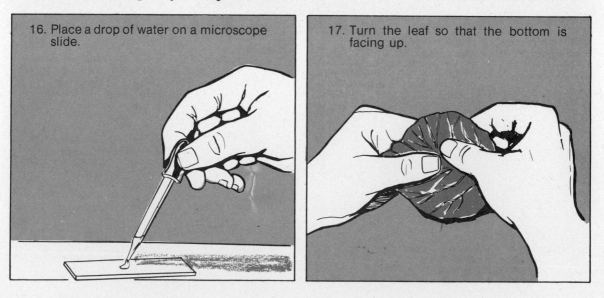

16. Place a drop of water on a microscope slide.

17. Turn the leaf so that the bottom is facing up.

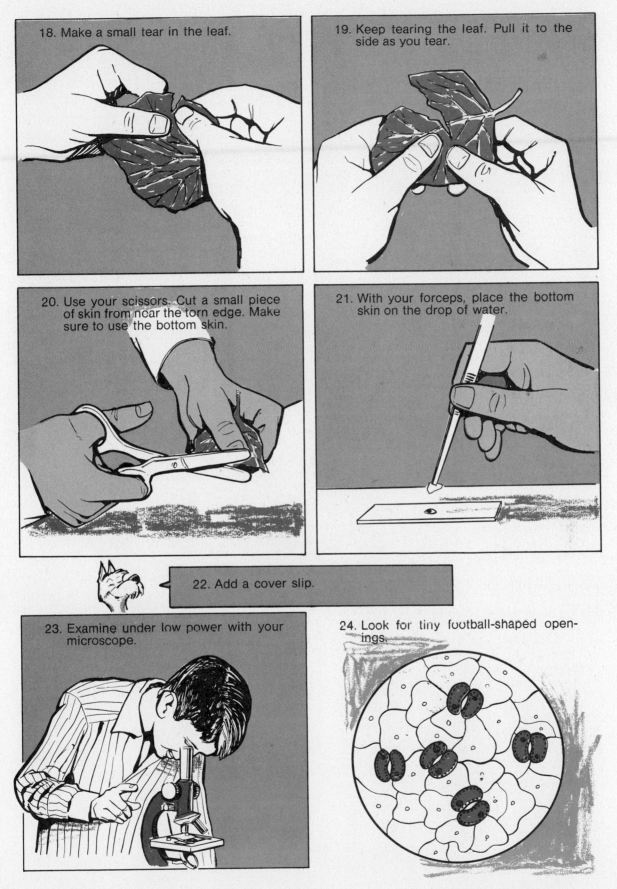

18. Make a small tear in the leaf.

19. Keep tearing the leaf. Pull it to the side as you tear.

20. Use your scissors. Cut a small piece of skin from near the torn edge. Make sure to use the bottom skin.

21. With your forceps, place the bottom skin on the drop of water.

22. Add a cover slip.

23. Examine under low power with your microscope.

24. Look for tiny football-shaped openings.

25. In Space **a** on your data sheet, draw what you see.

Scientists call these tiny openings *stomates*. Stomate means "little mouth." Of course these mouths have no teeth. That's what Phideau's uptight about.

• 26. How many stomates can you count?

• 27. Are the stomates bunched up or spread out over the leaf?

• 28. What job do you think the stomates have?

Let's test your prediction.

C. THAT'S A MOUTH-FULL

Your teacher will give you 2 seedlings.

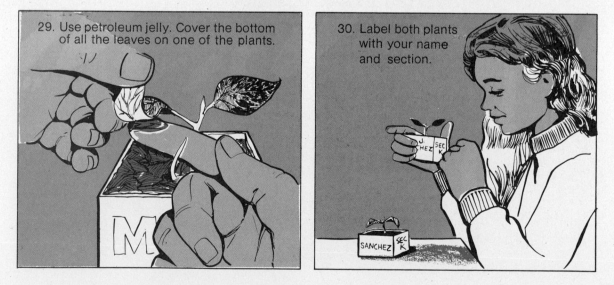

29. Use petroleum jelly. Cover the bottom of all the leaves on one of the plants.

30. Label both plants with your name and section.

31. Place both plants under a lamp. Do not disturb for 1 day.

32. After 1 day, compare the leaves of the 2 plants.

- 33. Describe the plant leaves that were not covered.

- 34. Describe the plant leaves that were covered with petroleum jelly.

- 35. On what part of the leaf were stomates found?

- 36. What did the petroleum jelly do?

- 37. What happened to the leaves?

- 38. What gas do the plants take in?

- 39. How does this gas enter the plant?

Re-read your answers to questions 38 and 39. Write the concept.

THE CONCEPT.

THE WILDEST RECIPE OF ALL

Let's put together what you've learned. In Investigation 1, you learned that plants take in water. In the last Investigation, you learned that plants take in carbon dioxide. Water and carbon dioxide are *raw materials*. They are taken in and used by plants. Plants use these raw materials to make food.

Phideau looks pretty upset, doesn't he? Something is on his mind. He's trying to solve a problem. Scientists have been trying to solve the same problem for many years.

Scientists are still trying to learn how green plants make food. They have learned that food-making takes place in the leaves of green plants. How this happens is still partly a mystery.

Food-making in green plants is called *photosynthesis*.

A. DID YOU STARCH MY COLLAR?

Sugar and starch are the foods that green plants make. These foods are made of carbon, hydrogen, and oxygen. They are called *carbohydrates*. During photosynthesis, plants make sugar. The sugar is then changed to starch and stored by the plant.

1. Place a few drops of water in a Petri dish.

2. Add enough starch to the water to make a paste.

Idea 4/Investigation 3   **139**

3. Mix the starch paste.

4. Add a few drops of iodine solution to the starch paste.

•5. What color is the starch alone?

•6. What color is the iodine solution alone?

•7. What color change takes place when the iodine is added to starch?

Iodine is used to test for starch. If iodine is mixed with starch, a blue-black color always results.

8. Add several drops of iodine to a sugar cube.

• 9. Describe what happens.

•10. What does this show?

11. Add several drops of iodine to a slice of potato.

•12. Describe what happens.

•13. What does this show?

B. I'M IN THE MOOD FOR FOOD

Your teacher will give you a plant leaf.

14. Crush the leaf in your hand.

15. With your forceps, place the leaf in a beaker of boiling water.

16. Boil the water for several minutes.

17. Shut off the flame.

18. Fill a test tube 1/2-full with alcohol.

CAUTION

ALCOHOL BURNS AND MUST NEVER BE USED NEAR AN OPEN FLAME!

19. Use your forceps. Place the leaf from the water into the alcohol.

20. Use your test tube holder. Put the test tube into the beaker of hot water.

21. Light your burner.

22. Heat your experiment for 5 minutes.

23. Shut off the flame.

24. Use your test tube holder to remove the test tube.

25. With your forceps, remove the leaf from the test tube.

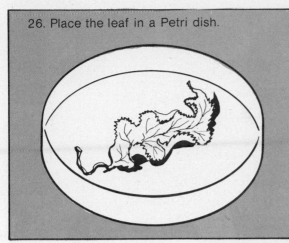
26. Place the leaf in a Petri dish.

• 27. What color change took place in the leaf?

• 28. What color change took place in the alcohol?

Congratulations! You've done a great job. You have removed the chlorophyll from the leaf. Now that the leaf is almost clear, you will be able to test for starch. With the chlorophyll taken out, your results will be easier to see.

C. NO STARCH, PLEASE.

JUST CLEAN 'EM! NO STARCH, PLEASE!

24 HOUR SERVICE

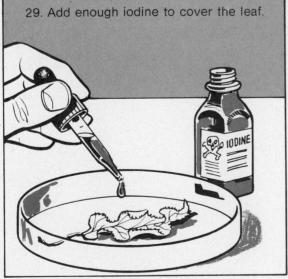
29. Add enough iodine to cover the leaf.

IODINE

• 30. What color change takes place?

• 31. What does this show?

• 32. What do we call food-making in green plants?

• 33. What raw materials does a plant need for photosynthesis?

• 34. What does a plant make from raw materials during photosynthesis?

Re-read your answers to questions 33 and 34.

THE CONCEPT.

Idea 4 Investigation 4

GREEN POWER

Carbon dioxide and water are important raw materials for food-making. They are like the nuts and bolts in the food factory. What about the tools used by plants? What does the plant use to put raw materials together?

A. THE MOD LEAF

In Idea 3, you studied the water plant, Elodea. You learned that the plant contains chlorophyll. Chlorophyll is important for photosynthesis. It is found in all green plants. Let's see if we can find out how important chlorophyll really is.

• 1. What is the name of the green material found in plants?

2. Get a leaf from your teacher.

3. Examine the leaf carefully.

•4. What do you notice about the leaf?

5. In Space **a** on your data sheet, make a drawing of the leaf.

6. Look at the green part of the leaf. Shade in this part on your drawing.

space **a**

6. ✓

•7. What material gives the leaf its green color?

•8. How do you know that chlorophyll is not all through the leaf?

•9. In which part of the leaf do you predict food is made?

Let's test your prediction.

B. GREEN ALCOHOL

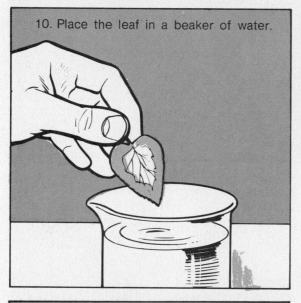

10. Place the leaf in a beaker of water.

11. Boil for 5 minutes.

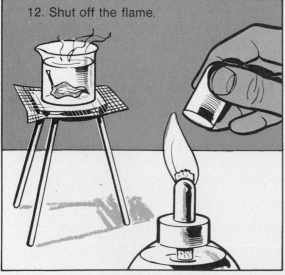

12. Shut off the flame.

CAUTION
ALCOHOL BURNS AND MUST NEVER BE USED NEAR AN OPEN FLAME!

13. Fill a test tube 1/2-full with alcohol.

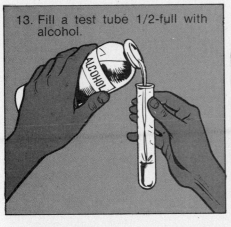

14. Use your forceps. Place your leaf into the test tube.

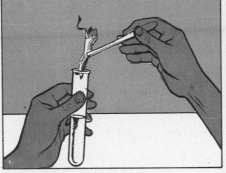

15. Use your test tube holder. Place the test tube in the beaker of hot water.

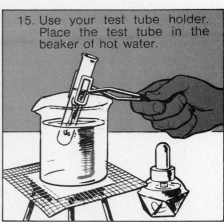

16. Heat your experiment for 5 minutes.

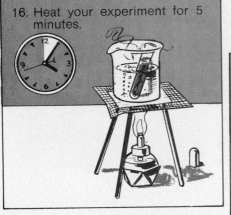

17. Shut off the flame.

18. Remove the leaf with your forceps.

19. Rinse the leaf in water.

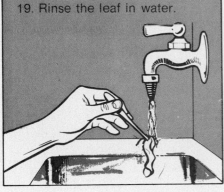

20. Gently blot the leaf with paper towels.

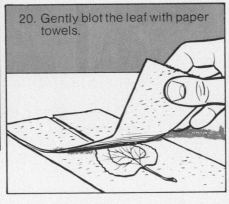

21. Place the leaf in a Petri dish.

•22. What color change took place in the alcohol?

•23. What color change took place in the leaf?

•24. What material did you remove from the leaf?

C. IODINE ISN'T ONLY FOR CUTS

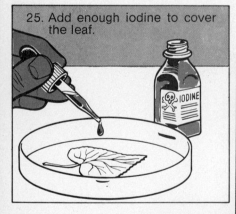

25. Add enough iodine to cover the leaf.

26. After 5 minutes, rinse the leaf in water.

27. Hold the leaf up to the light.

•28. Describe the leaf.

•29. What part of the leaf turned blue-black?

•30. What part of the leaf did not turn blue-black?

D. BACK TO THE DRAWING BOARD

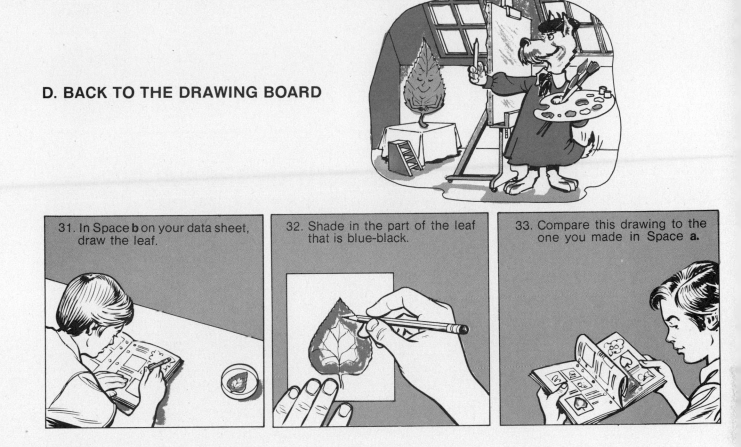

31. In Space **b** on your data sheet, draw the leaf.

32. Shade in the part of the leaf that is blue-black.

33. Compare this drawing to the one you made in Space **a.**

• 34. In Part A of this Investigation, you were given a leaf. What part of the leaf was green?

• 35. What did this part of the leaf contain?

• 36. What color is this part of the leaf now?

• 37. What is iodine used to test for?

• 38. What material is present in the part of the leaf that was green?

• 39. What do you think is the job of chlorophyll in green plants?

• 40. What part of the leaf did not contain chlorophyll?

• 41. What happened to this part of the leaf when iodine was added?

• 42. What does this show?

• 43. What is the job of chlorophyll?

Re-read your answers to questions 39 and 43. Write the concept.

THE CONCEPT.

LET'S THROW SOME LIGHT ON THE SUBJECT

Grant Heilman

In the last two Investigations, you learned that:

(a) Plants change raw materials into food.
(b) Chlorophyll is needed for photosynthesis.

You have also learned that the leaf is the food factory in plants.

The tools and the parts are there. But what about the *energy* to make the tools work? That's what is bugging David. In this Investigation, you will try to find the answer to David's problem.

A. A CRUSHING EXPERIENCE

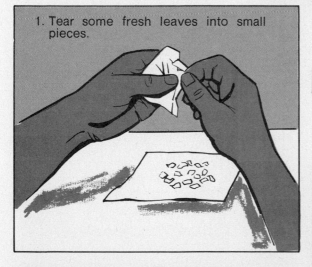

1. Tear some fresh leaves into small pieces.

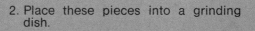

2. Place these pieces into a grinding dish.

3. Sprinkle a small amount of dry sand into the dish.

4. Pour in enough alcohol to cover the leaves.

5. Grind the leaves, alcohol, and sand.

• 6. What color change takes place in the alcohol?

• 7. What is being taken out of the leaves?

• 8. What is the job of the sand?

B. A CLEANER GREEN IS UP TO YOU

You are going to study chlorophyll. To do this, you will have to remove the sand and leaves.

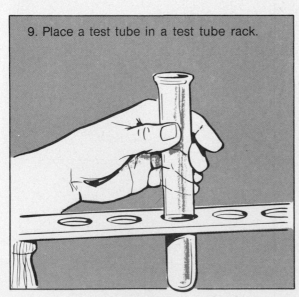
9. Place a test tube in a test tube rack.

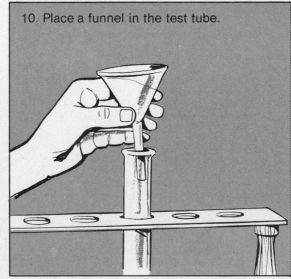
10. Place a funnel in the test tube.

Your teacher will show you how to use *filter paper*.
Filter paper has very small holes in it. It is like a
strainer.

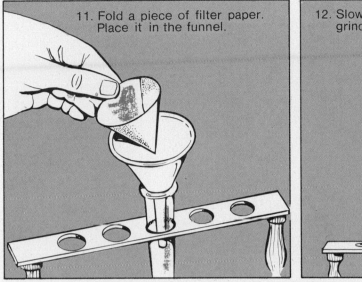

11. Fold a piece of filter paper. Place it in the funnel.

12. Slowly pour the material from the grinding dish into the filter paper.

- 13. What was trapped in the filter paper?

- 14. What color is the alcohol in the test tube?

- 15. What was taken out of the leaves?

- 16. What does the alcohol contain?

C. IT MUST BE MY EYES

17. Cut an 8-cm square from a piece of black construction paper.

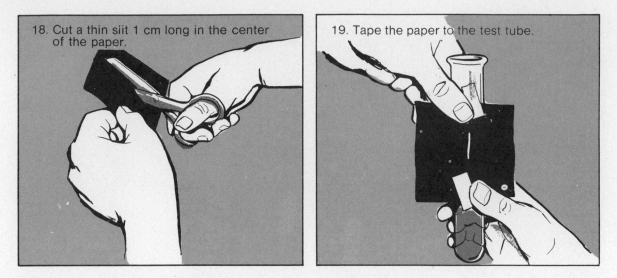

18. Cut a thin slit 1 cm long in the center of the paper.

19. Tape the paper to the test tube.

Make sure that the mixture of chlorophyll and alcohol can be seen through the slit.

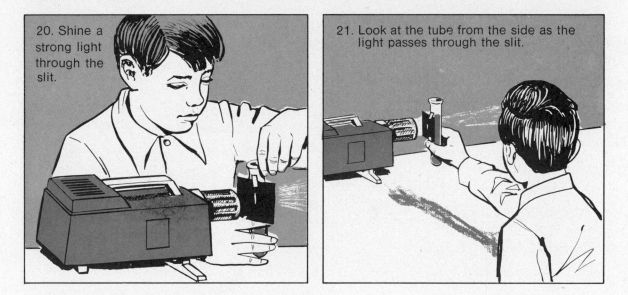

20. Shine a strong light through the slit.

21. Look at the tube from the side as the light passes through the slit.

•22. What color is the chlorophyll?

•23. What color was the chlorophyll before the light passed through it?

•24. What do you think made the chlorophyll give off another color?

•25. Light is a form of energy. What color light energy does the chlorophyll give off when the light hits it?

•26. How does light affect chlorophyll?

•27. When is the energy of the chlorophyll given off?

D. COVER ONE EYE, PLEASE

28. Cut a piece of black construction paper 5 cm long and 3 cm wide.

29. Write your name and section on the paper.

30. Fold the paper in half.

31. Use a paper clip to fasten the paper to a plant leaf. Do not remove the leaf from the plant.

Your teacher will place the plant under a strong light for 15 minutes.

32. After 15 minutes, remove your leaf from the plant.

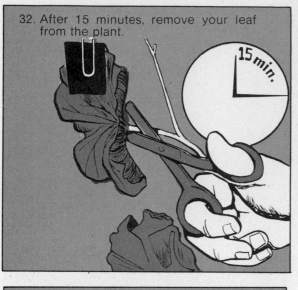

33. Remove the chlorophyll from the leaf. You did this in Part B of the last Investigation.

34. Place the leaf in a Petri dish. Test it for starch.

•35. What will you use to test for starch?

•36. What part of the leaf turns blue-black?

•37. What does this show?

•38. What part of the leaf did not change color?

•39. What part of the leaf did not make food?

•40. How can you explain this?

•41. What do plants need to make food?

•42. What kind of energy do plants need to make starch?

Re-read your answers to questions 27 and 42. Write the concept.

THE CONCEPT.

Idea 4 Investigation 6

THE BUSH THAT MADE IT

You've come a long way! You have learned that green plants do many things. You have seen that:

(a) Plant roots take in water.
(b) Plant leaves take in carbon dioxide.
(c) Plants use raw materials to make starch.
(d) Plants need chlorophyll to make starch.
(e) Plants need light energy to make starch.

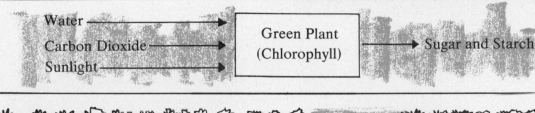

A. GOING UP

In Investigation 1, you learned that water moves through plants. Scientists are studying this water movement. They are trying to learn more about it. How does it happen?

Your teacher will give you a strip of cardboard, tape, a ruler, and some glass tubes.

WE DON'T GO TOO HIGH, BUT WE GO!

1. With your ruler, measure the lengths of the tubes.

2. Record your data in Table 1 on your data sheet.

• 3. What do you notice about the tube lengths?

4. Measure the opening in each of the tubes.

5. Record your data in Table 1.

• 6. What do you notice about the openings in each of the tubes?

• 7. How are the tubes the same?

• 8. How are the tubes different?

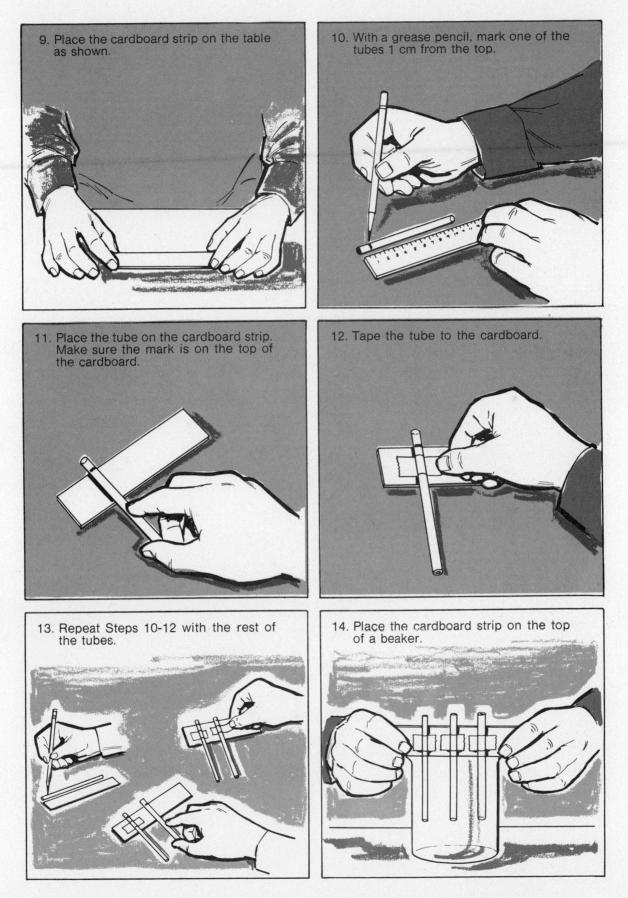

9. Place the cardboard strip on the table as shown.

10. With a grease pencil, mark one of the tubes 1 cm from the top.

11. Place the tube on the cardboard strip. Make sure the mark is on the top of the cardboard.

12. Tape the tube to the cardboard.

13. Repeat Steps 10-12 with the rest of the tubes.

14. Place the cardboard strip on the top of a beaker.

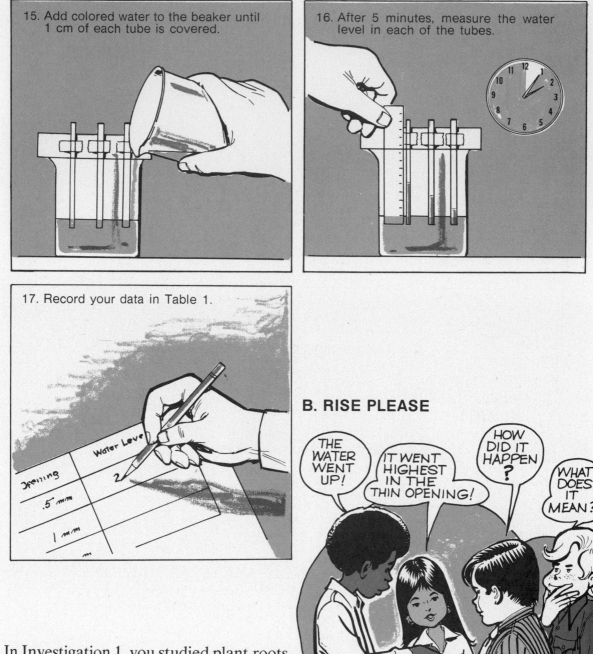

15. Add colored water to the beaker until 1 cm of each tube is covered.

16. After 5 minutes, measure the water level in each of the tubes.

17. Record your data in Table 1.

B. RISE PLEASE

THE WATER WENT UP!

IT WENT HIGHEST IN THE THIN OPENING!

HOW DID IT HAPPEN?

WHAT DOES IT MEAN?

In Investigation 1, you studied plant roots and stems. You learned that these plant parts have many tubes. These tubes have important jobs. Some of them carry food from the leaves. Other tubes are used to move water through the plant. It may sound strange, but plants do move materials.

Many trees are more than 100 feet tall. Yet water is carried to the highest leaf.

18. Look at your data in Table 1 on your data sheet.

• 19. In which tube did the water move the highest?

• 20. How high did the water move in this tube?

THE WATER MOVED ONLY A FEW CENTIMETERS!

THAT'S NOT ENOUGH FOR PLANTS!

WATER MOVES MUCH HIGHER IN PLANTS!

THERE MUST BE SOMETHING ELSE THAT GETS THE WATER SO HIGH!

THE PLANT REALLY HAS TO DO A JOB!

That's it, Phideau! The plant does have to do a job. A big job. And it takes work. Lots of work.

Most living things do some kind of work. To do work, living things need energy. Foods supply fuel for energy.

We need energy for work.

We need energy for play.

• 21. Plants also need energy. Why do plants need light energy?

• 22. Plants grow. What does that take?

• 23. Plants move materials. What does that take?

C. ROAST 'EM, TOAST 'EM

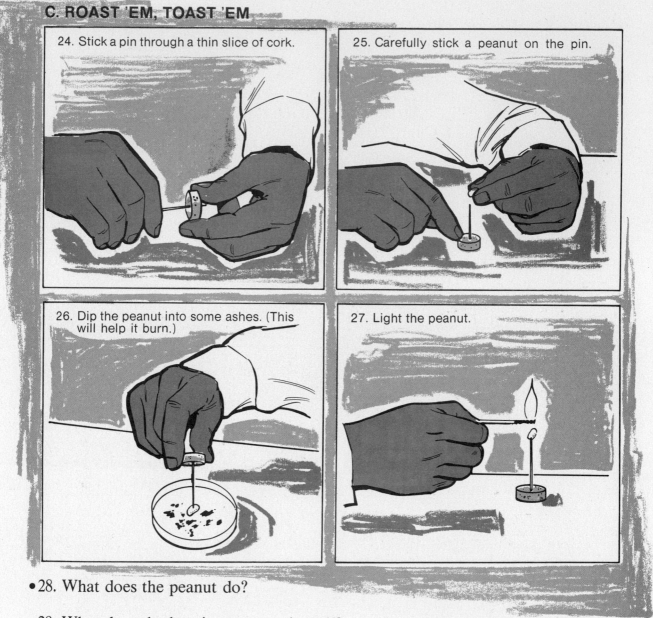

24. Stick a pin through a thin slice of cork.

25. Carefully stick a peanut on the pin.

26. Dip the peanut into some ashes. (This will help it burn.)

27. Light the peanut.

• 28. What does the peanut do?

• 29. What does the burning peanut give off?

• 30. What is light a form of?

• 31. What is heat a form of?

• 32. What do plants make?

• 33. What is food a form of?

• 34. What do plants use food for?

Re-read your answer to question 34. Write the concept.

THE CONCEPT.

GOT TO HAVE IT

You've made it! You've come to the end of another Idea. Green plants make it too! What do green plants make? Food!

WHAT ARE YOU DOING?

PHIDEAU, SOMETIMES I WONDER ABOUT YOU!

I'M HELPING THIS PLANT MAKE FOOD. I'M SUPPLYING IT WITH ENERGY!

In this Idea you learned that:

(a) Plant roots take in water.
(b) The stomates in plant leaves take in carbon dioxide.
(c) During photosynthesis, plants make carbohydrates from raw materials.
(d) Plants need chlorophyll to make starch.
(e) Plants need light energy to make starch.
(f) Plants use food for energy.

Energy is what this Idea has been all about. Energy and living things.

•35. What does food give plants?

Making food is quite a job. It takes a lot of work.

•36. To do work, what do plants use?

Animals cannot make their own food. They depend upon plants for their food supply.

•37. What does food give animals?

All living things must have food.

•38. What does food give all living things?

•39. What do all living things use food for?

•40. What must all living things obtain?

Write the Idea Summary.

THE IDEA.

Idea 5 Investigation 1

I TRIED IT AND I NEARLY DIED

That's right, Phideau. What does it take to stay alive? That will be the question for this new Idea.

A. COLOR ME WET

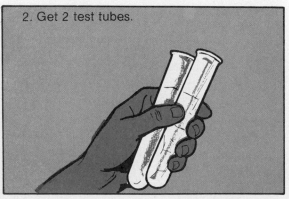

3. Put 5 bean seeds in each test tube.

A 2
D. SMITH

4. Push a piece of wet cotton 1/2-way into one tube. Use a pencil.

Wet cotton

5. Push a piece of dry cotton 1/2-way into the other tube.

Dry cotton

6. Turn both test tubes upside-down. Stand them in the beaker. Fill the beaker 1/4-full with water.

Five bean seeds

Dry cotton

Wet cotton

Beaker

A 2
D. SMITH

Water

7. Store your experiment at room temperature. Do not disturb for 2 days.

DEC. 1

DEC. 2

• 8. How are the 2 test tubes different?

• 9. Which test tube contains the control?

• 10. Which test tube contains the experiment?

• 11. What do you predict will happen after 2 days?

• 12. What is the experiment trying to test?

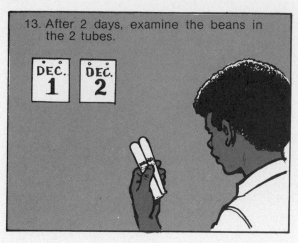

13. After 2 days, examine the beans in the 2 tubes.

DEC. 1 DEC. 2

When seeds sprout, we say they have *germinated.*

•14. What happened to the beans in the test tube with the wet cotton?

•15. What happened to the beans in the test tube with the dry cotton?

•16. Re-read your answers to questions 14 and 15. What do you predict all living things need to live?

B. GASP, GASP, GASP

OK, SO WE NEED WATER! WHAT ELSE?

EVERYONE'S TALKING ABOUT AIR POLLUTION!

SURE, MAYBE LIVING THINGS NEED AIR TOO!

ANY DOG KNOWS YOU NEED AIR AND WATER, DUMMIES! I THINK I'LL GO TAKE A SHOWER!

MAN

17. Label a beaker **B.** Add your name and section.

B 2 D. SMITH

18. Push equal size pieces of wet steel wool into the bottom of 2 test tubes.

Wet steel wool

B 2 D. SMITH

Wet steel wool

19. Add 5 bean seeds to one test tube.

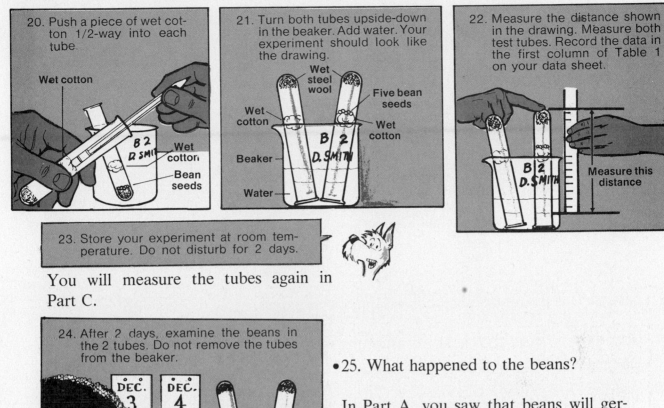

20. Push a piece of wet cotton 1/2-way into each tube.

Wet cotton

B 2
D. SMITH

Wet cotton

Bean seeds

21. Turn both tubes upside-down in the beaker. Add water. Your experiment should look like the drawing.

Wet steel wool

Wet cotton

Five bean seeds

Wet cotton

Beaker

Water

B 2
D. SMITH

22. Measure the distance shown in the drawing. Measure both test tubes. Record the data in the first column of Table 1 on your data sheet.

B 2
D. SMITH

Measure this distance

23. Store your experiment at room temperature. Do not disturb for 2 days.

You will measure the tubes again in Part C.

24. After 2 days, examine the beans in the 2 tubes. Do not remove the tubes from the beaker.

DEC. 3   DEC. 4

A 2
D. SMITH

•25. What happened to the beans?

In Part A, you saw that beans will germinate on wet cotton. But, the beans will not germinate in the tube with wet steel wool.

•26. What do you think keeps the bean seeds from germinating? List your predictions on your data sheet.

•27. Which one of your predictions do you think is the correct one? Why?

C. WHERE DID THE FIFTH GO?

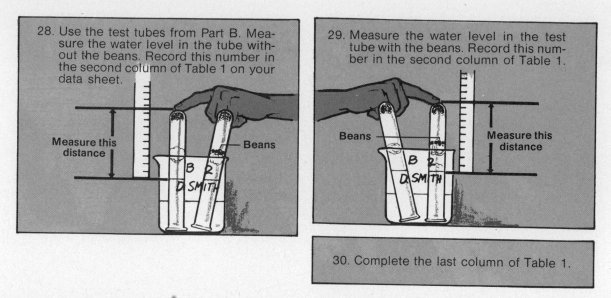

28. Use the test tubes from Part B. Measure the water level in the tube without the beans. Record this number in the second column of Table 1 on your data sheet.

Measure this distance

Beans

29. Measure the water level in the test tube with the beans. Record this number in the second column of Table 1.

Beans

Measure this distance

30. Complete the last column of Table 1.

•31. In which tube or tubes did the water level move?

•32. Did the steel wool or beans cause the water level to move? Explain.

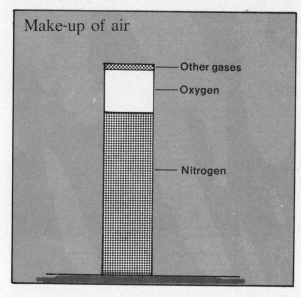

Make-up of air

Other gases

Oxygen

Nitrogen

Some part of the air must have been used up. This part was needed by the seeds to germinate. Study this diagram.

It shows that the air you breathe is a mixture of different gases. It also shows how much of each gas is present. Compare your data in Table 1 with the diagram.

•33. What gas is the steel wool using up?

•34. What gas do you think seeds need to germinate?

•35. You've observed only bean seeds in this experiment. But what gas do you think living things need to stay alive?

•36. Re-read questions 16 and 35. What two substances are needed by living things?

THE CONCEPT.

Idea 5 Investigation 2

IT'S A REAL GASSER

A. WHY OXYGEN?

In the last Investigation, you learned that:

Living things need water and oxygen.

In this Investigation, you'll find out if living things give off anything.

1. Label a tall, thin jar with your name and section.

2. Put 10 seedlings inside a syringe.

10 seedlings

3. Put the piston into the syringe. Push it to the 30 mark.

4. Place the syringe in the jar with a little water.

The water is used to keep the room air from getting to the seedlings. In other words, the seedlings are now trapped inside the syringe.

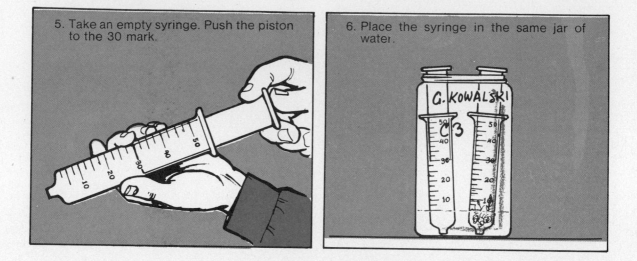

5. Take an empty syringe. Push the piston to the 30 mark.

6. Place the syringe in the same jar of water.

This is what you have set up. You have 10 seedlings in one syringe. You have no seedlings in another syringe. There is air trapped inside both syringes. Water is in the jar.

• 7. Which syringe contains the control?

• 8. Which syringe contains the experiment?

• 9. Predict what will happen to the air inside the syringe with the seedlings.

10. Store your experiment at room temperature. Do not disturb it for 1 day.

DEC. 7

CAUTION

DO NOT LIFT OR TOUCH THE SYRINGES. YOU NEED THE TRAPPED AIR FOR PART B!

When you started, all of the water was outside the syringe. Now, look at the level of the water inside the syringe with the seedlings.

- •11. What happened to the level of the water in the syringe with the seedlings?

- •12. What happened to the level of the water in the syringe without the seedlings?

- •13. Compare your answers to questions 11 and 12. Why did the level of the water change in the syringe with the seedlings?

- •14. What gas do you think the seedlings used?

B. NO, NOT ANOTHER PROBLEM

You saw the seedlings grow inside the syringe. Do you think this caused anything to happen to the air inside the syringe? Let's run another experiment and find out.

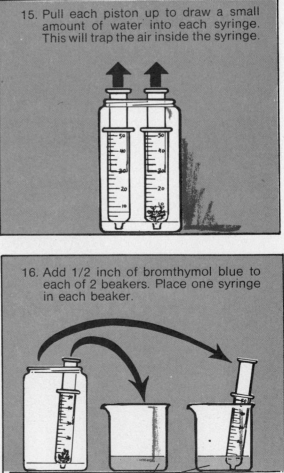

15. Pull each piston up to draw a small amount of water into each syringe. This will trap the air inside the syringe.

16. Add 1/2 inch of bromthymol blue to each of 2 beakers. Place one syringe in each beaker.

Bromthymol blue

DO NOT TIP OR TURN THE SYRINGES UPSIDE-DOWN! KEEP THE AIR TRAPPED INSIDE THE SYRINGES!

You used bromthymol blue in the last Idea. It is a carbon dioxide detector. If carbon dioxide is bubbled through the bromthymol blue, it will turn yellow.

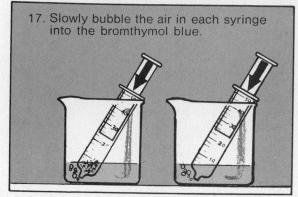

17. Slowly bubble the air in each syringe into the bromthymol blue.

•18. What happened to the bromthymol blue in the tube with the seedlings?

•19. What happened to the bromthymol blue in the tube without the seedlings?

•20. Compare your answers to questions 18 and 19. What did the seedlings do to the air in the syringe?

•21. What gas did the seedlings produce?

Well, it seems you haven't solved a problem. Instead, you've raised a new question. But that's all right. This sometimes happens in science. Scientists raise more questions than they answer. You will too!

WOW! I'VE ASKED ANOTHER QUESTION!

You have learned that living things need water and oxygen to stay alive.

•22. Now you have learned that seedlings (and maybe other living things) produce __?__

THE CONCEPT.

Idea 5 Investigation 3

SOUNDS FISHY TO ME

YES, IT'S CALLED BROMTHYMOL BLUE!

WAIT! WE DIDN'T TEST THE AIR FOR OXYGEN IN THE FIRST INVESTIGATION!

RIGHT! WE NEED AN OXYGEN DETECTOR!

In the last Investigation, you learned that seedlings give off carbon dioxide. You did this by testing the air with a "carbon dioxide detector." Do you remember what it was?

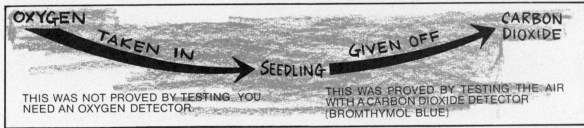

OXYGEN

TAKEN IN

SEEDLING

GIVEN OFF

CARBON DIOXIDE

THIS WAS NOT PROVED BY TESTING. YOU NEED AN OXYGEN DETECTOR.

THIS WAS PROVED BY TESTING THE AIR WITH A CARBON DIOXIDE DETECTOR (BROMTHYMOL BLUE)

A. A HAIRY FIZZLER

In this Investigation, you will do another chemical test. You will see if living things remove oxygen from air and water.

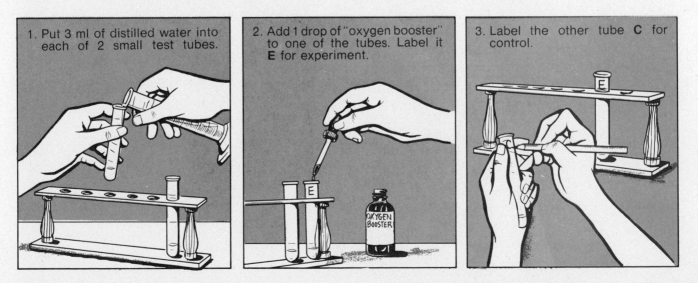

1. Put 3 ml of distilled water into each of 2 small test tubes.

2. Add 1 drop of "oxygen booster" to one of the tubes. Label it **E** for experiment.

3. Label the other tube **C** for control.

The "oxygen booster" you used is common household hydrogen peroxide. Most people call it peroxide. It is used to clean wounds or to bleach hair. Peroxide can be broken apart into water and oxygen gas.

Steps 4-8 are your oxygen test.

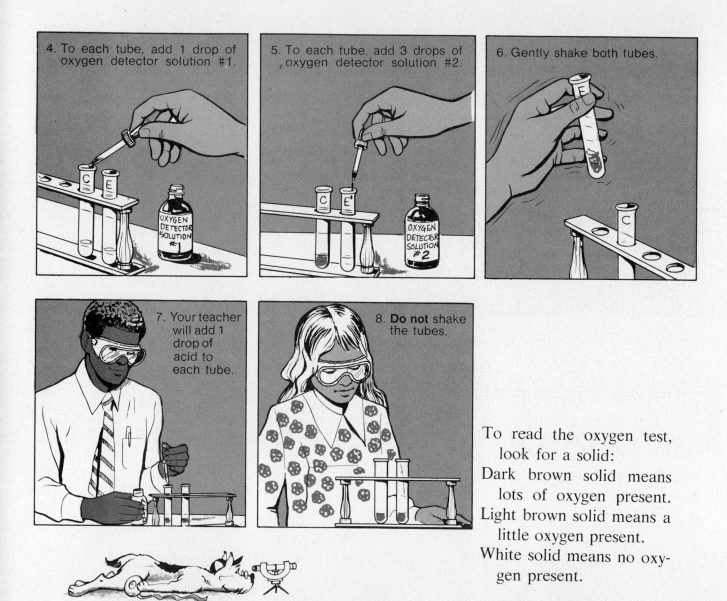

4. To each tube, add 1 drop of oxygen detector solution #1.

5. To each tube, add 3 drops of oxygen detector solution #2.

6. Gently shake both tubes.

7. Your teacher will add 1 drop of acid to each tube.

8. **Do not** shake the tubes.

To read the oxygen test, look for a solid:
Dark brown solid means lots of oxygen present.
Light brown solid means a little oxygen present.
White solid means no oxygen present.

Describe the color of the solid in your two tubes. Tell what these colors mean. Record your data in Table 1 on your data sheet.

Now you have learned how to test for oxygen. You know all that's needed to carry out the rest of the Investigation.

B. BRING ON THE FISHES

9. Read Steps 10-14 and Steps 21-28 first. If you do not understand the directions, ask your teacher.

10. Fill 2 clean jars about 3/4-full with water.

11. Add 4 drops of "oxygen booster" to each jar.

12. Gently net a fish. Quickly transfer it to one of your jars. Transfer a second fish to the same jar.

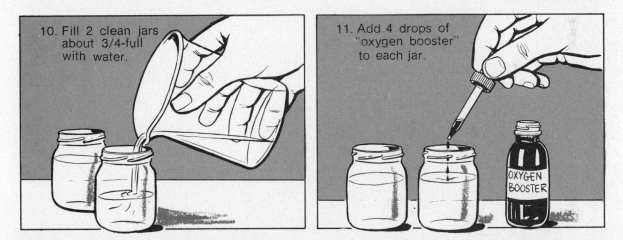

13. Add water to the very top of both jars. Try not to leave an air space. Tightly cap each jar.

14. Wait 20 minutes before going on to Step 21. Answer questions 15-19 while waiting.

•15. Record the time on your data sheet.

•16. What will the time be 20 minutes from now?

•17. Which jar holds the control?

•18. Which jar holds the experiment?

•19. What do you predict will happen to the water in the experimental jar?

•20. What do you predict will happen to the water in the control jar?

Now that you have waited 20 minutes, do Step 21.

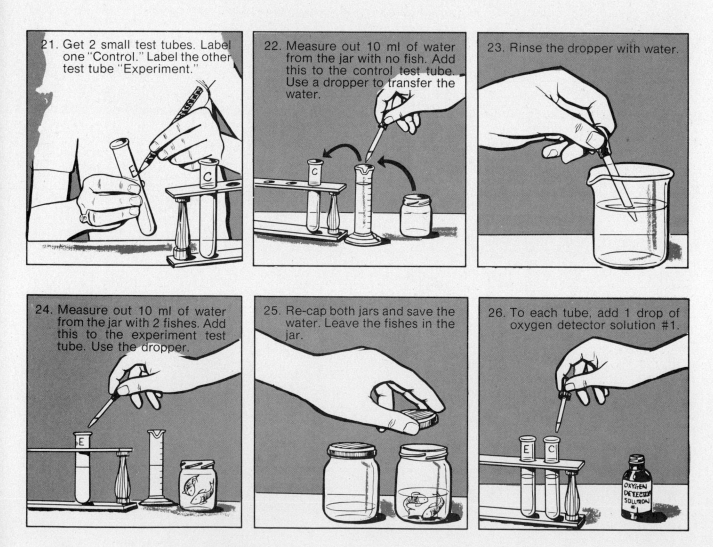

21. Get 2 small test tubes. Label one "Control." Label the other test tube "Experiment."

22. Measure out 10 ml of water from the jar with no fish. Add this to the control test tube. Use a dropper to transfer the water.

23. Rinse the dropper with water.

24. Measure out 10 ml of water from the jar with 2 fishes. Add this to the experiment test tube. Use the dropper.

25. Re-cap both jars and save the water. Leave the fishes in the jar.

26. To each tube, add 1 drop of oxygen detector solution #1.

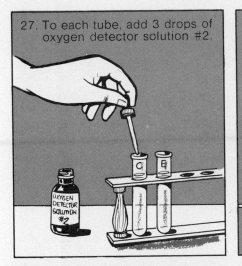

27. To each tube, add 3 drops of oxygen detector solution #2.

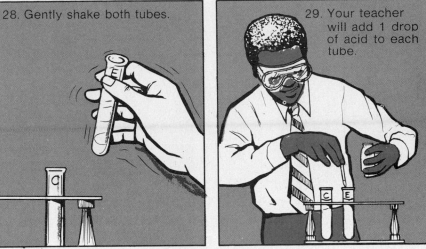

28. Gently shake both tubes.

29. Your teacher will add 1 drop of acid to each tube.

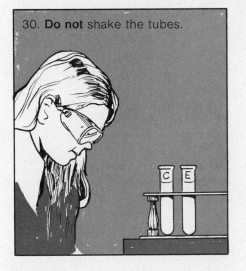

30. **Do not** shake the tubes.

•31. In which tube did the darker solid form?

Check back to page 173 to read your oxygen test.

•32. Which jar has more oxygen?

•33. What happened to the oxygen in the jar with the fishes?

C. DOES ANYTHING COME OUT?

You have just seen that a fish uses up some of the oxygen in water.

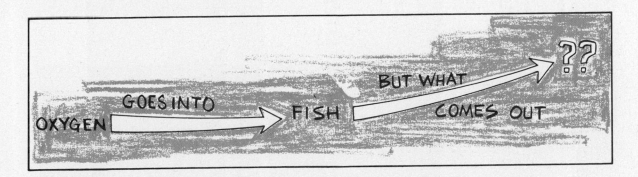

OXYGEN GOES INTO → FISH BUT WHAT COMES OUT → ??

•34. What gas do you predict is produced by the fish?

•35. What test can you run to check your answer to question 34?

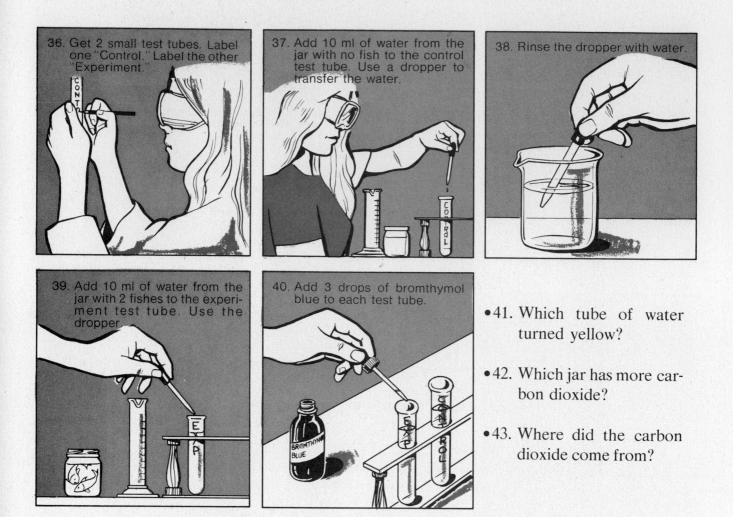

36. Get 2 small test tubes. Label one "Control." Label the other "Experiment."

37. Add 10 ml of water from the jar with no fish to the control test tube. Use a dropper to transfer the water.

38. Rinse the dropper with water.

39. Add 10 ml of water from the jar with 2 fishes to the experiment test tube. Use the dropper.

40. Add 3 drops of bromthymol blue to each test tube.

• 41. Which tube of water turned yellow?

• 42. Which jar has more carbon dioxide?

• 43. Where did the carbon dioxide come from?

Review what you have learned in the last three Investigations.

• 44. What gas is needed by living things?

• 45. What gas is produced by living things?

Gently pour fish into a net over a sink.

Quickly transfer to an aquarium.

THE CONCEPT.

Idea 5 Investigation 4

YOU'LL GET A RISE OUT OF THIS

Congratulations! After three Investigations, you have learned that:

- (a) Living things need water and oxygen.
- (b) Living things take in oxygen.
- (c) Living things produce carbon dioxide.

WHY DO LIVING THINGS NEED OXYGEN AND WATER?

HOW DOES A LIVING THING PRODUCE CARBON DIOXIDE?

DON'T ASK ME; ASK THE BEANS AND FISHES!

These three concepts can be combined in a diagram.

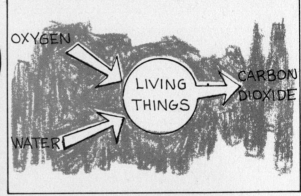

A. THAT BEAST, THE YEAST

Yeast is easy to find in most grocery stores. It is sold in small "cakes" or in thin packets. Yeast is commonly used in baking bread.

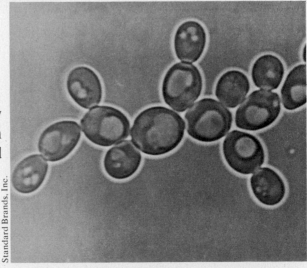

Standard Brands, Inc.

Bread dough rises as it sets at room temperature. This is caused by the carbon dioxide gas made by the yeast cells in the dough. You studied yeast in Idea 2. Yeast cells are like the seedlings and fishes. They are alive and can produce carbon dioxide.

This brings up some questions.

WHAT DO YEAST CELLS NEED TO MAKE CARBON DIOXIDE?

HOW DO YEAST CELLS MAKE CARBON DIOXIDE?

WHAT'S IN IT FOR THE YEAST?

You will answer these questions in this Investigation.

B. BRING ON THOSE BEASTS

1. Read Steps 2-8 before starting.

2. Get 2 large test tubes. Label one "Control." Label the other "Experiment."

3. Fill both test tubes 1/2-full with warm yeast mixture.

4. Weigh out 1 gram of sugar.

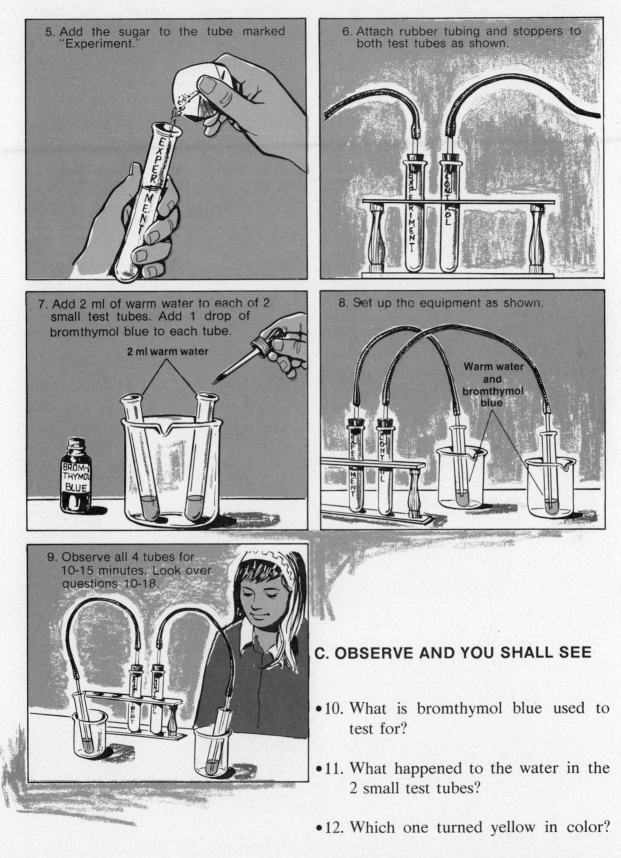

5. Add the sugar to the tube marked "Experiment."

6. Attach rubber tubing and stoppers to both test tubes as shown.

7. Add 2 ml of warm water to each of 2 small test tubes. Add 1 drop of bromthymol blue to each tube.

2 ml warm water

BROM-THYMOL BLUE

8. Set up the equipment as shown.

Warm water and bromthymol blue

9. Observe all 4 tubes for 10-15 minutes. Look over questions 10-18.

C. OBSERVE AND YOU SHALL SEE

• 10. What is bromthymol blue used to test for?

• 11. What happened to the water in the 2 small test tubes?

• 12. Which one turned yellow in color?

• 13. What does the yellow color tell you?

• 14. What is different between the experiment and the control tubes?

• 15. Observe the 2 large test tubes. Which yeast cells are more active?

• 16. What do you think the more active yeast cells are doing?

• 17. Why is one group of yeast cells more active than the other?

• 18. For yeast cells to produce carbon dioxide, what must they have?

Yeast cells certainly don't take in sugar for the fun of it. Nor do they give off carbon dioxide without reason. Yes, what's in it for the yeast? The sugar is food for the yeast. Just as you need food to stay alive, the yeast plants need sugar.

• 19. What do you think living things use up when they produce carbon dioxide?

THE CONCEPT.

Idea 5

LET'S BREAK IT APART

Say, you are really going places. In the last two Investigations, you have learned that:

(a) Living things produce carbon dioxide.

(b) Living things produce carbon dioxide from sugar.

A. WHAT'S WITH SUGAR?

Yes, Phideau, what's so special about sugar? Why do living things need sugar? To find out, you must learn how to test for sugar first.

1. Measure 5 ml of prepared sugar solution into a test tube.

2. Rinse the graduated cylinder with water.

3. Add 5 ml of Benedict's solution. This is a "sugar detector" solution.

4. Heat gently over a flame. Use your test tube holder.

CAUTION

DO NOT POINT THE MOUTH OF THE TEST TUBE AT YOURSELF OR ANYONE ELSE!

5. Look for an orange color. This tells you that the sugar is present.

You are now on your own. Your teacher will give you different foods. Write the names of the foods in the first column of Table 1 on your data sheet. After you test each food for sugar, write "yes" or "no" in the second column.

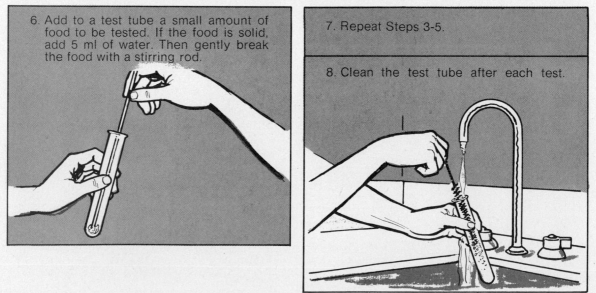

6. Add to a test tube a small amount of food to be tested. If the food is solid, add 5 ml of water. Then gently break the food with a stirring rod.

7. Repeat Steps 3-5.

8. Clean the test tube after each test.

There are three major kinds of foods: *proteins, fats,* and *carbohydrates.* Examples of foods that contain proteins are meat, milk, and cheese.

National Dairy Council

Fats include oil, butter, and the fat from meat.

And carbohydrates include bread, potatoes, and corn.

Charles D. Druss

National Dairy Council

• 9. Look at your data in Table 1. Which proteins or fats have sugar?

• 10. Which of the carbohydrates have sugar?

In Idea 4, you learned that sugar and starch are carbohydrates. Both are made of carbon, hydrogen, and oxygen. Starch is nothing more than many sugars joined together.

SUGAR SUGAR SUGAR SUGAR SUGAR SUGAR

STARCH

YOU MEAN STARCH IS JUST A LOT OF SUGARS JOINED TOGETHER!

B. WHAT'S WITH STARCH?

You have just read that starch is many sugars joined together.

• 11. If this is true, then you should be able to break up starch and get _____?_____

Let's test this.

12. Put a cracker in your mouth.

14. What change in taste do you notice?

Here's what happened. There is a chemical in your saliva. It broke the starch in the cracker into many sugars.

LOOK, A CHEMICAL IN THE SALIVA BROKE THE STARCH INTO SUGARS!

Another chemical in your intestine also helps break up the starch into sugar. Then, what does your body do with the sugar?

C. DON'T BURN THE CANDY

Your teacher will do this next part. Watch what happens and be ready to answer questions 17 and 18.

•17. What did the acid do to the sugar?

Look for a white gas. Most of this is steam.

•18. What other gas is the sugar giving off? (*Hint:* What gas comes from a fire extinguisher?)

Leo Choplin/Black Star

Notice the black hunk that is left. It is carbon. This helps explain, where the word "carbohydrate" comes· from. The "carbo" comes from the carbon. "Hydrate" means water. The carbon and a part of the water can be given off as a gas. The gas is called carbon dioxide.

D. WHAT HAPPENED?

Let's review what you have learned so far. In Investigation 3, you learned that:

Living things produce carbon dioxide.

In Investigation 4, you learned that:

Living things produce carbon dioxide from sugar.

And, in this Investigation, you have learned *how* carbon dioxide comes from sugar.

Review Parts B and C. In Part B you chewed on a cracker.

•19. What did the saliva do to the cracker to get sugar?

In Part C your teacher added acid to sugar.

•20. What did the acid do to sugar to produce carbon dioxide?

•21. What must a living thing do to sugar to produce carbon dioxide?

THE CONCEPT.

THE LITTLE OLD HEATMAKER, ME

Your experiments have shown you that living things use up and give off things. Thus far, you have seen that:

(a) Living things need water.
(b) Living things need oxygen.
(c) Living things produce carbon dioxide.
(d) Living things produce carbon dioxide from sugar.
(e) When living things break apart sugar, carbon dioxide is given off.

Putting these concepts together, this is what you have.

In Investigation 4, you saw something that looked like this diagram.

A. DOES IT WORK IN A LIVING THING?

You will be shown two styrofoam cups. Each has been prepared in a different way.

One cup has 100 ml of sugar-water. The other cup has the same, plus yeast.

• 1. Which cup is the control?

• 2. Which cup has a living thing in it?

• 3. What is the temperature of the control cup?

• 4. What is the temperature of the experimental cup?

• 5. What is causing the difference in temperature?

• 6. What do you predict the yeast is doing to cause the difference?

You already know that yeast breaks apart sugar to produce carbon dioxide. Now you know that yeast reacts with sugar to produce heat. When a living thing breaks down food, heat is produced. You can do it—yourself.

7. Hold a thermometer in the air. Do not wave it around.

•8. What is the temperature of the air?

9. Place the thermometer as shown. Wait 2 minutes before reading it.

•10. What is the skin temperature of your body at the elbow?

•11. What is your body producing?

•12. How do you think your body produces heat?

B. WHAT'S THE HEAT FOR?

You must have energy if you are to do any work. Energy is the ability to do work. You are working when you breathe, move an arm, or think. For these tasks, you must have energy. Where does the energy come from?

There are many forms of energy. One common form is heat. You learned this in Idea 4. When you burn gasoline, you produce heat. When you burn gasoline inside an engine, you produce heat energy for work. The car moves.

A living thing produces heat in the same way. Instead of burning gasoline, however, it slowly burns or breaks apart food. You can get an idea of the heat energy produced by a living thing. You will do this by burning a marshmallow, a food that is mostly sugar.

13. Thread 3 mini-marshmallows on a nail.

14. Fill a 50 ml beaker 1/2-full with water.

15. Record the temperature of the water in Table 1 on your data sheet.

16. Arrange the materials as shown.

17. Light all of the marshmallows over a flame.

18. Quickly set the burning marshmallows under the beaker of water.

CAUTION
DO NOT KNOCK OVER THERMOMETER OR BEAKER!

19. Put the can over the whole set-up.

20. After the 3 marshmallows burn out, measure the temperature of the water. Record this in Table 1.

•21. What work was done in this experiment?

•22. What kind of energy was produced to do this work?

•23. Where did the heat come from?

> Your body does the same thing with food to produce heat. The more you eat, the more energy you produce. Except, if you eat too much and your body does not need the extra energy, you store it. Then everybody calls you chubby.

•24. Describe what happens to the marshmallow in your body to produce energy.

C. ON A CLEAR DAY, YOU CAN SEE A BETTER ANSWER

In conclusion:

•25. Why is energy necessary?

•26. Name one thing all living things need to stay alive.

•27. What does sugar supply?

•28. Therefore, what must a living thing do to release energy from the sugar it receives?

THE CONCEPT.

RIGHT ON, AGAIN

You are right on, again! Another Idea finished! This Idea was about how living things use energy. How do living things get energy from food?

You have learned that:
(a) Living things need water and oxygen.
(b) Living things produce carbon dioxide.
(c) Living things take in oxygen and produce carbon dioxide.
(d) Living things produce carbon dioxide from sugar.
(e) When living things break apart sugar, carbon dioxide is released.
(f) When living things break apart sugar, energy is released.

In Idea 4, you learned that living things need to get energy. Plants get their energy from the sun. Plants then make food. Animals get their energy by eating food.

Once the plant or animal gets the food, how is the energy released? That has been the question for this Idea.

•29. Why does Phideau need to eat?

•30. What do living things get out of food?

•31. How do living things get energy from food?

•32. To stay alive, what must all living things use?

Re-read question 31 and summarize the entire Idea.

THE IDEA.

Idea 6 Investigation 1

YOU'LL WIND UP BROKE, EVERY TIME

At the beginning of this course, you learned about the idea of inquiry. Inquiry is a way of thinking and finding out about things. Scientists use the inquiry method to find out more about the world. You have used inquiry to learn the following Ideas:

Idea: Living things have certain characteristics.
Idea: Living things are made of cells.
Idea: Living things must obtain energy.
Idea: Living things use energy.

We eat to stay alive. The raw material of life is food. Other than water and salt, we usually eat food that was once alive. Thus, food is made up of the same materials as we are. These materials are of three kinds: proteins, fats, and carbohydrates. You learned this in Idea 5.

A. YOU BREAK ME UP

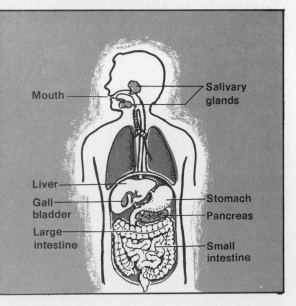

There is a 30-foot long tube inside your body. It is coiled to fit inside. This is your food tube. It is an organ system. Every part has a job. To begin, let's see one job of the mouth.

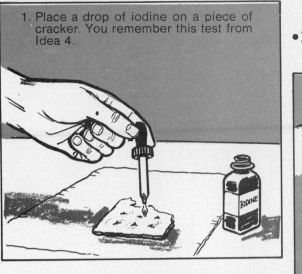

1. Place a drop of iodine on a piece of cracker. You remember this test from Idea 4.

• 2. What does your test show?

3. Break a different piece of cracker into one test tube.

4. Rinse your mouth. Then put some saliva into a second test tube.

5. Chew another cracker for 2 minutes. Do not swallow.

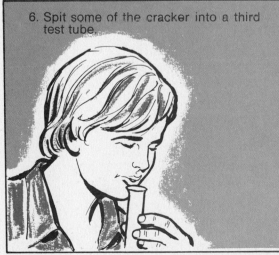

6. Spit some of the cracker into a third test tube.

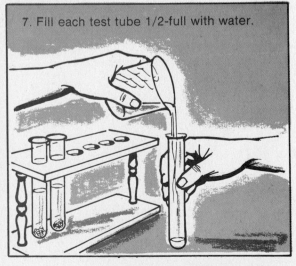

7. Fill each test tube 1/2-full with water.

Idea 6/Investigation 1   **195**

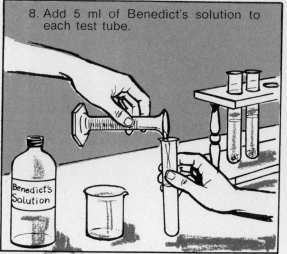

8. Add 5 ml of Benedict's solution to each test tube.

9. Use your test tube holder. Heat each tube gently over a flame.

CAUTION

DO NOT POINT THE MOUTH OF THE TEST TUBE AT YOURSELF OR ANYONE ELSE!

You used Benedict's solution in Idea 5. If an orange color appears, sugar is present.

• 10. What happened in the test tube with the cracker alone?

• 11. What happened in the test tube with the saliva only?

• 12. What happened in the test tube with the cracker and saliva?

There must be something in the saliva that changed the starch. The substance is a *digestive juice*. A digestive juice can break food down from larger particles into smaller particles.

• 13. What changed the cracker from starch to sugar?

B. LET'S BREAK THIS ONE, TOO

Breaking down food into smaller particles is called *digestion*. The body makes chemicals that help digest food. Different digestive juices do different jobs. There are starch-breaking juices, fat-breaking juices, and protein-breaking juices.

Your teacher will give you some digestive juices. These are like the kinds found in the small intestine.

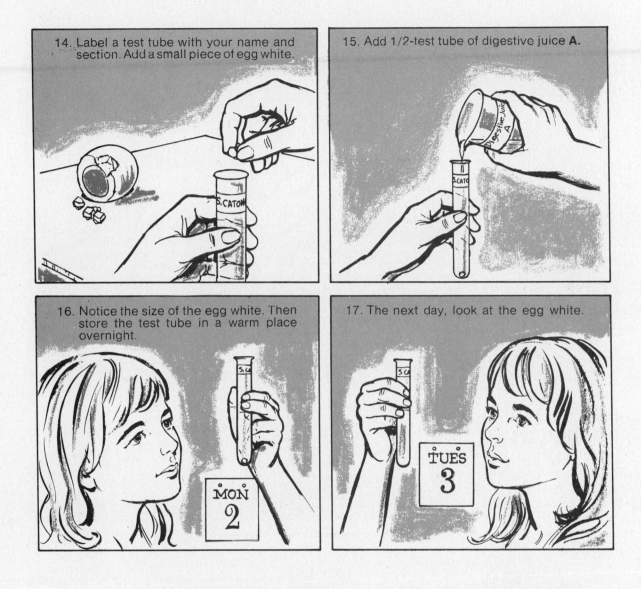

14. Label a test tube with your name and section. Add a small piece of egg white.

15. Add 1/2-test tube of digestive juice **A**.

16. Notice the size of the egg white. Then store the test tube in a warm place overnight.

17. The next day, look at the egg white.

- 18. What happened to the egg white?

- 19. What do you think caused the change?

- 20. What do digestive juices do to food?

- 21. What is digestion?

C. IT'S A FOUR-HOUR TRIP

Your teacher will give you some other digestive juices.
These are also found in the small intestine.

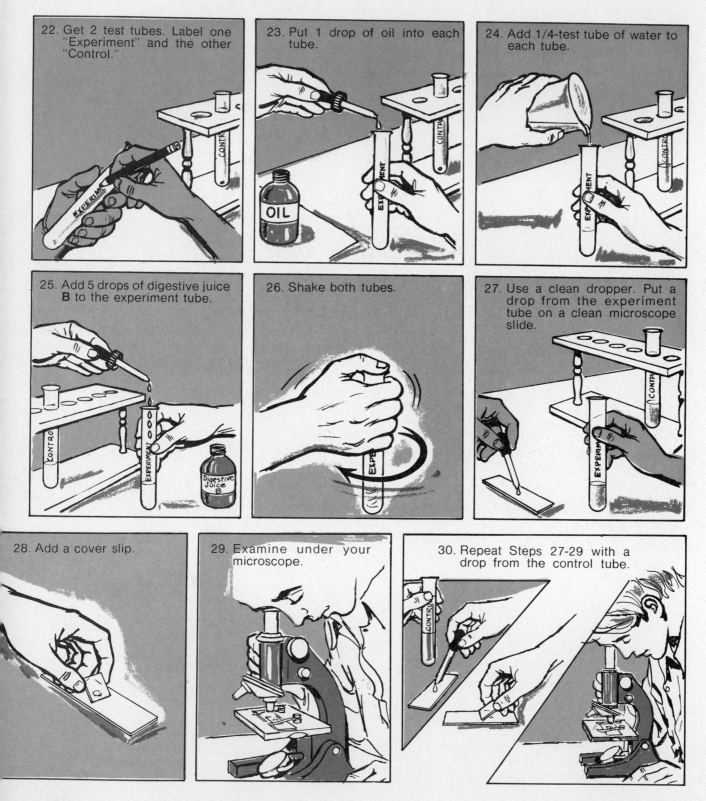

22. Get 2 test tubes. Label one "Experiment" and the other "Control."

23. Put 1 drop of oil into each tube.

24. Add 1/4-test tube of water to each tube.

25. Add 5 drops of digestive juice **B** to the experiment tube.

26. Shake both tubes.

27. Use a clean dropper. Put a drop from the experiment tube on a clean microscope slide.

28. Add a cover slip.

29. Examine under your microscope.

30. Repeat Steps 27-29 with a drop from the control tube.

•31. What difference do you see in the size of the oil particles?

•32. What caused the difference?

•33. What do digestive juices do to food?

•34. What is digestion?

D. DON'T BREAK IT DOWN; PUT IT TOGETHER

What you saw in Parts B and C takes place mostly in the small intestine. Most of the digestion takes place here. Twenty of the 30 feet in the food tube are small intestine. Many different kinds of digestive juices pour into the food tube.

Look at the diagram of your digestive system again.

•35. What do digestive juices do to food as it moves through the food tube?

Finally, the food that cannot be digested moves into the *large intestine*. No digestion takes place there. Instead, water is squeezed out of the food and returned to the body. Then the unwanted part of the food is passed out of the body.

•36. What is digestion?

THE CONCEPT.

GETTING IT THROUGH TO YOU

In the last Investigation, you learned that food is digested. Digestion breaks food down into smaller particles. Somehow the particles have to make their way to the cells.

There are finger-like projections, the *villi*, inside the intestine. It's as if someone took a long hose and squeezed it like an accordion. This packs a lot of surface into a small space.

Tiny tubes of blood flow into and out of each of the villi. The digested food must pass out of the intestine and into the blood tubes. The trick is how to cross the border.

A. CAN YOU CROSS THE BORDER?

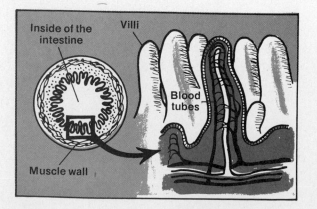

Your teacher will show you two jars of raisins. There is water in one jar. The raisins in this jar have been soaking overnight. Your group will be given one raisin from each jar.

1. Carefully blot the raisins dry. Do not break the skin.

• 2. How do the soaked and unsoaked raisins differ?

• 3. Why do you think they differ?

4. Use a toothpick to poke a hole in one end of each raisin.

5. Gently squeeze both raisins.

• 6. What difference do you see?

• 7. What do you think is coming out of one raisin?

• 8. How do you think this liquid got into the raisin?

B. DOES YOUR TUBING LEAK?

WHAT DO YOU MEAN, DO MY TUBES LEAK? HERE'S A TUBE OF WATER! LOOK, IT DOESN'T LEAK! SO IF WATER CAN'T GET OUT, IT CAN'T GET IN! RIGHT?

THAT'S WHAT YOU THINK!

9. You will be given a piece of tubing. Tie a knot at one end; then fill it 1/4-full with water.

• 10. Does the tube leak?

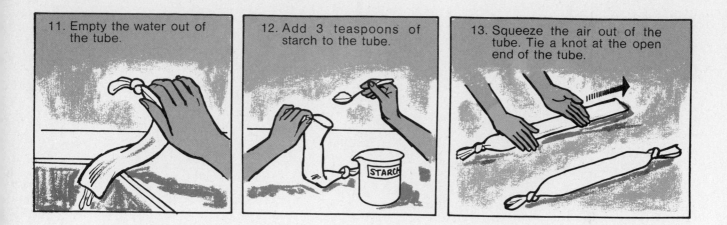

11. Empty the water out of the tube.

12. Add 3 teaspoons of starch to the tube.

13. Squeeze the air out of the tube. Tie a knot at the open end of the tube.

• 14. Feel the tube of starch. How is it like a dried raisin?

• 15. What do you think would happen if the tube were soaked in water?

In the last Investigation, you tested for starch. If starch is mixed with iodine, the mixture turns blue-black. You can use this test to help you answer question 15.

16. Label a beaker with your name and section.

17. Fill the beaker 3/4-full with water. Add 5 drops of iodine and stir.

18. Tie a paper clip around each knot in the tube. Hang the tube in the beaker of water as shown.

Answer the next four questions before stopping for the day.

• 19. If the starch turns blue, what happened?

• 20. If the iodine and water turn blue, what happened?

• 21. If both the iodine and starch turn blue, what happened?

• 22. What do you predict will happen?

NEXT DAY

• 23. What happened in your experiment?

• 24. How would you explain what happened?

C. WHY DOES MY TUBING LEAK?

You remember learning about the cell membrane in Idea 3. The cell membrane is the outside of the cell. A membrane is like a border. Cell membranes keep particles apart.

• 25. What part of the raisin is like a membrane?

• 26. How is the tubing like a membrane?

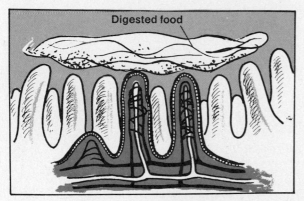

Digested food

• 27. Study the picture. There is digested food in the intestine. It must pass out of the intestine and into the blood tubes. What parts are like membranes?

Hey gang, let's see if we can find some answers.

•28. Study the two cartoons. Define the word "diffusion."

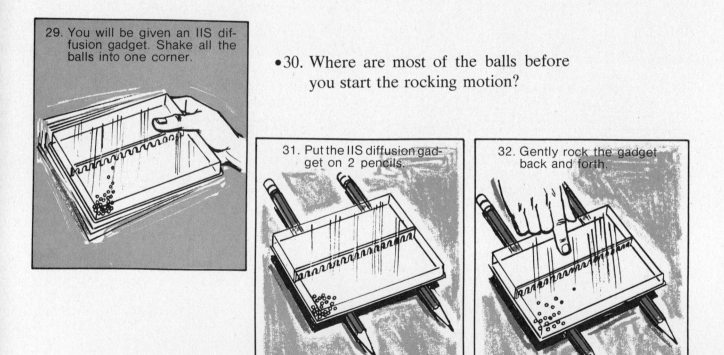

•30. Where are most of the balls before you start the rocking motion?

•33. What happens to the balls as you rock the gadget?

•34. Where are the balls after you rock the gadget for at least 2 minutes?

35. Shake all the balls info one corner again.

• 36. Where are most of the particles before you start the rocking motion?

• 37. Where are the particles after you rock the gadget for at least 2 minutes?

You have just seen an example of diffusion. During diffusion the particles bounce around. They move from where it's crowded to where it's not so crowded.

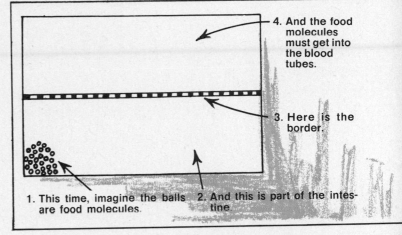

4. And the food molecules must get into the blood tubes.

3. Here is the border.

1. This time, imagine the balls are food molecules.

2. And this is part of the intestine

• 38. What is diffusion?

• 39. How do materials get from one place to another?

I FEEL SICK! I THINK MY INTESTINES ARE SHAKING THE FOOD AROUND!

NO, YOUR INTESTINES DON'T SHAKE!

IN REAL LIFE THE PARTICLES BOUNCE AROUND ON THEIR OWN! THEY HAVE TO USE THEIR OWN ENERGY!

Let's bring this whole thing up to date. In the last Investigation, you learned that food is broken down during digestion. The digested food changes into a watery liquid inside the intestine. The food has to move into the blood tubes. But the blood tubes are outside of the intestine. How is the food going to cross the border at the villi?

• 40. How does digested food pass out of the intestine to the blood tubes?

• 41. What is one way that materials move from one part of your body to another part?

THE CONCEPT.

IT GETS IT ALL AROUND

You are doing very well. You have learned that:

(a) Digestion breaks food down into smaller particles.
(b) Food particles can diffuse through a membrane.

This is great; but how is the food carried through the body?

A. WHICH WAY DID HE GO?

Over 350 years ago in England, William Harvey published his discoveries about circulation. The heart is a bag of muscles. Its job is to keep blood going around and around.

National Portrait Gallery, London

You have all played with mazes. (Do not draw on this one.)

On your data sheet is a different kind of maze. The maze is in the shape of a heart. There are four rooms or chambers in the maze.

START HERE

1. Begin at "Start" and trace a line to "Finish."

Congratulations. You have just traced the flow of blood through the heart. When the heart squeezes, blood flows.

- 2. How many chambers are in the heart?

- 3. What other organ must blood pass through before going to the body?

- 4. What do you think the blood picks up there?

Your bloodstream is like a maze. Tubes called *arteries* leave the heart and branch out to all the cells. The maze of tubes then join together to return blood to the heart. The tubes that return the blood to the heart are called *veins*.

On your data sheet is another maze. It is in the shape of a human body.

5. Trace the flow of blood from the heart to the head. Then trace it back to the heart. Begin at "Start" and return to "Start."

6. Trace the flow of blood from the heart to an arm. Then trace it back to the heart. Begin at "Start" and return to "Start."

7. Trace the flow of blood from the heart to a leg. Then trace it back to the heart. Begin at "Start" and return to "Start."

Congratulations! You have just traced blood through the circulatory system.

- 8. What makes the blood go around and around?

- 9. How many heart chambers must blood always go through?

- 10. What are the tubes called that lead out of the heart?

WHAT'S CIRCULATION?

THAT MEANS TO CIRCULATE -- TO GO AROUND AND AROUND!

THAT'S THE TROUBLE! WE JUST GO AROUND AND AROUND!

- 11. What are the tubes called that return blood to the heart?

- 12. What do you think carries food throughout the body?

B. DO YOU KNOW THE LUB-DUB DANCE?

HEY, PHIDEAU, NEW DANCE?

YEAH MAN! IT'S THE LUB-DUB STEP!

What does the doctor hear when he listens with a stethoscope?

13. Have your partner rest his head on the table.

14. Place the stethoscope on your partner's back. Move it around until you hear a "lub-dub" sound.

What you hear are the opening and closing of the valves inside the heart. The valves are like one-way trap doors. Blood can go in only one direction.

You will hear "lub" when the heart squeezes and "dub" when it relaxes. Therefore, count each "lub-dub" as one beat.

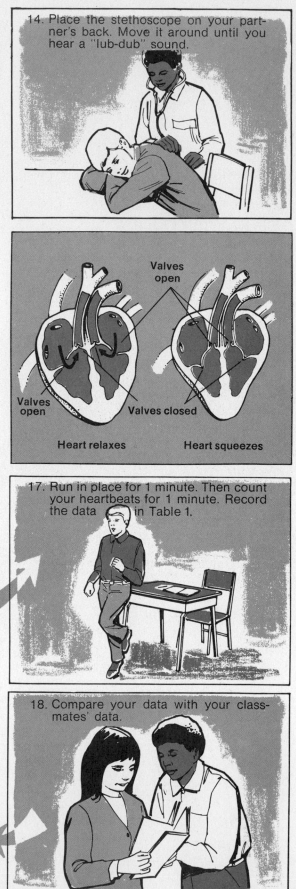

Valves open

Valves open

Valves closed

Heart relaxes

Heart squeezes

15. Count the number of heartbeats you hear in 1 minute. Record the data in Table 1 on your data sheet.

16. Have your partner repeat this count on you. Record the data in Table 1.

17. Run in place for 1 minute. Then count your heartbeats for 1 minute. Record the data in Table 1.

18. Compare your data with your classmates' data.

• 19. Does everyone have the same heartbeat rate?

• 20. How does exercising affect the heartbeat rate?

C. IT GOES TO YOUR HEAD FAST

Number of cocktails or Bottles of beer	Effects on average person:
	Gay, happy, moody
	Warm, relaxed
	Talkative, noisy
	Awkward, clumsy
	BOMBED!

Can you balance on one foot? Or walk a straight line? That's what the policeman will have you do if you drive after drinking. Alcohol gets into the bloodstream very fast. It is not digested by the stomach or small intestine.

• 21. What happens to the body as the amount of alcohol goes up?

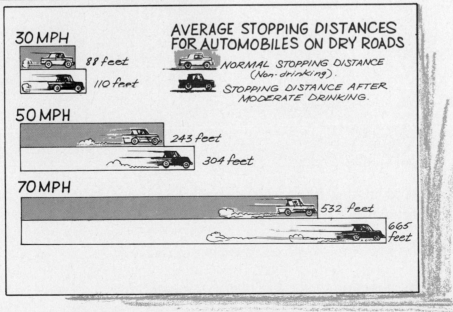

• 22. According to the graph, who can stop a car more quickly?

The moderately drinking driver needs over 3 more car lengths than the non-drinking driver to stop at 50 mph.

So you see, each drink makes a person more dangerous. Is it any wonder that 50,000 people are killed each year by drunken drivers?

D. KEEP TRUCKING ALONG

This Investigation began with a question. How is food carried throughout the body? You should be able to answer this question now. Let's review what you've learned.

• 23. In the first Investigation, you learned about digestion. What is digestion?

• 24. In the last Investigation, you learned that food molecules can pass through a membrane. What is this process called?

Now you know how food and water get from the intestine to the blood tubes.

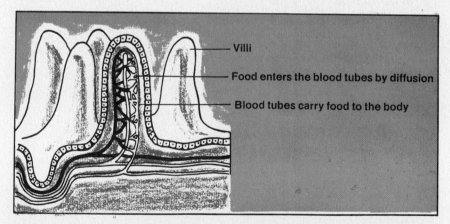

Villi

Food enters the blood tubes by diffusion

Blood tubes carry food to the body

And in this Investigation, you've learned that blood tubes branch out to all the cells.

• 25. Therefore, how is food carried throughout the body?

• 26. What is the function of the circulatory system?

THE CONCEPT.

Idea 6 Investigation 4

SMOKE AND MAKE THE DOCTORS RICH

In the last Investigation, you learned that:

> The circulatory system carries materials to all parts of the body.

You have learned that blood carries food and water. The digested food and water diffuse into the bloodstream from the intestine.

You will remember that arteries and veins carry blood. One big artery leaves the heart, then branches. The branches become smaller and smaller. Finally they are about the size of cells. These tiny tubes are called *capillaries*.

If the webbed foot of a frog is examined under a microscope, you can see the capillaries.

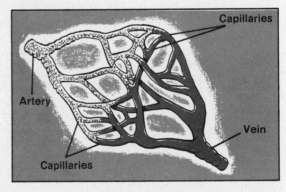

A. STOP ME WHEN THE COLOR TURNS

Air enters your nose or mouth and travels down the windpipe. The windpipe branches and enters both lungs. The tubes branch and become microscopic in size. At the end of each tube is a tiny air sac. There are millions of these tiny air sacs in each lung.

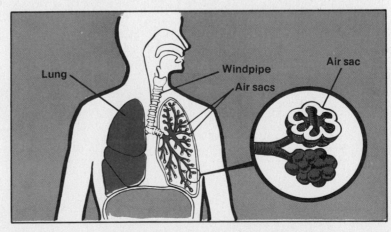

Around each tiny air sac are capillaries. The air diffuses from the air sacs to the capillaries. Unwanted air diffuses from the capillaries to the air sacs. This air is breathed out of the lungs.

• 7. Read the labels on the jars. In which jar did the color change?

• 8. Why do you think the color changed?

• 9. What gas do you breathe out?

•10. What gas do you think was bubbling into the jar that did not change color?

•11. What gas do you breathe in?

•12. How do these gases·get to and from your blood tubes?

•13. Where does the blood take the gases?

•14. For the cells to stay alive, what two gases must be exchanged?

This constant exchange of gases is part of a process called *respiration*.

B. OLD WHAT'S-HIS-NAME SMOKED

Cigarette smoke is an example of polluted air. Let's see what one puff can do.

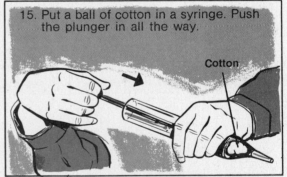

15. Put a ball of cotton in a syringe. Push the plunger in all the way.

Cotton

16. Tape a cigarette to one end of a piece of tubing.

17. Attach the tubing to the syringe. Light the cigarette.

18. Slowly pull the plunger all the way out.

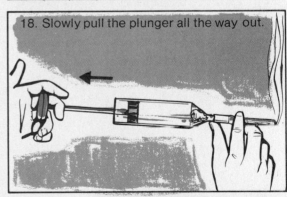

19. Put out the cigarette. Then take out the ball of cotton and examine it.

•20. Describe what one puff did to the cotton.

21. Put 10 ml of water into a clean jar.

10 ml water

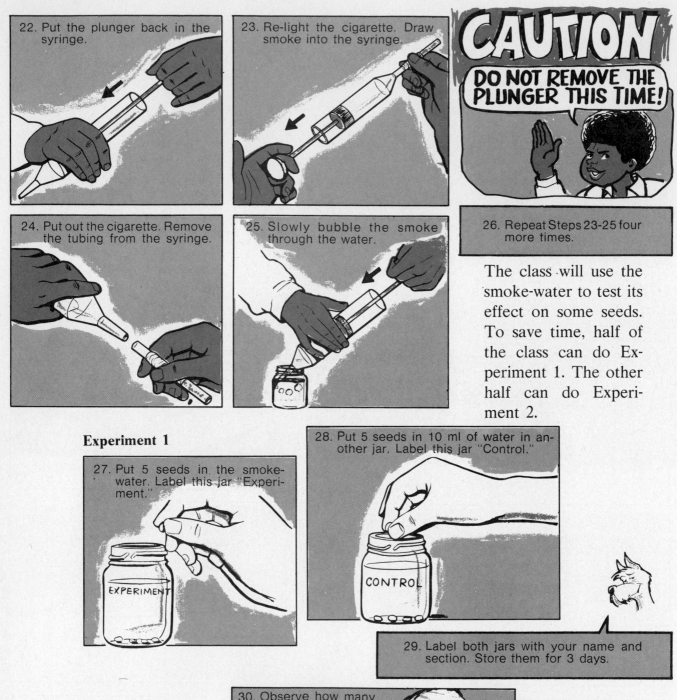

22. Put the plunger back in the syringe.

23. Re-light the cigarette. Draw smoke into the syringe.

CAUTION
DO NOT REMOVE THE PLUNGER THIS TIME!

24. Put out the cigarette. Remove the tubing from the syringe.

25. Slowly bubble the smoke through the water.

26. Repeat Steps 23-25 four more times.

The class will use the smoke-water to test its effect on some seeds. To save time, half of the class can do Experiment 1. The other half can do Experiment 2.

Experiment 1

27. Put 5 seeds in the smoke-water. Label this jar "Experiment."

EXPERIMENT

28. Put 5 seeds in 10 ml of water in another jar. Label this jar "Control."

CONTROL

29. Label both jars with your name and section. Store them for 3 days.

30. Observe how many seeds germinate in 3 days. Record the data in Table 1.

MON 1 TUES 2 WED 3

214   Idea 6/Investigation 4

Experiment 2

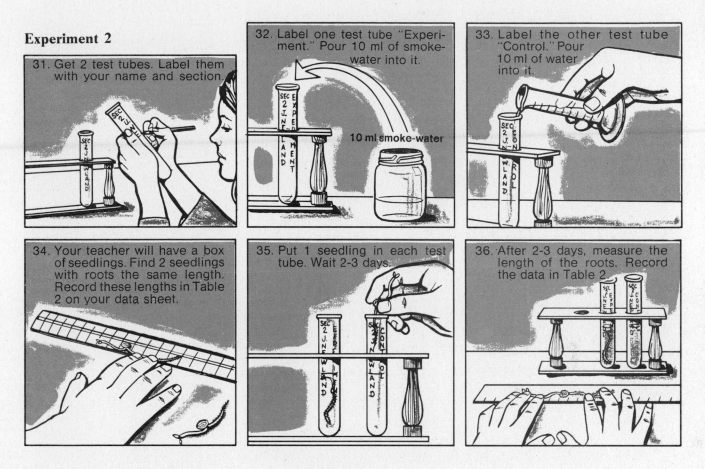

31. Get 2 test tubes. Label them with your name and section.

32. Label one test tube "Experiment." Pour 10 ml of smoke-water into it.

10 ml smoke-water

33. Label the other test tube "Control." Pour 10 ml of water into it.

34. Your teacher will have a box of seedlings. Find 2 seedlings with roots the same length. Record these lengths in Table 2 on your data sheet.

35. Put 1 seedling in each test tube. Wait 2-3 days.

36. After 2-3 days, measure the length of the roots. Record the data in Table 2.

Discuss both experiments with your classmates.

• 37. How did the cigarette smoke-water affect the germination of the seeds?

• 38. How did the cigarette smoke-water affect the length of the roots?

C. THE FAMILY THAT SMOKES TOGETHER CHOKES TOGETHER

You've seen what cigarette smoke can do to seeds. Now, what does it do to people?

Your lung is a big bag of millions of tiny tubes and air sacs. The walls of the tubes are usually very thin and soft. Cigarette smoke, coal dust, or air pollution can cause changes in these tubes. The tube walls become thicker and harder. Examination of the lungs of smokers after death shows this. Look at the difference in these pictures.

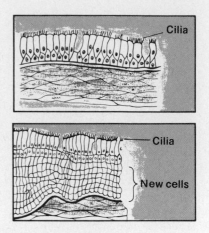

Materials begin to pile up in the tubes. The smoker tries to get rid of these materials by coughing them out. This is sometimes called "smoker's cough." A summary of five studies shows:

TABLE **3**
COMPARISON OF SMOKERS AND NON-SMOKERS

Percent With	Smokers	Non-Smokers
Cough	24	7
Other Respiratory Problems	26	15

As smoking continues, the insides of the tubes become smaller. The smoker coughs, but the air can't come out. Some of the air sacs break. Then more and more air sacs break.

•39. What happens to the amount of air a person can breathe now?

•40. How does smoking affect respiration?

D. SMOKING PAYS the tobacco company, the hospital, the undertaker

You spent most of your time in this Investigation experimenting on smoking. But the larger concept has to do with respiration. All living things must carry on respiration.

•41. What is exchanged during respiration?

•42. How does the air get from the outside to the capillaries?

•43. What is respiration?

Re-read questions 14, 42, and 43 before writing the concept.

THE CONCEPT.

Idea 6 Investigation 5

THE AMEBA AND THE OSMOND BROTHERS

Osbro Productions, Inc.

Grant Heilman

Carolina Biological Supply Co.

Donny Osmond, a maple tree, and this ameba all have something in common. They are all alive. They carry on certain activities necessary for life. A tiny ameba, a tall tree, and a large animal all carry on the activities of:

(a) digestion
(b) circulation
(c) respiration
(d) diffusion.

WAIT! WHAT REGULATES MY BODY ACTIVITIES?

YES! WHY DOES MY BLOOD FLOW FAST OR SLOW?

WHAT ABOUT MY BREATHING RATE?

WHO TELLS ME WHEN I'M HUNGRY?

A. IS THERE A TIGER IN YOUR TANK?

If you look inside the carburetor, you will see a float. This float regulates the amount of gasoline going into the engine.

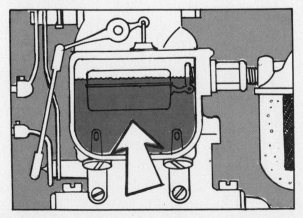

The thermostat on the wall regulates the amount of heat in a room.

"Regulate" means to control.

Idea 6/Investigation 5 **217**

1. Put 2 pea seedlings into each of 2 milk cartons. Label the cartons with your name and section. Be sure to water the seedlings.

C. MIGNOSA C-2

C. MIGNOSA C-2

2. Put one carton in a dark box.

C-2

3. Leave the other carton out in the light.

● 4. Which plants do you predict will grow taller?

5. Wait 3 days. Then open the dark box.

MAY 1   MAY 2   MAY 3

●6. Surprise! Which plants grew taller?

Just because a plant is taller does not mean that it is healthier.

7. Feel the plants. Squeeze the stems. Bend the stems.

A. MIGNONE

●8. Which plants are stronger? In what way?

We know what regulates the height of a plant. It is a chemical called a *hormone*. Hormones are chemicals that regulate activities. In the experiment you just did, the sun affects the amount of hormone. The amount of hormone regulates the height of the plant.

● 9. What does the word "regulate" mean?

●10. How are different activities regulated in an organism?

B. THE SHORT AND TALL OF IT

The first plant hormone was discovered in 1926. Plant hormones are made by the cells in the growing tips of plants. Hormones cause plants to bend toward light. Hormones cause roots to grow down and stems up. Hormones regulate the dropping of leaves. Why do some plants grow tall or short?

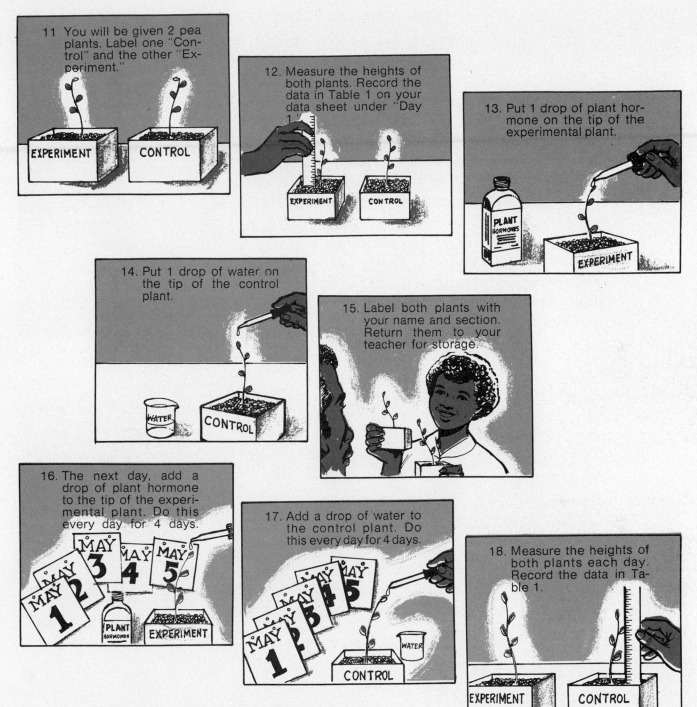

11. You will be given 2 pea plants. Label one "Control" and the other "Experiment."

EXPERIMENT   CONTROL

12. Measure the heights of both plants. Record the data in Table 1 on your data sheet under "Day 1."

EXPERIMENT   CONTROL

13. Put 1 drop of plant hormone on the tip of the experimental plant.

PLANT HORMONES

EXPERIMENT

14. Put 1 drop of water on the tip of the control plant.

WATER   CONTROL

15. Label both plants with your name and section. Return them to your teacher for storage.

16. The next day, add a drop of plant hormone to the tip of the experimental plant. Do this every day for 4 days.

MAY 1   MAY 2   MAY 3   MAY 4   MAY 5   PLANT HORMONES   EXPERIMENT

17. Add a drop of water to the control plant. Do this every day for 4 days.

MAY 1   MAY 2   MAY 3   MAY 4   MAY 5   WATER   CONTROL

18. Measure the heights of both plants each day. Record the data in Table 1.

EXPERIMENT   CONTROL

• 19. What happened to the experimental plant?

• 20. What happened to the control plant?

• 21. What do you think caused the difference?

• 22. What do you think this hormone regulates?

• 23. What do hormones do?

C. LET'S REGULATE THIS WHOLE SCENE

What makes people fat or skinny, tall or short, bony or stocky? What makes some people slow-moving and others nervous and jumpy? What tells the heart to beat faster or slower?

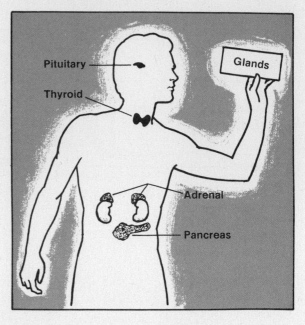

There are many kinds of hormones. Some hormones make the heart beat faster or slower. Other hormones keep the amount of sugar in the blood steady. Maybe you know of people who do not have the right amount of body sugar. These people have a disease called *diabetes*. They have to take *insulin*. Insulin is a hormone that regulates the body sugar.

Hormones are chemicals that regulate activities in the body. Hormones are made in organs called glands. Some of your major glands are shown.

Hormones diffuse directly into the bloodstream. The hormones are then carried to where they do their work.

You have learned that a living thing carries on certain activities. Some of these activities are digestion, circulation, respiration, and diffusion. As long as they are performed, the living thing stays alive.

And now you have learned what regulates these activities.

• 24. What chemicals regulate activities in a living thing?

• 25. Where are hormones made in animals?

• 26. What do hormones do?

Re-read questions 23 and 26.

THE CONCEPT.

Idea 6 Investigation 6

THE DEBBIL MADE ME DO IT

NBC Television Network

When Flip Wilson plays Geraldine, she has her shopping problems. "The Debbil made me buy dis dress!" she cries. "I didn't want to buy it. But old Debbil, he made me!"

Does the Debbil make you do things, too? Or do you figure out things for yourself?

A. WHAT A MEMORY, EXCEPT AT TEST TIME

Let's take a closer look at that thinking machine in your head. You've got a computer between your ears. Scientists tell us that your computer makes a man-made computer look like a toy. Your brain takes up the space of a large fist. Yet, the brain can remember more than any computer. Man could make a computer with the memory of a brain. But, he'd need a room larger than your school.

It's a staggering thought. Every sound, every taste, every smell, every sight, every motion is recorded forever in the "deep-freeze" of the mind. What you decide to do may depend on what is stored in your brain. Here is an example.

1. Write your name on line 1 of Table 1. Use your left hand if you are right-handed. Use your right hand if you are left-handed.

2. Write your name with the same hand on line 2.

3. Write your name again with the same hand on lines 3, 4, and 5.

Each time you write your name, it looks better. It becomes easier each time. Your brain remembers what you did. It has a memory and stores information. Thus it helps you control how you do things. This ability to do things from experience and memory is called *coordination*.

- •4. Why was it easier to write your name each time?

- •5. What is your memory?

- •6. What is coordination?

- •7. How does memory help coordination?

- •8. What part of your body controls what you do?

B. ARE YOU COORDINATED?

Black Star

Maybe you've heard the phrase, "She's very coordinated." Just what does that mean?

You probably take eating with a fork for granted. But eating with a fork takes coordination. You learned this coordination when you were young.

There are millions of children who eat with chopsticks. They use chopsticks as easily as you use a fork. All it takes is coordination.

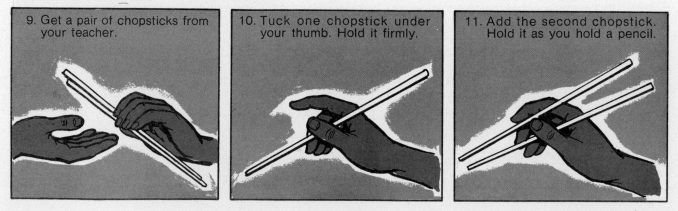

9. Get a pair of chopsticks from your teacher.

10. Tuck one chopstick under your thumb. Hold it firmly.

11. Add the second chopstick. Hold it as you hold a pencil.

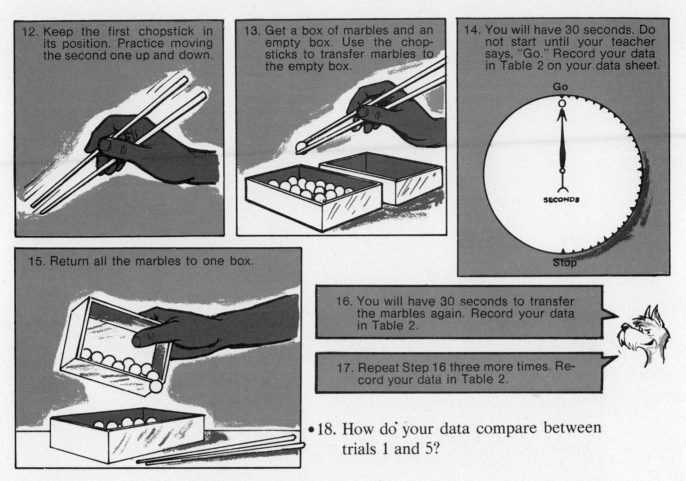

12. Keep the first chopstick in its position. Practice moving the second one up and down.

13. Get a box of marbles and an empty box. Use the chopsticks to transfer marbles to the empty box.

14. You will have 30 seconds. Do not start until your teacher says, "Go." Record your data in Table 2 on your data sheet.

Go

SECONDS

Stop

15. Return all the marbles to one box.

16. You will have 30 seconds to transfer the marbles again. Record your data in Table 2.

17. Repeat Step 16 three more times. Record your data in Table 2.

• 18. How do your data compare between trials 1 and 5?

• 19. Why was it easier to pick up more marbles each time?

• 20. What is coordination?

• 21. What part of your body coordinates your activities?

C. DO YOU SEE THE PATTERN?

Let's play a game. There are 40 numbers printed on page 224.

22. You are to touch each number in order, starting at 1. You will have 1 minute. Start when your teacher says, "Go."

• 23. What number did you reach after 1 minute?

Your teacher will ask you to do it again. But this time see if you can recognize a pattern. This means the numbers have been arranged in a certain way.

24. Touch each number in order, starting at 1. Start when your teacher says, "Go." Again, you will have 1 minute.

Idea 6/Investigation 6   **223**

•25. What number did you reach after 1 minute?

•26. How are the numbers arranged? (Discuss this in class.)

27. Now that you see the pattern, do Step 24 again.

•28. What number did you reach this time?

•29. How do your results compare between the first and third trials?

•30. Why did you reach a higher number each time?

•31. What part of your body coordinates your activities?

•32. What is the job of your brain?

D. LET'S COORDINATE THINGS

In this Idea, you have learned the following concepts:

(a) Digestion is the taking in, breaking down, and use of food.
(b) Respiration is the constant exchange of gases.
(c) The circulatory system transports materials to all parts of the body.
(d) For life to continue, materials must enter and leave the cell (diffusion).
(e) Hormones regulate the life activities of living things.

And in this Investigation, you have learned what coordinates this whole show.

•33. What is the function of the brain?

•34. What coordinates the life activities of living things?

THE CONCEPT.

GET REALLY STONED

We think you should know as much as the average pusher.

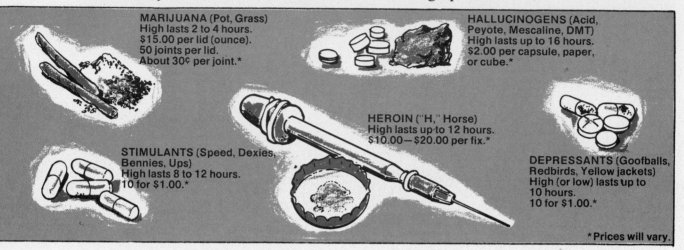

MARIJUANA (Pot, Grass)
High lasts 2 to 4 hours.
$15.00 per lid (ounce).
50 joints per lid.
About 30¢ per joint.*

HALLUCINOGENS (Acid, Peyote, Mescaline, DMT)
High lasts up to 16 hours.
$2.00 per capsule, paper, or cube.*

HEROIN ("H," Horse)
High lasts up to 12 hours.
$10.00—$20.00 per fix.*

STIMULANTS (Speed, Dexies, Bennies, Ups)
High lasts 8 to 12 hours.
10 for $1.00.*

DEPRESSANTS (Goofballs, Redbirds, Yellow jackets)
High (or low) lasts up to 10 hours.
10 for $1.00.*

*Prices will vary.

• 1. If you smoke one joint a day, what will it cost you?

• 2. Someone who is hooked on heroin needs at least two fixes a day. What does this habit cost each week?

• 3. How will the heroin addict usually get this money?

• 4. What do you think the drug user gets for the money he spends?

A. GET REALLY STONED; DRINK WET CEMENT

In order to support their habits, drug addicts steal billions of dollars each year. They steal 1-1/2 billion dollars each year in New York City alone. Most people hide the fact that they use drugs. We do not know exactly how many drug users there are in the United States. But good estimates show:

Drugs	Estimated Users
Stimulants, barbiturates	25 to 30 million
Marijuana	12 to 20 million
Heroin	100 to 200 thousand

With so many people using drugs, we think you should know what the average user knows. He knows what marijuana smells like. Do you?

5. Your teacher will give you an artificial marijuana wafer. It is not harmful.

6. Break the wafer into two pieces. Place the larger piece on top of the smaller piece in a glass dish.

7. Light the top piece. Notice the odor.

• 8. Describe the odor of marijuana.

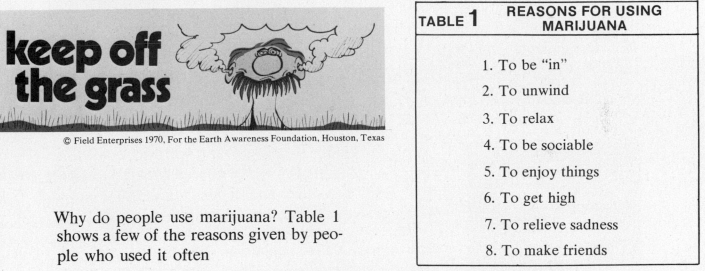

keep off the grass

© Field Enterprises 1970, For the Earth Awareness Foundation, Houston, Texas

TABLE 1	REASONS FOR USING MARIJUANA
	1. To be "in"
	2. To unwind
	3. To relax
	4. To be sociable
	5. To enjoy things
	6. To get high
	7. To relieve sadness
	8. To make friends

Why do people use marijuana? Table 1 shows a few of the reasons given by people who used it often

• 9. Which reasons were used to escape from problems?

All the others are social reasons. Most teenagers begin using drugs to get into a "cool group." The desire "to belong," to be part of an "in group," is strong. In fact, many teenagers buy "grass" and give it away.

•10. Why do many teenagers give away drugs? What are they looking for in return?

•11. The average teenager is not after the drugs themselves. What is he after?

B. COLD TURKEY IS NOT A THANKSGIVING TRIP

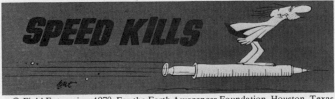

SPEED KILLS

© Field Enterprises 1970, For the Earth Awareness Foundation, Houston, Texas

You may have heard the line, "Pot is not harmful." Or, "Pot does not lead to stronger drugs." This may be true; but have you ever met a "speed freak" who had not blown pot?

What is it like to be a speed freak?

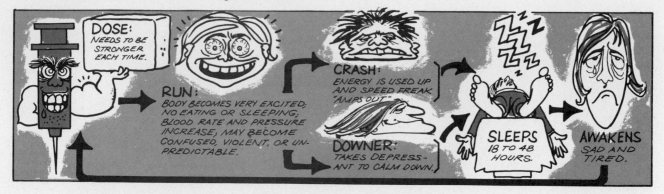

"Speed," that's the same as methamphetamine. You can inject it or take it as pills. Speed is not addicting. The body does not have to have it. But the body does become tolerant. This means that the user needs a larger and larger dose to get turned on.

• 12. Why do speed freaks go from a few pills to many?

• 13. Why do speed freaks go from many pills to injections?

Speed may not be addicting, but heroin is. This means your body must have it. And when you don't get heroin, you get cold turkey.

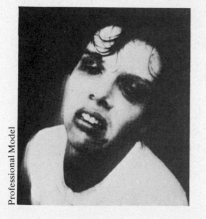

Professional Model

You get a terrible headache. You feel very cold. But you also run a high fever. You can't think straight. You vomit. You shiver and shake. You thrash around. And you do all this for three days, maybe more.

Do you want this to happen to you? Not on your life, huh? So let's talk about drugs. Because if we don't, the pusher will.

C. HEROIN, THE EXTRA PAIN STRENGTH RELIEVER

14. Do you believe that drugs are **not** harmful? If so, write your reasons in Space **a** on your data sheet. If you believe that drugs **are** harmful, write those reasons in the space.

There are no right or wrong answers to what you are about to do. Be a free spirit. Just state your opinions. Then the class can have a rap session.

15. Cut out an ad that tells you how a product can make you happier. Attach it to your data sheet.

• 16. How are these ads like turning on with drugs?

17. A part of a newspaper article is shown in Space **b** on your data sheet. Finish the article. Write some of the other things people might say about drugs.

18. Suppose you had to write a letter to the editor. What would you say about the article? Do this in Space **c** on your data sheet.

Here are two situations. What would you say?

Carl is 12 and in the 7th grade. He's been blowing a little pot lately. One day, Steve says, "Grass is for babies. Try some speed. It's the greatest!"

Carl is not sure. He has heard that speed can cause serious illnesses. Steve says, "Go on. Try it."

Jim has invited Beverly to the school dance. They meet Ronald and Carol there. During the dance, the four sneak out. Jim makes a reefer. Ronald and Carol are eager to begin. Beverly has never smoked grass before. Jim offers her a puff.

• 19. If you were Carl, what would you say?

• 20. If you were Beverly, what would you say?

D. WILL THE REAL PILLHEADS PLEASE ROLL OVER

Here are some sayings for you to think about. Comment on each, if you want.

"The happy that I am when I'm straight is so much more beautiful than the happy that I seem to be when I'm stoned."

"Get high with life and turn on with sunshine."

21. Write your own saying in Space **d** on your data sheet. Write a poem. Draw a picture. Make a collage. Be yourself.

Look at your poem, or your picture, or your collage. What are you trying to tell yourself? What are you trying to tell the world?

THE CONCEPT.

Shazam! You've completed another Idea. You're doing so well. This Idea had to do with those activities living things must do to stay alive. Yes, what are the activities of living things?

To find out what activities all living things must have, you did seven Investigations. You learned that:

(a) Digestion breaks down food into smaller particles.
(b) Diffusion is the way in which materials enter cells.
(c) The circulatory system transports materials to all parts of the body.
(d) Respiration is the constant exchange of gases.
(e) Hormones regulate the life activities of living things.
(f) The brain coordinates the life activities of living things.
(g) Drugs disrupt the brain's ability to coordinate.

A snake, mouse, dog, flea, and even man have many things in common.

•22. They all have to eat and break down food. What is this activity called?

•23. All the cells in a living thing must have food. How do cells get food?

•24. How do the cells in a living thing get gases?

These are just three activities. There are many other activities going on in a living thing.

•25. Why do living things need to perform activities?

Re-read the seven concepts and question 25. Then summarize the entire Idea.

THE IDEA.

COME LOOK AT MY GOOSE TREE

Have you ever seen a goose tree? Sounds silly, doesn't it? Some people didn't think so 700 years ago. In fact, some people still believed in the goose tree 250 years ago.

People in the Orient talked about another kind of tree. This tree had fruits that looked like melons. These melons were said to contain full-grown lambs.

GOOSE TREES?

LAMBS FROM MELONS?

MAYBE I DID COME FROM A CABBAGE PATCH!

YOU GUYS CAN CLOWN AROUND, BUT WHERE *DID* WE COME FROM?

Where do all living things come from? Do living things come from air, dust, fire, or water? Is there some kind of magic energy? Some kind of unknown force? That's what this Investigation is all about.

A. THERE'S A FLY IN YOUR WHAT?

In Idea 2, you learned that living things grow. You also learned that organisms change as they grow. This happens to many insects. Very young flies do not look like adult flies. They look like tiny worms. These worms are called *maggots*.

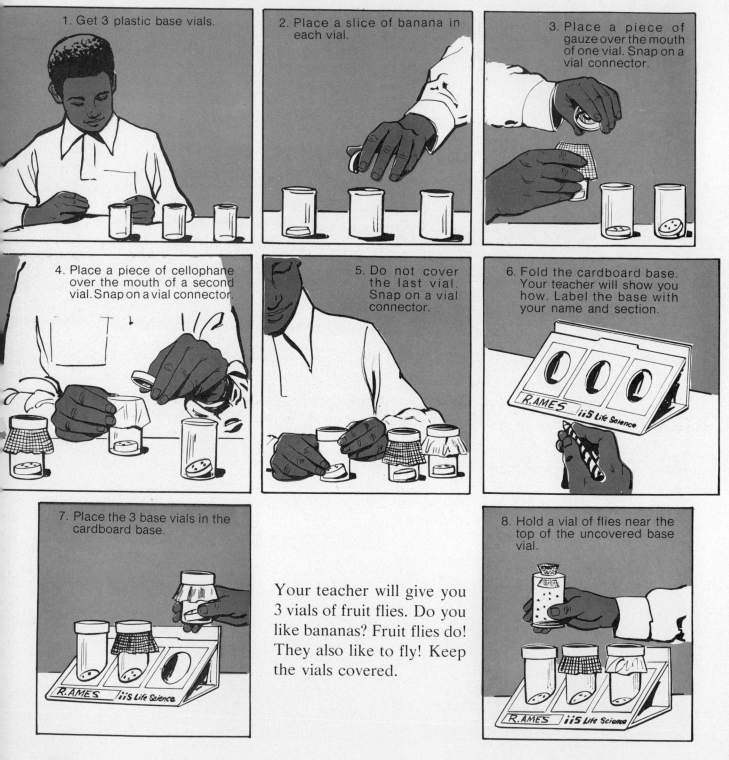

1. Get 3 plastic base vials.

2. Place a slice of banana in each vial.

3. Place a piece of gauze over the mouth of one vial. Snap on a vial connector.

4. Place a piece of cellophane over the mouth of a second vial. Snap on a vial connector.

5. Do not cover the last vial. Snap on a vial connector.

6. Fold the cardboard base. Your teacher will show you how. Label the base with your name and section.

7. Place the 3 base vials in the cardboard base.

8. Hold a vial of flies near the top of the uncovered base vial.

Your teacher will give you 3 vials of fruit flies. Do you like bananas? Fruit flies do! They also like to fly! Keep the vials covered.

9. Loosen the cover. But do not let any flies escape.

10. Quickly remove the cover and snap the upper vial onto the vial connector.

11. Number this vial **1**.

• 12. Observe the flies. What are they doing?

• 13. Why do you think they are doing this?

14. Hold another vial of flies over the gauze-covered base vial.

15. Loosen the cover.

16. Quickly remove the cover and snap the upper vial onto the vial connector.

17. Number this vial **2**.

• 18. Observe the flies. What are they doing?

• 19. Why do you think they are doing this?

• 20. Where are most of the flies?

• 21. What is the gauze doing?

• 22. How many flies have gotten through the gauze?

23. Hold the last vial of flies over the cellophane-covered base vial.

24. Loosen the cover.

25. Quickly remove the cover and snap the upper vial onto the vial connector.

26. Number this vial **3**.

• 27. What are the flies doing?

• 28. Where are most of the flies?

• 29. How can you explain this?

• 30. How many flies have gotten through the cellophane?

• 31. What is the cellophane doing?

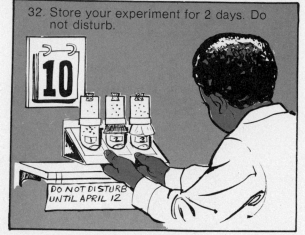

32. Store your experiment for 2 days. Do not disturb.

DO NOT DISTURB UNTIL APRIL 12

B. YOU GET CABBAGE FROM A CABBAGE PATCH

I KNEW THAT GOOSE STORY WAS FOR THE BIRDS!

33. After 2 days, examine your vials.

• 34. Carefully observe the banana in vial **1.** Describe what you see.

• 35. How has the banana changed?

• 36. What do you think caused this change?

•37. Carefully observe the banana in vial **2**. Describe what you see.

•38. How has the banana changed?

•39. How many flies got through the gauze?

•40. What do you think caused the change in the banana?

•41. How do you think this happened?

•42. Carefully observe the banana in vial **3**. Describe what you see.

•43. How is the banana in vials **1** and **2** different from the banana in vial **3**?

•44. How can you explain this?

C. JUST PASSING THROUGH

•45. How many maggots can you see on the banana in vial **1**?

•46. Where do you think these came from?

•47. How many maggots can you see on the banana in vial **2**?

•48. Where do you think these came from?

•49. How did they reach the banana?

•50. How many maggots can you see on the banana in vial **3**?

•51. How can you explain this?

•52. Maggots are living things. Where do they come from?

•53. Why are there living things in vial **1**?

•54. Why are there living things in vial **2**?

•55. Why aren't there living things in vial **3**?

•56. Where must maggots come from?

•57. Where must living things come from?

THE CONCEPT.

Idea 7 Investigation 2

THIS WILL BREAK YOU UP

That's right, Phideau. David doesn't have to get uptight. You've already seen that living things come from other living things.

That's what it's all about, Peter! Reproduction. Organisms making more organisms. But making the same kind of organisms.

How does it happen? That's what this Investigation is all about.

A. WHO HIT THE YEAST?

You've worked with yeast before. Yeast cells are one-celled microscopic plants. Let's see how the yeast cell reproduces.

1. Get a jar containing yeast mixture.

2. Use your dropper. Place a drop of yeast mixture on a microscope slide.

3. Add a cover slip.

4. Examine the slide under low power with your microscope.

5. In Space **a** on your data sheet, draw some of the yeast cells.

•6. What shape do most of the yeast cells have?

7. Examine the slide carefully. You may have to move it. Try to find a cell that looks like a bowling pin.

8. Draw one of these cells in Space **b** on your data sheet.

• 9. How is this cell different from the ones you drew in Space **a**?

Look at the cell you drew in Space **b**. The larger part of the cell is the parent cell. The smaller part is the new organism. It is called a *bud*.

•10. What is the new organism attached to?

•11. What is the new organism growing out of?

•12. In time, what do you predict will happen to the bud?

•13. How do yeast cells reproduce?

•14. How can reproduction take place in some living things?

•15. How many parents are needed for reproduction in yeast?

•16. How many cells are needed for reproduction in yeast?

B. THE BEASTIES ARE BREAKING UP

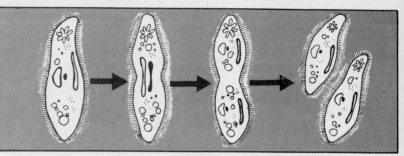

Look at these drawings.

In Idea 3, you studied one-celled animals. Like other living things, they reproduce. Let's see how.

These are pictures of a one-celled animal. The animal is reproducing.

• 17. How many parent cells are needed for reproduction here?

• 18. How many cells does the parent cell produce?

The cells produced by the parent cell are called *daughter cells*.

• 19. How are the daughter cells different from the parent cell?

• 20. How do the daughter cells compare with each other in size and shape?

In time, each daughter cell will grow as large as the parent cell.

• 21. What do you predict they will do then?

• 22. How will they do this?

• 23. How many cells are needed for reproduction in this organism?

• 24. How do these one-celled organisms reproduce?

Look at these drawings.

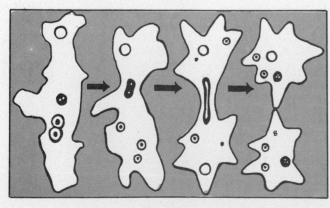

These are pictures of another one-celled animal. The animal is reproducing.

• 25. How many parent cells are needed for reproduction in this organism?

• 26. How many cells does the parent cell produce?

• 27. How are the daughter cells different from the parent cell?

• 28. How do the daughter cells compare with each other in size and shape?

• 29. In time, what do you predict each of the daughter cells will do?

• 30. How will they do this?

• 31. How many cells are needed for reproduction in this organism?

• 32. How do these one-celled organisms reproduce?

• 33. How can reproduction take place in some living things?

C. CAN CELLS DO MATH?

An organism carries on its life activities, and cells wear out and die. Other cells may be injured. When you cut yourself, the cut heals. Cells that are injured or worn out are replaced.

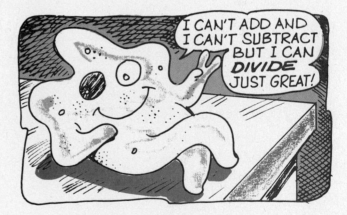

• 34. Where do you think new cells come from?

• 35. How do you think skin cells reproduce?

• 36. How does reproduction take place in yeast?

• 37. How does reproduction take place in some one-celled animals?

• 38. What can you say about how reproduction may begin in some living things?

THE CONCEPT.

Idea 7 Investigation 3

LET'S GET TOGETHER

You've learned that reproduction can begin with the splitting of a single cell. Many one-celled organisms reproduce this way. The parent cell divides and forms two daughter cells. These cells are alike. They are the same size and shape. But there is only one parent. This type of reproduction is called *asexual reproduction*.

Asexual reproduction usually takes place in one-celled organisms. But reproduction may also take place in another way. Two parent cells may take part in producing a new organism. This type of reproduction usually takes place in many-celled organisms. It is called *sexual reproduction*.

By the way, you are a many-celled organism.

A. LET'S BUILD A BRIDGE

In the summer, water in many ponds looks green. This color may be caused by a plant. The plant looks like a piece of green sewing thread. The cells of this plant are attached end to end, forming a thread.

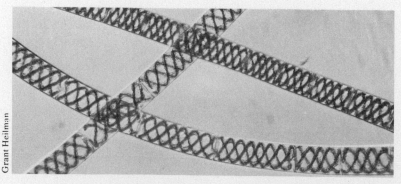

Grant Heilman

Let's examine how reproduction takes place in this plant.

Look at Drawing (a).

• 1. How are the threads arranged?

• 2. How are the cells in each thread arranged?

Look at Drawing (b).

• 3. What is happening to the wall of the thread?

• 4. What is happening to the cell wall?

Look at Drawing (c).

• 5. What do you notice about the bridge between the two cells?

• 6. How is this different from the bridge in Drawing (b)?

• 7. What is the bridge doing?

• 8. In what direction did the arms of the bridge move?

Look at Drawing (d).

• 9. What has happened to the wall between the two arms?

•10. What is happening to the material in one of the cells?

•11. Where do you think this material is moving?

Look at Drawing (e).

•12. Where did the material from the empty cell go?

•13. How many cells do you see now?

•14. What do you think the material from both cells did?

•15. How many new cells were formed?

•16. How many parent cells were needed to form the new cell?

Look at Drawing (f).

•17. What is happening to the new cell that was formed?

•18. What does this cell look like?

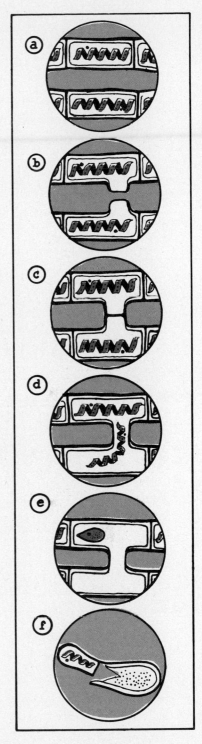

In time, this new cell will divide. The daughter cells will divide several times to form a new thread. Then sexual reproduction will begin again.

• 19. How many new cells are formed in sexual reproduction?

• 20. How many parent cells are needed?

• 21. What happens to the material from each parent cell?

B. I HEARD THAT FISH STORY BEFORE

In one-celled organisms, different sexes are not found. There is no male. There is no female. This is not true in most many-celled organisms. There are male and female organisms. The male organism produces male reproductive cells. These are called *sperm*. The female organism produces female reproductive cells. These are called *eggs*.

Let's see what this means.

There are male and female fish. How do they reproduce?

The female fish may drop thousands of eggs at a time.

The male fish swims over these cells. He drops millions of sperm to cover the eggs.

• 22. What do you predict will happen between each of the sperm and eggs?

Remember, sperm and eggs are reproductive cells. In Part A, you learned how parent cells in plants behave.

• 23. How many parent cells are needed?

• 24. How many new cells will form from these?

• 25. What happens to the material from the parent cells?

C. THAT'S THE STORY

SEXUAL RE-PRODUCTION IS EASY TO UNDERSTAND!

THERE ARE TWO PARENT CELLS!

AND THEY JOIN TO FORM A NEW CELL!

• 26. How many parent cells are needed in sexual reproduction?

• 27. How many new cells are produced?

• 28. What happens to the material from parent cells in some plants?

• 29. What happens to the material from parent cells in some animals?

• 30. How can reproduction begin in some organisms?

THE CONCEPT.

YOU CAN'T BUY PARTS FOR IT

In Investigations 2 and 3, you learned that:

    (a) Reproduction can begin with the splitting of a cell.
    (b) Reproduction can begin with the joining of two cells.

There's more to the story of reproduction. There is another very special kind. Not all organisms can do it. In fact, much of what happens is still a mystery.

A. DON'T LOSE YOUR SKIN

Your teacher will give you a jar with some one-celled organisms.

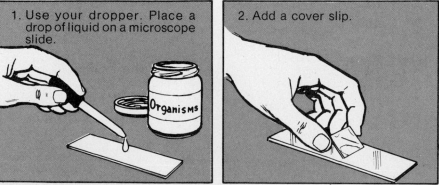

1. Use your dropper. Place a drop of liquid on a microscope slide.

2. Add a cover slip.

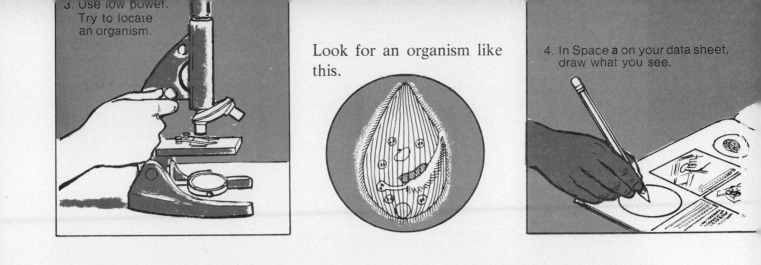

3. Use low power. Try to locate an organism.

Look for an organism like this.

4. In Space **a** on your data sheet, draw what you see.

5. Label the nucleus.

6. Label the cell membrane.

- 7. Describe what you see.

- 8. What does the cell membrane look like?

Your teacher will give you a bottle of very weak acid. You may have seen bottles of acid in your classroom. Most acids are harmful to skin and other tissues.

What effect will the acid have on your organism?

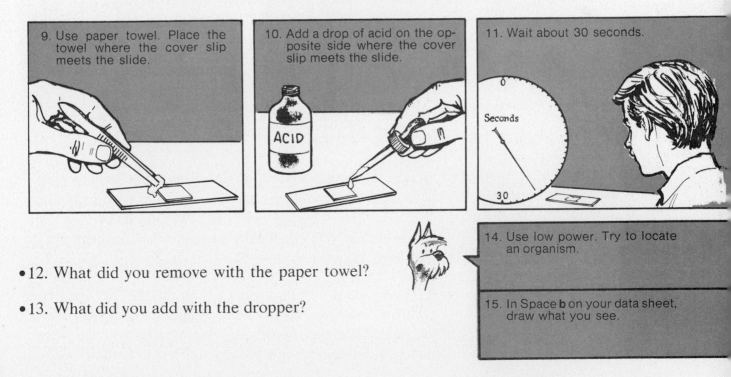

9. Use paper towel. Place the towel where the cover slip meets the slide.

10. Add a drop of acid on the opposite side where the cover slip meets the slide.

11. Wait about 30 seconds.

Seconds

14. Use low power. Try to locate an organism.

- 12. What did you remove with the paper towel?

- 13. What did you add with the dropper?

15. In Space **b** on your data sheet, draw what you see.

• 16. Look at the cell membrane. What do you see?

• 17. How is this drawing different from the one you made in Space **a**?

• 18. What happened to the cell membrane?

• 19. How can you explain this?

20. Use paper towel. Place the towel where the cover slip meets the slide.

21. Use a clean dropper. Add a drop of clean water on the opposite side of the cover slip.

22. Use low power. Try to locate an organism. Observe it for several seconds.

23. In Space **c** on your data sheet, draw what you see.

• 24. Look at the cell membrane. What do you see?

• 25. How is this drawing different from the one you made in Space **b**?

• 26. What happened to the cell membrane?

• 27. What did the organism do?

B. HOW ABOUT THAT SPONGE FARM?

Florida News Bureau

You have seen that a one-celled animal can reproduce one of its parts. There are several other organisms that can do this. This special type of reproduction is called *regeneration.* Let's look at regeneration in some other living things.

Did you know that a sponge is an animal? Sponges can be grown. A sponge is cut into many small pieces. These pieces are planted in shallow water. When the pieces grow large, they are picked.

The starfish is another animal that regenerates a part of its body.

Starfish feed on oysters. Many years ago, angry fishermen who caught starfish would cut them up. Then they threw them back into the sea. They thought this destroyed the animal.

• 28. Why was this an unwise thing to do?

Have you ever seen lobsters or crabs? These animals can also regenerate missing parts. When you walk on the beach, you may see the claws of these animals. The claws have broken off.

• 29. What do you think these animals can do?

• 30. What special type of reproduction lets them do this?

Skin cells can also regenerate themselves.

• 31. What happens to a cut after a few days?

• 32. What do you think the skin cells are doing?

• 33. What kind of special reproduction have you studied in this Investigation?

• 34. What does regeneration mean?

THE CONCEPT.

Idea 7
Investigation 5

THE WORLD'S FULL COURT PRESS

Mickey Palmer/DPI

In this Idea, you have studied reproduction. You have learned that:

(a) All living things come from other living things.
(b) Reproduction may begin with the splitting of a cell.
(c) Reproduction may begin with the joining of two cells.
(d) Some organisms can reproduce new parts.

MAN, THAT'S A LOT OF OYSTERS!

THAT'S A LOT OF PEARLS!

BOY, MORE PEARLS OF WISDOM!

In Investigation 3, you learned that some fish may produce thousands of eggs. A single female oyster can produce more than 100 million eggs in one year. What would happen if all these eggs grew into adults? In two years, the earth would be covered with a layer of oysters several miles thick!

David has a point. That's a lot of oysters. How would they affect each other: Would there be any pressure on the organisms in the group? In fact, how does the number of organisms in any group affect that group? That is the question for this Investigation.

Your teacher will give you 4 closed Petri dishes. These dishes contain food for microscopic organisms. Your teacher will also give you 4 cotton-plugged test tubes. Do not open the dishes or tubes until you are ready to use them.

A. HE ISN'T SO BIG

THAT GUY MUST HAVE BEEN RAISED ON A FARM!

1. Label the dishes **A, B, C,** and **D.**

2. Label the cotton-plugged test tubes **A, B, C,** and **D.**

3. Remove the cotton plug from tube **A**. Add 10 ml of water to the tube. Do this also with tubes **B, C,** and **D.**

4. Dip the loop into the jar marked "Organisms." Make sure that water fills the loop.

5. Stir the loop into the water in tube **A**.

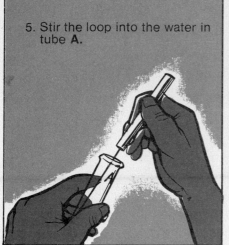

6. Mix tube **A** by rolling it between your hands.

8. Use your dropper. Add 20 drops of water from tube **A** to tube **B**.

•7. What did you add to the water in tube **A**?

9. Mix tube **B** by rolling it between your hands.

•10. What did you add to the water in tube **B**?

•11. Where does this water come from?

•12. What does this water contain?

•13. What does tube **B** now contain?

•14. Which tube do you think contains more organisms?

15. Use your dropper. Add 20 drops of water from tube **B** to tube **C**.

16. Mix tube **C** by rolling it between your hands.

•17. What did you add to the water in tube **C**?

•18. What does the water in tube **B** contain?

•19. What does tube **C** now contain?

•20. Which of the 3 tubes do you think contains the most organisms?

•21. Which of the 3 tubes do you think contains the fewest organisms?

22. Do not add anything to tube **D**.

•23. What does tube **D** contain?

•24. Which tube is your control?

25. Use your dropper. Add 20 drops of liquid from tube **A** to dish **A**.

26. Use a cotton swab. Gently smear the liquid over all of the food in the dish.

Your teacher will give you a jar containing a liquid. Place *each* cotton swab in the jar *after* you use it.

27. Rinse your dropper. Add 20 drops of liquid from tube **B** to dish **B**.

28. Use a clean cotton swab. Gently smear the liquid over all of the food.

29. Rinse your dropper. Add 20 drops of liquid from tube **C** to dish **C**.

30. Use a clean cotton swab. Gently smear the liquid over all of the food.

31. Use a clean dropper. Add 20 drops of liquid from tube **D** to dish **D**.

32. Use a clean cotton swab. Gently smear the liquid over all of the food.

33. Label the dishes with your name and section. Store them in a warm, dark place for 2 days.

B. LET'S CHECK IT OUT

I'M READY TO CHECK OUT!

NOTES

34. After 2 days, carefully observe your dishes.

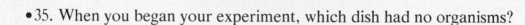

- 35. When you began your experiment, which dish had no organisms?

- 36. Which dish had the fewest organisms?

- 37. Which dish had the most organisms?

- 38. How many groups of organisms are now in dish **A**?

- 39. How many groups of organisms are now in dish **B**?

- 40. How many groups of organisms are now in dish **C**?

- 41. How many groups of organisms are now in dish **D**?

- 42. How can you explain the difference between dishes **A** and **C**?

•43. What is the average size of the groups in dish **A**?

•44. What is the average size of the groups in dish **C**?

45. Enter all of your data in Table 1 on your data sheet.

•46. How can you explain the difference?

•47. Which dish started with the most organisms?

•48. Which dish was the most crowded?

•49. Which dish started with the fewest organisms?

•50. Which dish was the least crowded?

•51. How did crowding affect growth in dish **A**?

•52. How did crowding affect growth in dish **C**?

•53. How did crowding affect your organisms?

•54. What can you say about crowding and living things?

C. DENSENESS BREEDS TENSENESS

Dr. John Calhoun examined the effects of crowding on rats. He placed several rats in a large cage. He gave them more than enough food. Dr. Calhoun figured that in two years there would be 50,000 rats. But after two years, he counted only 200. There was no over-population. Why was this so?

During the two years, Dr. Calhoun and his staff watched the rats closely. These are some of the things they saw.

(a) The rats formed groups and "rat slums."
(b) Fighting became common. Groups attacked other groups.
(c) Mothers neglected their young.
(d) Older rats attacked younger ones.
(e) Fewer babies were born. Many died soon after birth.
(f) Males and females were not interested in mating.
(g) The rats wandered around in a daze.
(h) Some rats just mysteriously died.
(i) The death rate reached 90 percent.

Why were so many rats dying?   When the dead rats were examined, the scientists found great changes in the organs. The changes had been caused by *emotional stress*. Emotional stress means being worried and upset. The body was no longer able to work properly.

• 55. What do you think would happen if 10 rabbits had to live inside a room for two years?

• 56. What do you think would happen if 10 people had to live inside a house for two years?

• 57. How did crowding affect your organisms?

• 58. How did crowding affect the rats?

• 59. What can you say about crowding and living things?

THE CONCEPT.

WE ALL HAVE AN AUNT CESTOR

Wow! Another one done! Hang in, you're doing great! This Idea has been about reproduction. Why must living things reproduce? Why is reproduction important?

You have learned that:

(a) All living things come from other living things.
(b) Reproduction may begin with the splitting of a cell.
(c) Reproduction may begin with the joining of two cells.
(d) Some organisms can produce new parts.
(e) The number of organisms in a group can pressure the group.

• 60. What do all living things come from?

• 61. What must plants be able to do to continue their own kind?

• 62. What must animals be able to do to continue their own kind?

• 63. What is this process called?

• 64. What must living things be able to do to continue their own kind?

Summarize the Idea.

THE IDEA.

THE DRIP OF LIFE

U.S. Forest Service

These trees are the same age. One group is tall and healthy. The other group is short and weak. Why are they different?

USDA

U.S. Forest Service

These rats are the same age. One is large and healthy. The other is smaller and weak. Why are they different?

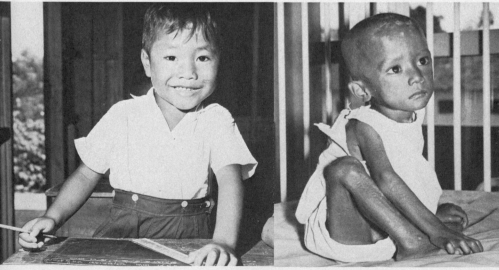

UNICEF

UNICEF

These children are the same age. Why are they different?

These questions·are not hard to answer. We just need some information. We must know more about the surroundings of these living things. We call the surroundings of living things their *environment*.

A. A CONTROLLED MOLD

You have probably seen molds. They are small plants that can grow on bread, cheese, or fruit. They are in the air around us. Let's experiment with a mold's environment.

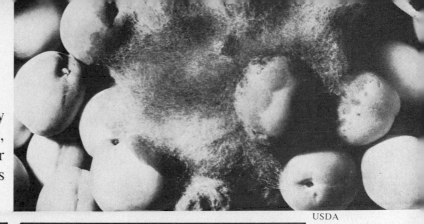

USDA

1. Get 2 jars. Write your name and section on each.

2. Label one jar "Control." Label the other jar "Experiment."

3. Place a small piece of bread in the control jar.

4. Wet a small piece of paper towel. Place it in the experiment jar. Add a small piece of bread.

Wet paper towel

5. At the end of the period, cover both jars. Store them in a dark place for 2 days.

- 6. What did you place in the control jar?

- 7. What did you place in the experiment jar?

- 8. How are the jars the same?

- 9. How are the jars different?

•10. What is the environment in the control jar?

•11. What is the environment in the experiment jar?

•12. What do you predict will happen in the control jar?

•13. What do you predict will happen in the experiment jar?

B. I WOULDN'T BUY THAT BREAD

•15. What do you see in the control jar?

•16. What do you see in the experiment jar?

•17. How are the pieces of bread different?

•18. What do you think caused this difference?

•19. What do molds need in order to grow?

•20. Where must the water come from?

•21. What do you think happens to molds if the environment doesn't supply water?

> You began this Investigation by looking at some pictures of trees. One group was short and weak.

•22. What do you think was missing from their environment?

•23. What do you think living things must get from their environment?

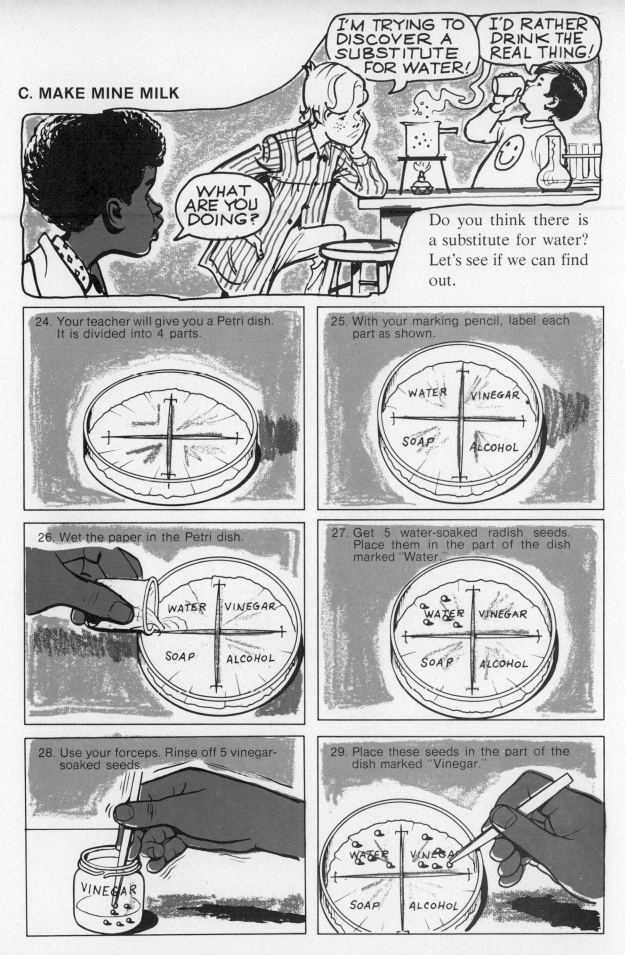

C. MAKE MINE MILK

30. Rinse off 5 soap-soaked seeds. Place them in the part of the dish marked "Soap."

31. Rinse off 5 alcohol-soaked seeds. Place them in the part of the dish marked "Alcohol."

32. Cover the seeds with a wet paper towel circle.

33. Cover the Petri dish. Write your name and section on the cover.

34. Your teacher will give you another Petri dish.

35. Place 5 dry seeds in this dish. These seeds have not been soaked in anything.

36. Cover this Petri dish. Write your name and section on the cover. Label this dish "Dry."

37. Store your experiment for 2 days. Do not disturb.

• 38. What were the five environments of your seeds?

• 39. Which seeds are the control?

• 40. Which seeds do you predict will not grow?

• 41. Which seeds do you predict will grow?

D. WHERE ARE THOSE WILD SEEDS?

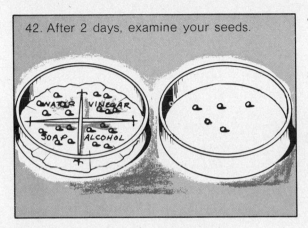

42. After 2 days, examine your seeds.

• 43. What happened to the vinegar-soaked seeds?

• 44. What happened to the soap-soaked seeds?

• 45. What happened to the alcohol-soaked seeds?

• 46. What happened to the water-soaked seeds?

• 47. What happened to the dry seeds?

• 48. What do seeds need to grow?

• 49. Where does this come from?

Myers/Black Star

Massar/Black Star

E. DRINKING IT ALL UP

• 50. Why do you think these animals are here?

• 51. Why do you think nothing has grown here?

• 52. What must the environment supply for mold to grow?

• 53. What must the environment supply for seeds to grow?

• 54. What must all living things get from their environment?

Re-read your answers to questions 23 and 54. Write the concept.

THE CONCEPT.

Idea 8 Investigation 2

WHEN YOU'RE HOT, YOU'RE HOT

Grant Heilman

In the last Investigation, you learned how important water is to living things. Water is a non-living part of the environment. Non-living parts of the environment are called *physical factors*.

Let's see if we can find out what else the environment is made of.

A. PLEASE DON'T SLIT MY GILLS

Your teacher will give you a jar of water containing a fish.

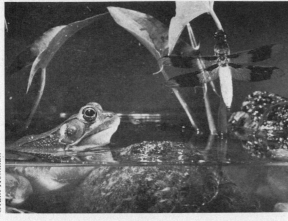

I HOPE YOU GET HEARTBURN!

1. Look at the gill slits of your fish.

Mouth

Gill slit

• 2. What are the gill slits doing?

Fishes breathe through their gills. Water moves into the mouth and out through the gill slits. The gills of a fish are like your lungs. Your lungs take oxygen from the air you breathe. A fish's gills take oxygen from the water.

You are going to count the number of gill movements of your fish. You will count for one minute. The number of gill movements in one minute is the breathing rate. Your fish will be moving, so watch closely.

3. Read the temperature of the water. Enter this temperature in Table 1 on your data sheet.

4. Count the number of gill movements of your fish. Remember to count for 1 minute. Enter this count in Table 1.

•5. What is the breathing rate of your fish?

6. Gently place 2 ice cubes in the water.

7. Wait 2 minutes. Read the temperature. Enter the data in Table 1.

8. Count the number of gill movements in 1 minute. Enter this in Table 1.

9. Gently place 2 more ice cubes in the water.

•10. What is the total number of ice cubes you have added?

11. After 2 minutes, take the water temperature. Enter this in Table 1.

12. Count the number of gill movements in 1 minute. Enter this in Table 1.

•13. What is the breathing rate of your fish now?

•14. What was the water temperature at the start of the experiment?

•15. What is the water temperature now?

•16. What has happened to the water temperature?

•17. What was the breathing rate of your fish at the start of the experiment?

•18. What was the breathing rate of your fish at the end?

•19. Why do you think it changed?

•20. What change in the fish's environment caused the breathing rate to slow down?

•21. What physical factor might affect living things?

•22. Besides water, what is another physical factor found in the environment?

B. DO YEAST CELLS BLUSH?

In Part A, you found that temperature can affect a fish. Let's find out what temperature changes can do to yeast cells. Your teacher will give you a test tube of yeast mixture.

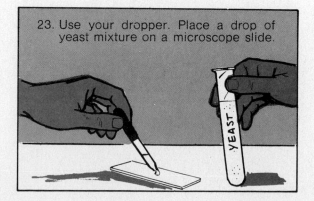

23. Use your dropper. Place a drop of yeast mixture on a microscope slide.

24. Add a cover slip.

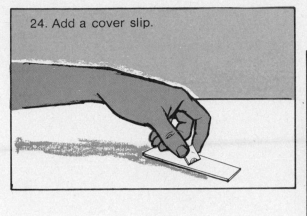

25. Examine the yeast cells under low power with your microscope.

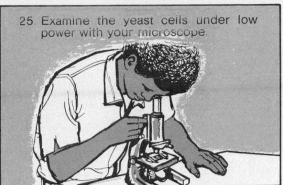

• 26. What color are the yeast cells?

27. Add 5 drops of red dye to the yeast mixture.

Dye

YEAST

DYE

28. Shake the tube gently.

YEAST

29. Rinse your dropper. Place a drop of the red yeast mixture on a slide.

30. Add a cover slip.

31. Examine the mixture under low power.

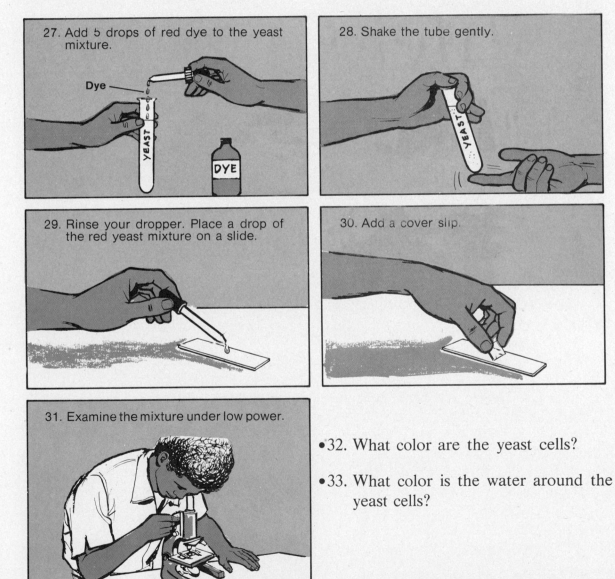

• 32. What color are the yeast cells?

• 33. What color is the water around the yeast cells?

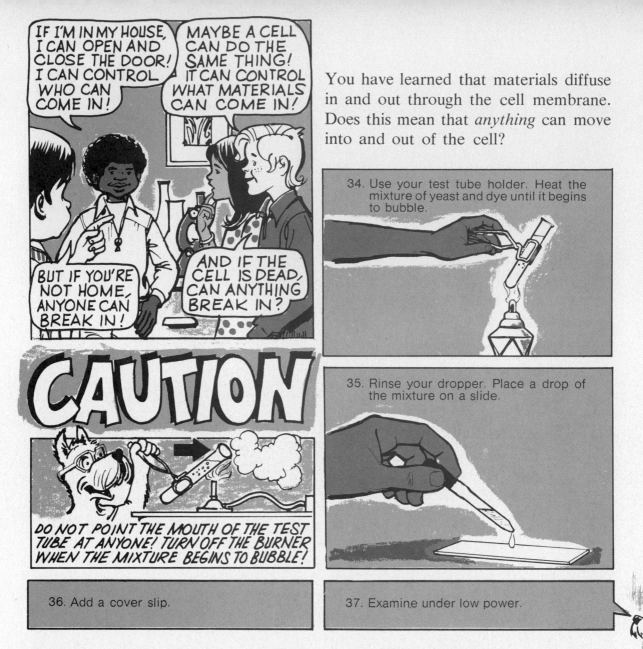

You have learned that materials diffuse in and out through the cell membrane. Does this mean that *anything* can move into and out of the cell?

34. Use your test tube holder. Heat the mixture of yeast and dye until it begins to bubble.

35. Rinse your dropper. Place a drop of the mixture on a slide.

36. Add a cover slip.

37. Examine under low power.

•38. What color is the water around the yeast cells?

•39. What color are the yeast cells?

•40. What color were the yeast cells before heating?

The red dye is unwanted material. As long as the yeast is alive, it can keep the red dye out. When the cell dies, materials are free to enter it.

•41. What did heating do to the yeast cells?

•42. What is the job of the cell membrane?

•43. What can you say about temperature and living things?

•44. What physical factor might affect living things?

•45. Water is one physical factor in the environment. What is another physical factor?

Re-read questions 44 and 45.

THE CONCEPT.

264   Idea 8/Investigation 2

Idea 8 Investigation 3

YOU'VE GOT TO SEE THE LIGHT

You have just learned that:

(a) Living things must obtain water from the environment.
(b) Living things are affected by the temperature of the environment.

Water and temperature are two physical factors that can affect life.

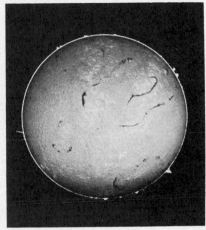

This is a close-up view of our sun. Energy from the sun can affect the environment in many ways.

High Altitude Observatory, Boulder, Col.

A. DON'T KEEP ME IN THE DARK

HOW DOES LIGHT AFFECT LIVING THINGS?

THIS CALLS FOR ANOTHER CONTROLLED EXPERIMENT!

I'VE GOT AN IDEA! LET'S KEEP HALF OF PHIDEAU IN THE DARK AND THE OTHER HALF IN THE LIGHT FOR TWO DAYS!

MAY I SUGGEST RADISHES? THEN WE CAN EAT THE EXPERIMENT!

Phideau has a good idea. Radish seeds grow fast. How are they affected by light?

1. Get 2 Petri dishes. Write your name and section on both dishes.

L. TAYLOR *1
L. TAYLOR #1

2. Label one dish "Dark" and the other "Light."

L. TAYLOR *1 DARK
TAYLOR *1 LIGHT

3. Get 20 radish seeds and 4 paper towel circles.

TAYLOR #1 DARK

TAYLOR #1 LIGHT

4. Place 2 wet paper towel circles in each dish.

TAYLOR #1 DARK

TAYLOR #1 LIGHT

5. Use your forceps. Place 10 radish seeds in each dish.

TAYLOR #1 DARK

TAYLOR #1 LIGHT

6. Cover both dishes.

L.TAYLOR #1 LIGHT

TAYLOR #1 DARK

7. Place the "Dark" dish in a dark place.

YLOR #1 DAR

8. Place the "Light" dish under a bright light.

TAYLOR #1 LIGHT

• 9. What is the only difference in the environments of the radish seeds?

10. Wait 2 days. Then observe the seeds.

MARCH 4

MARCH 3

MARCH 2

• 11. How many radish seeds grew in the dark?

• 12. How many radish seeds grew in the light?

• 13. What color are the seedlings grown in the dark?

• 14. What color are the seedlings grown in the light?

●15. Which seedlings have the longer stems?

●16. Which seedlings have the longer roots?

17. Examine the root hairs with a magnifying glass.

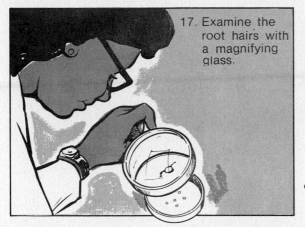

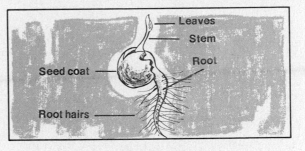

●18. Which seedlings have more root hairs?

●19. What other differences can you observe between the two groups of seedlings?

●20. What was the difference in the environments of the radish seeds?

●21. What factor affects the growth of radish seedlings?

●22. What factor can affect the growth of living things?

B. I'D RATHER BE BRIGHT

I DIDN'T REALIZE I WAS SUCH AN IMPORTANT PHYSICAL FACTOR!

Elodea is a water plant. You've worked with it before. How is it affected by light?

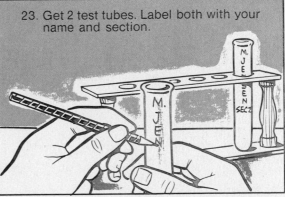

23. Get 2 test tubes. Label both with your name and section.

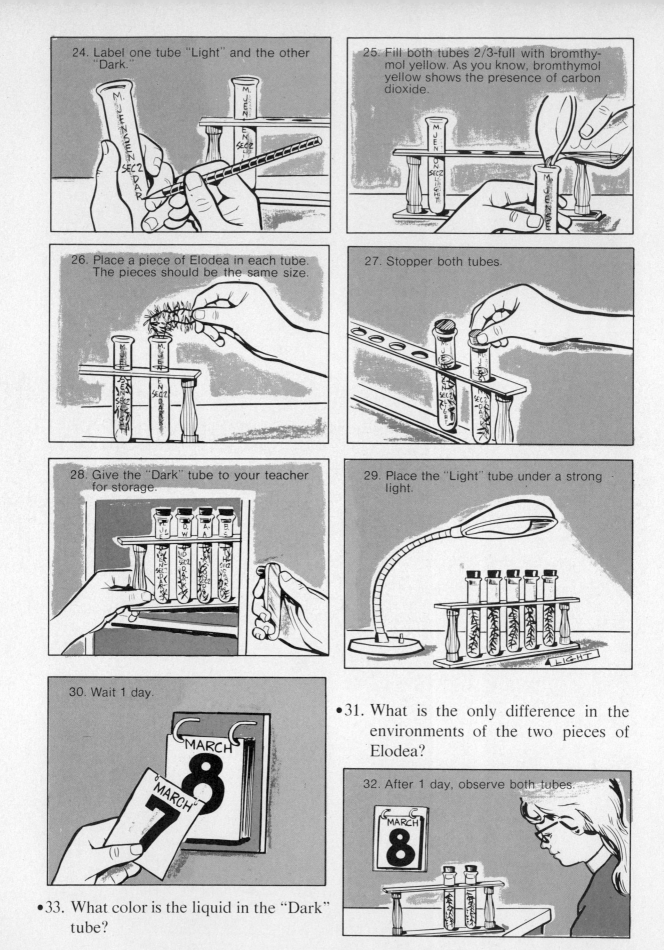

24. Label one tube "Light" and the other "Dark."

25. Fill both tubes 2/3-full with bromthymol yellow. As you know, bromthymol yellow shows the presence of carbon dioxide.

26. Place a piece of Elodea in each tube. The pieces should be the same size.

27. Stopper both tubes.

28. Give the "Dark" tube to your teacher for storage.

29. Place the "Light" tube under a strong light.

30. Wait 1 day.

•31. What is the only difference in the environments of the two pieces of Elodea?

32. After 1 day, observe both tubes.

•33. What color is the liquid in the "Dark" tube?

• 34. What does this mean?

• 35. What color is the liquid in the "Light" tube?

• 36. What does this mean?

• 37. What physical factor must be present for Elodea to remove carbon dioxide?

• 38. What physical factor can affect plants?

• 39. What factor in the environment might affect living things?

C. ARE ALL THE LIGHTS ON?

Light conditions affect living things in many ways.

Rue/Monkmeyer

Both owls and mice prefer doing their thing in the dark.

Some plants turn to face the sun as it moves in the sky.

• 40. What environmental factor can affect radish seeds and Elodea?

• 41. Water and temperature are two physical factors in the environment. What is a third factor in the environment?

• 42. What factor in the environment might affect living things?

Re-read questions 39 and 42. Write the concept.

THE CONCEPT.

SOUL FOOD SPECIAL

You've learned that water, temperature, and light can affect life.

Ancient man hunted for something else in his environment.

David is hunting for the same thing.

How does the food supply in an environment affect living things?

A. BACK TO BACTERIA

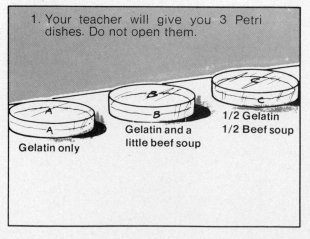

1. Your teacher will give you 3 Petri dishes. Do not open them.

A — Gelatin only

B — Gelatin and a little beef soup

C — 1/2 Gelatin 1/2 Beef soup

The dishes are marked **A** **B**, and **C**. **A** contains gelatin. **B** has mostly gelatin and a little beef soup. **C** is about half gelatin and half beef soup.

You will try to grow bacteria and molds in each dish. Bacteria and molds are microscopic living things. They are on you and all around you. Beef soup is food for bacteria and molds. Gelatin is *not*.

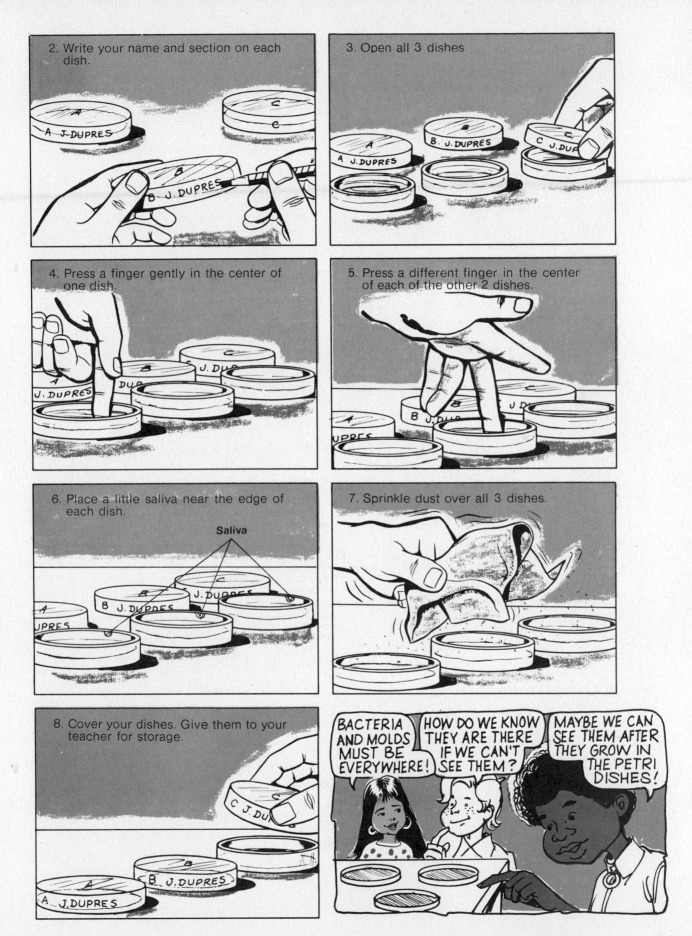

2. Write your name and section on each dish.

3. Open all 3 dishes.

4. Press a finger gently in the center of one dish.

5. Press a different finger in the center of each of the other 2 dishes.

6. Place a little saliva near the edge of each dish.

Saliva

7. Sprinkle dust over all 3 dishes.

8. Cover your dishes. Give them to your teacher for storage.

BACTERIA AND MOLDS MUST BE EVERYWHERE!

HOW DO WE KNOW THEY ARE THERE IF WE CAN'T SEE THEM?

MAYBE WE CAN SEE THEM AFTER THEY GROW IN THE PETRI DISHES!

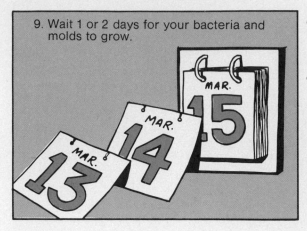

9. Wait 1 or 2 days for your bacteria and molds to grow.

10. What two kinds of living things are you trying to grow?

11. What is the only difference in the environments in the dishes?

12. After 1 or 2 days, examine your 3 dishes.

The spots you see are called *colonies*. Each colony may contain millions of organisms. The number of organisms in any colony is its *population*.

13. How much food was in dish **A**?

14. What do you observe in dish **A**?

15. How much food was in dish **B**?

16. What do you observe in dish **B**?

17. How much food was in dish **C**?

18. What do you observe in dish **C**?

19. Which dish has the most growth?

20. How much food was in this dish?

21. Each colony is a population of millions of organisms. Which dish has the greatest population? Why?

22. What do populations of bacteria and molds need to grow?

23. What do populations of living things need to grow?

B. IT'S NOT ALL THE SAME

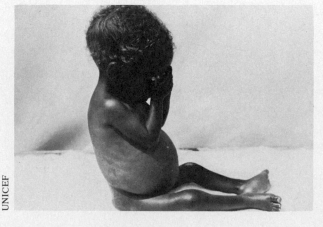

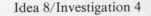
UNICEF

This child is sick. He has a disease common in poor countries where most food is starchy. He needs protein in his diet. Protein can help this child grow normally.

You've already learned how to test foods for starch and sugar. How can we test foods for protein?

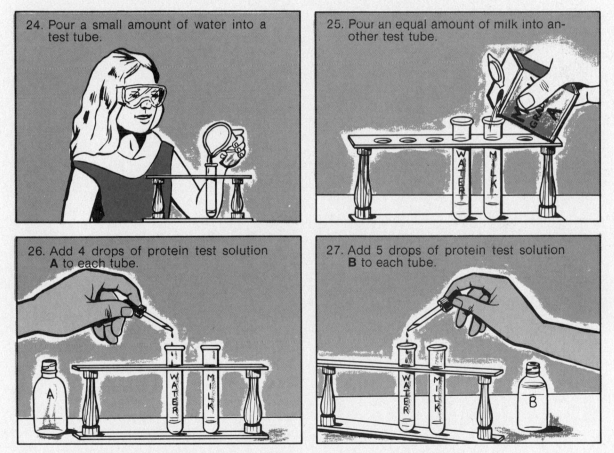

24. Pour a small amount of water into a test tube.

25. Pour an equal amount of milk into another test tube.

26. Add 4 drops of protein test solution **A** to each tube.

27. Add 5 drops of protein test solution **B** to each tube.

• 28. What change did you observe with the water?

• 29. What change did you observe with the milk?

The violet color shows that protein is present. If the violet color does not appear, protein is not present. Now try some other foods.

30. Pour a little egg white into a test tube.

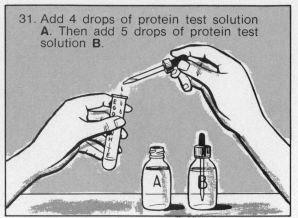

31. Add 4 drops of protein test solution **A**. Then add 5 drops of protein test solution **B**.

• 32. What change do you observe?

• 33. What type of food is in egg white?

34. Pour a little bean soup into a test tube.

35. Add water until the test tube is 1/2-full. Shake it gently.

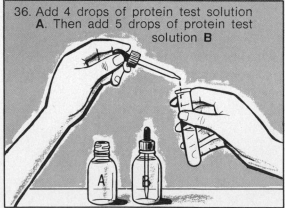

36. Add 4 drops of protein test solution **A**. Then add 5 drops of protein test solution **B**

• 37. What change do you observe?

• 38. What type of food is in bean soup?

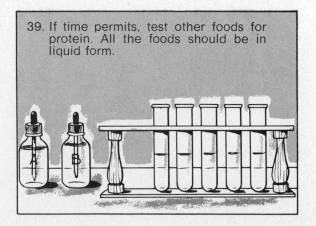

39. If time permits, test other foods for protein. All the foods should be in liquid form.

• 40. What foods have you found that have protein?

• 41. What is missing in the diet of the sick child on page 272?

•42. How can lack of protein in the diet affect a population?

•43. What do populations of living things need to grow?

C. WHO DO YOU SUPPORT?

There is very little food for cattle in this environment.

Wettach/Black Star

USDA

USDA

This environment gives cattle all the food they can eat.

•44. Which environment can support a larger cattle population?

The plants on the right were fed with fertilizer. The plants on the left were not. Fertilizer is a plant food.

•45. Which environment can support a larger plant population?

•46. How did the amount of food affect your bacteria and mold populations?

•47. What factor influences the size of a population?

•48. What do populations of living things need to grow?

Re-read questions 23 and 48. Write the concept.

THE CONCEPT.

Investigation 5

CHANGE IS THE NAME OF THE GAME

I'M NOT SURE I LIKE THIS CHANGE!

You're becoming an environmental expert! Here's what you've learned about living things and their environment:

(a) Living things must obtain water.
(b) Living things are affected by temperature changes.
(c) Living things are affected by light conditions.
(d) The food supply influences the size of a population.

What else is happening in the environment?

A. RAIN, RAIN, GO AWAY

This mountain environment is in Hawaii. Over 470 inches of rain may fall here each year. That is about 8 times your height.

This desert environment is in Death Valley, California. About 4 inches of rain fall here each year.

TABLE 1 AVERAGE MONTHLY RAINFALL (OR SNOWFALL) FOR NEW YORK CITY IN 1969

Month	Inches of Rain
Jan.	1.1
Feb.	3.1
March	3.7
April	4.0
May	2.7
June	3.2
July	7.4
Aug.	2.5
Sept.	8.3
Oct.	2.0
Nov.	3.6
Dec.	7.1

U.S. Department of Commerce
Environmental Data Service

Study Table 1. It shows the average monthly rainfall (or snowfall) for New York City in 1969.

• 1. Which month had the most rain?

• 2. How much rain fell in that month?

• 3. Which month had the least rain?

• 4. How much rain fell in that month?

• 5. How much difference in rain was there between the wettest and the driest months? (Subtract your answer to question 4 from your answer to question 2.)

• 6. How many months had the same amount of rain?

• 7. The spring months are March, April, and May. How much rain fell during the spring?

• 8. The summer months are June, July, and August. How much rain fell during the summer?

• 9. How much difference in rain was there between summer and spring? (Subtract your answer to question 7 from your answer to question 8.)

• 10. What factor in an environment can change from season to season?

• 11. What can you say about the amount of rain in any one environment?

B. SOME LIKE IT HOT; SOME LIKE IT COLD

Is the amount of rainfall in an environment the only factor that changes?

TABLE 2
AVERAGE MONTHLY TEMPERATURE FOR LOS ANGELES IN 1970

Month	Average Temperature
Jan.	58°F.
Feb.	61°
March	61°
April	61°
May	67°
June	70°
July	75°
Aug.	76°
Sept.	74°
Oct.	68°
Nov.	63°
Dec.	57°

U.S. Department of Commerce
Environmental Data Service

TABLE 3
HIGHEST DAILY TEMPERATURE FOR CHICAGO, JULY, 1971

July	Highest Temp	July	Highest Temp
1	84° F	17	75° F
2	80°	18	83°
3	89°	19	74°
4	94°	20	82°
5	86°	21	86°
6	88°	22	89°
7	90°	23	80°
8	86°	24	79°
9	79°	25	85°
10	81°	26	74°
11	71°	27	76°
12	86°	28	76°
13	90°	29	72°
14	83°	30	69°
15	84°	31	73°
16	90°		

U.S. Department of Commerce
National Weather Service

Study Table 2. It shows the average monthly temperature for Los Angeles in 1970.

• 12. Which month had the highest average temperature?

• 13. What was the average temperature for that month?

• 14. Which month had the lowest average temperature?

• 15. What was the average temperature for that month?

• 16. What was the difference in average temperature between the hottest and coldest months? (Subtract your answer to question 15 from your answer to question 13.)

• 17. How many months had the same average temperature?

• 18. Besides rain, what factor in the environment can change from month to month?

___

Study Table 3. It shows the highest daily temperature in Chicago for one month.

• 19. What date had the highest temperature?

• 20. What was the temperature on that date?

• 21. What date had the lowest temperature?

• 22. What was the temperature on that date?

• 23. How much difference in temperature was there between these two dates? (Subtract your answer to question 22 from your answer to question 20.)

•24. How many dates had the same 86° temperature?

•25. What factor in the environment can change from day to day?

•26. What can you say about the temperature in any one environment?

C. DOES EVERYTHING CHANGE?

Phideau can be sure the environment will change. These changes will affect Phideau and all other living things.

•27. This is the same tree in summer and winter. What environmental changes could have caused these differences?

•28. What can you say about the amount of rain in any one environment?

•29. What can you say about the temperature in any one environment?

•30. What is constantly happening to the environment?

THE CONCEPT.

WHERE ON EARTH IS LIFE?

NASA

This is the planet Earth seen from space. Earth is the environment for billions of organisms.

You've learned that this environment is constantly changing. Living things are affected by these changes.

No trace of life has been discovered on any other planet. The environments on other planets do not seem to have what living things need.

Can life exist everywhere on Earth?

A. FINDERS KEEPERS

I SEE LIFE ALL OVER THE EARTH!

BUT IS THERE LIFE DEEP IN THE OCEANS?

WHAT ABOUT MILES UP IN THE AIR?

ANYONE SEE A McDONALD'S?

Grant Heilman

•1. What kinds of living things are found in an ocean environment?

Thomas/Black Star

•2. What kinds of living things are found in an air environment?

Wenzel/Black Star

Monroe/DPI

•3. What living things are found in the mountain parts of a land environment?

•4. What kinds of living things are found under the ground?

Frauca/Monkmeyer

•5. In what environments can you find turtles?

Photo Researchers

•6. In what environments can you find pigeons?

•7. In what kinds of environments can you find people?

•8. In what kinds of environments can you find living things?

B. MY ENVIRONMENT IS BETTER THAN YOUR ENVIRONMENT

Environments are not all the same. The amount of light, heat, water, and food changes from place to place.

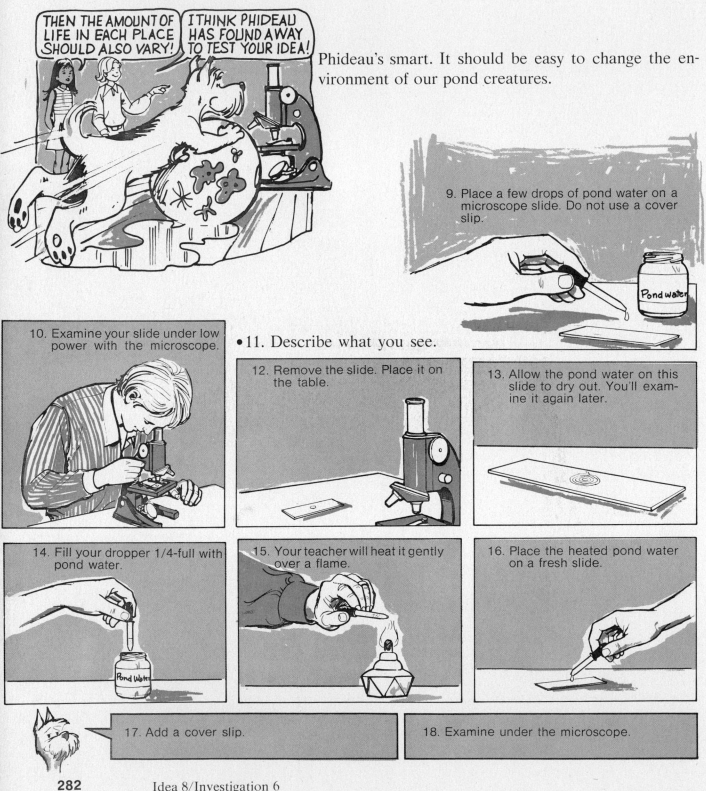

Phideau's smart. It should be easy to change the environment of our pond creatures.

9. Place a few drops of pond water on a microscope slide. Do not use a cover slip.

10. Examine your slide under low power with the microscope.

•11. Describe what you see.

12. Remove the slide. Place it on the table.

13. Allow the pond water on this slide to dry out. You'll examine it again later.

14. Fill your dropper 1/4-full with pond water.

15. Your teacher will heat it gently over a flame.

16. Place the heated pond water on a fresh slide.

17. Add a cover slip.

18. Examine under the microscope.

• 19. Describe what you see.

• 20. What factor has changed for this pond life?

• 21. What can very hot temperatures do to pond life?

• 22. What might very hot temperatures do to living things?

23. Get some frozen pond water from your teacher. It was frozen overnight and then melted.

24. Place a few drops of this pond water on a slide. Use a clean dropper.

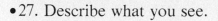

25. Add a cover slip.

26. Examine under the microscope.

• 27. Describe what you see.

• 28. What factor has changed for this pond life?

• 29. What can very cold temperatures do to pond life?

• 30. What might very cold temperatures do to living things?

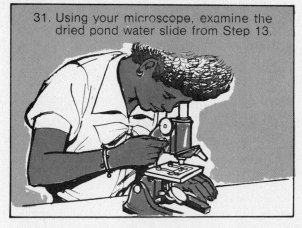

31. Using your microscope, examine the dried pond water slide from Step 13.

• 32. Describe what you see.

• 33. What factor has changed for this pond life?

• 34. What can lack of water do to pond life?

• 35. What might lack of water do to living things?

• 36. What kinds of environments might harm living things?

C. THE BIOSPHERE IS WHERE IT'S AT

I KNOW "BIO" MEANS "LIFE", BUT WHAT'S A SPHERE?

A BASKETBALL IS A SPHERE!

I GET IT! "BIOSPHERE" MEANS LIFE ON A BASKETBALL!

Paul's only half right. The earth is also a sphere. The *biosphere* is a layer around the earth. We find life only in the biosphere.

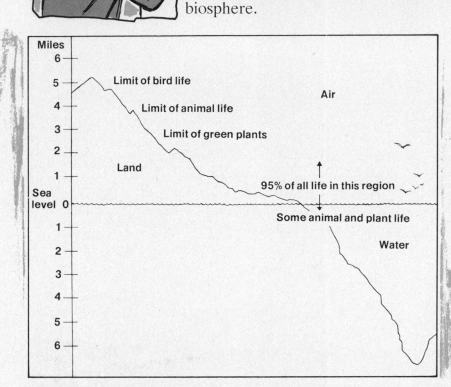

This chart shows the limits of the earth's biosphere. Some life can be found very high in the air. Some life can be found very deep in the ocean.

Most fish are found just below the water's surface. The environment near the surface provides most of their needs.

William H. Amos

This hatchet fish lives miles below the ocean surface. Very few other fish live at these great depths. The deep environment cannot supply their needs.

• 37. What part of the ocean supports the most life?

Few plants grow high in the mountains.

•38. What factors in a mountain environment might keep plants from growing?

•39. If few plants grow on mountain tops, would you expect many animals there? Why?

•40. What part of the land supports the least life?

•41. Would you expect much life high in the air? Why?

•42. What is the layer of life around the earth called?

•43. Would you expect much life at the top and bottom of the biosphere? Why?

•44. In what part of the biosphere is most life found?

D. WRAPPING UP THE BIOSPHERE

•45. The oceans are several miles deep. Where would you find the most life in the oceans?

•46. Birds have been seen several miles high in the air. But where would you find most birds?

•47. Plants have been found several miles up on the mountains. But where would you find most plants on land?

•48. What is the biosphere?

•49. In what part of the biosphere is most life found?

THE CONCEPT.

THE GOOD EARTH

You made it again! This Idea was about the environment. What is the environment made of?

To answer this question, you did six Investigations. You learned that:

(a) Living things must obtain water from their environment.

(b) Living things are affected by temperature changes in the environment.

(c) Living things are affected by light conditions in the environment.

(d) The food supply influences the size of a population.

(e) The environment is constantly changing.

(f) Most life exists near the middle of the biosphere.

Here's what the environment looks like on the moon. There is no life on the moon.

• 50. Is there a biosphere on the moon? Why?

• 51. What factors are missing in the moon's environment?

• 52. What are the surroundings of living things called?

• 53. What factors must be in these surroundings to maintain life?

• 54. What is the environment?

THE IDEA.

Idea 9 Investigation 1

AN OCEAN OF LIFE

In Idea 8, you learned that water is important to living things. Plants and animals need water. Their cells contain large amounts of water. In fact, without water there would be no life on earth.

Water has many other uses. It is so important that man builds his cities near water.

• 1. On your data sheet, list some uses of water.

A. THE WATER GAME

You can play the water game, too. Look at the picture.

Do you notice anything strange? Is something missing?

• 2. What has been left out of the picture?

You don't have to be an expert to know that water and fish are missing. Fish live in water. Some plants do too. In fact, many different living things make water their home.

Your teacher will give you a sheet of blue paper. You will also need scissors and some paste.

3. Look at the photographs in your data book.

4. Cut out the picture of the fish.

• 5. Where do fish live?

6. Cut out the pictures of all living things that live in water.

7. Place your pictures on the blue paper. Try to make an ocean scene.

8. Paste the pictures on the paper.

All the living things whose pictures you cut out share something. They all live in the same environment.

• 9. Where do they all live?

B. THE MICRO-MINI ZOO

Have you ever gone to the zoo? You can see many animals there. You probably have a zoo right in your science room. Do you know about it?

If you're looking for animals, you don't have to go far. All you need is some pond water and a microscope.

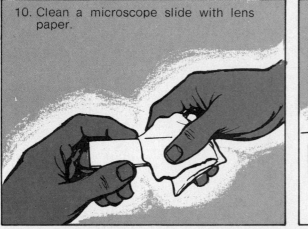

10. Clean a microscope slide with lens paper.

11. Use a toothpick and petroleum jelly. Draw a circle about the size of a dime on your slide.

When you finish Step 11, show the slide to your teacher. Do not go on to Step 12 until your slide has been checked.

12. With your dropper, place 2 or 3 drops of pond water inside the circle.

13. Carefully place a cover slip on the circle.

14. Examine your slide under low power.

15. In Space **a** on your data sheet, draw what you see.

• 16. How many living things did you see?

• 17. Describe the size of some of the organisms.

• 18. Describe the shape of some of the organisms.

• 19. Where do all of these organisms live?

C. HOME IS A WET PLACE

You have made an ocean scene. You have also studied the life in pond water. All of these organisms, large and small, plant and animal, share the same environment.

• 20. What environment do these organisms share?

• 21. What environment do these organisms need to stay alive?

• 22. What do you think will happen if these organisms are taken out of their environment?

Look at your answers to question 1 on your data sheet. Can you add anything to this list?

• 23. Why is water important to living things?

• 24. What environment do some organisms need to stay alive?

Re-read your answers to questions 21, 23, and 24. Write the concept.

THE CONCEPT.

DON'T BUG ME

In the last Investigation, you learned that many organisms live in water. Water is their home. It supplies these organisms with everything they need to stay alive.

Water is not the only home for living things. In this Investigation, you will learn about another place to live.

A. DON'T LITTER

THERE'S SOMEONE ON THE ROOF, DEAR!

NO Litter $50 FINE

New Jersey Dept. of Transportation

You have probably seen signs like this many times. They are on roads, on streets, and in parks. What do they mean?

Wide World Photos

LITTERING IS UNLAWFUL DROP LITTER HERE D.S.N.Y.

Here is a well-known object. It's called a litter basket. Most people know what litter baskets are used for; but do most people use them?

Wouldn't it be strange to find litter signs in a forest? You would be surprised to find a litter basket in a forest. But there is litter in a forest. It's a special kind of litter.

Leaves and twigs cover a forest floor. Branches and pieces of bark are also present. Scientists call this *forest litter*. It's not dirt. It's part of the soil.

Grant Heilman

B. MEET A REAL LITTER BUG

1. Get a jar. Label it with your name and section.

2. Add a small amount of water to the jar.

3. Press a piece of screen into a funnel.

4. Place the funnel in the jar.

5. Carefully break some forest litter into small pieces. Do this over a piece of paper.

6. Place this material in the funnel.

• 9. What do you see in the jar?

• 15. What collected in the water?

• 16. How many organisms did you collect?

• 17. What does forest litter contain?

• 18. Where did these organisms come from?

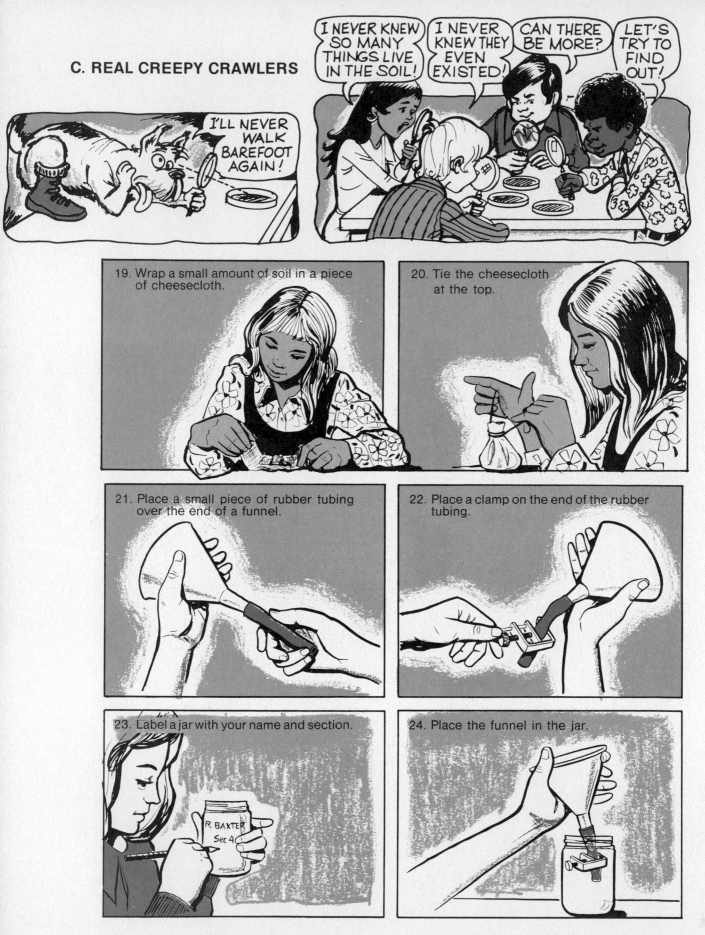

C. REAL CREEPY CRAWLERS

25. Set the bag of soil in the funnel.

26. Add enough water to almost fill the funnel.

27. Store your experiment. Do not disturb for 1 day.

DO NOT DISTURB UNTIL APRIL 26

•28. What do you predict will collect in the rubber tubing?

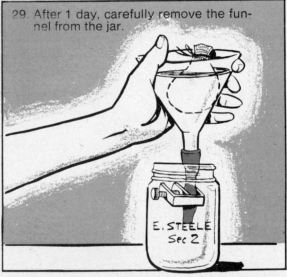

29. After 1 day, carefully remove the funnel from the jar.

30. Hold the funnel over a Petri dish.

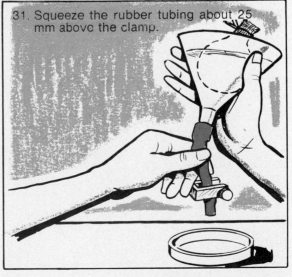

31. Squeeze the rubber tubing about 25 mm above the clamp.

32. Have your partner open the clamp.

33. Collect the water in the Petri dish.

34. Use your dropper. Place a drop of the water on a clean microscope slide.

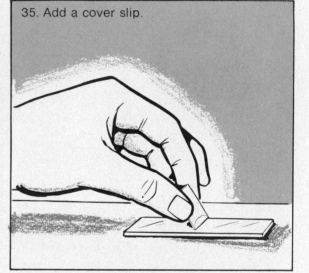

35. Add a cover slip.

36. Examine under low power with the microscope.

37. In Space **b** on your data sheet, draw what you see.

38. Compare your results with those of your classmates.

• 39. What do these organisms look like?

• 40. How many organisms did you collect?

• 41. What environment do these organisms live in?

D. HOME SWEET HOME

• 42. What materials did you examine in Part B?

• 43. In Part C, you looked at some living things. Where did these organisms come from?

• 44. How many different kinds of organisms did you see?

• 45. What can you say about some living things and their environment?

Re-read questions 18, 41, and 45. Write the concept.

THE CONCEPT.

IT PAYS TO HAVE A BACKBONE

Congratulations! Without leaving your classroom, you've visited many homes. You've met water and soil organisms. Their homes are important to them. But there are other kinds of homes too.

Leonard Lee Rue/National Audubon Society

Henderson/Rapho-Guillumette

Rue/Rapho-Guillumette

Landre/National Audubon Society

David has a point. Many organisms can make their home almost anywhere. Man is one of these organisms. Why is man so special?

A. JOIN THE CLUB

That's easy, Peter. You're in the club because you have a backbone. Animals that have backbones are called *vertebrates*. Man is a vertebrate.

Some vertebrates live in cold places on the earth.

Information Canada Phototheque

The National Film Board of Canada

Here is another vertebrate, the polar bear.

Myers/Black Star

Vertebrates can also live in warm places.

Do you know what animals these are?

- 1. Where do these animals live?

B. WHAT COLOR AND SIZE?

Vertebrates come in different colors and sizes. Here is a picture of one of the largest vertebrates.

Statile/DPI

Clark & Handley/National Audubon Society

- 2. What animal is this?

- 3. Where does this animal live?

Other vertebrates are small. They can live in fields or in big cities.

Some vertebrates are green.

Bernard L. Gluck/National Aucubon Society

•4. What animal is this?

•5. Where does this animal live?

Some have spots.

Rue/Monkmeyer

•6. What animal is this?

•7. Where does this animal live?

Some are yellow.

Some are black.

Koch/Rapho-Guillumette

Brack/Black Star

Idea 9/Investigation 3   **301**

Some are white.

No matter what size or color, they all share something. They all have something in common.

- 8. What do all of these animals have?

- 9. What do we call these animals?

- 10. Where do these animals live?

C. MOVE ME, BABY

You have learned that vertebrates live in places that are hot or cold. You have also learned that vertebrates can be large or small, colored or spotted.

Vertebrates also have different ways of moving from place to place in their environment.

Some fly...

Some run...

Some crawl...

Some walk...

Staffan/National Audubon Society

John H. Gerard/National Audubon Society

Some swim...

A. W. Ambler/National Audubon Society

•11. Why are vertebrates found in so many environments?

•12. Why is movement important to vertebrates?

•13. In what environments do you find vertebrates?

In the last Investigation, you studied soil organisms. These organisms do not have backbones. In Investigation 1, you studied small organisms in water. The organisms also do not have backbones.

•14. Why must soil and water organisms live where they do?

•15. What organisms did you study in this Investigation?

•16. Why are most vertebrates able to live where they want?

•17. What helps them do this?

•18. What can you say about vertebrates and where they live?

•19. Where do vertebrates live?

THE CONCEPT.

Idea 9 Investigation 4

STICK WITH ME

Everybody's going places. You are too. After three Investigations, you have learned that:

(a) Many organisms live in water.
(b) Many organisms live in soil.
(c) Vertebrates can make their home almost anywhere.

That's a good question, David. It will be the question for this Investigation.

A. EVEN SQUARES CAN FLY

1. You will be given 5 squares of paper.

2. Hold the squares at waist level in front of you.

3. Let the squares fall.

4. Measure the distance from your feet to the nearest and farthest squares.

5. Enter your results in Table 1 on your data sheet.

6. Repeat Steps 2-4 a second time. Record your results in Table 1.

7. Drop the squares a third time. Record your results.

• 8. Look at Table 1. How far away did the nearest square land when dropped from waist level?

• 9. How far away did the farthest square land?

Idea 9/Investigation 4   **305**

10. Hold the squares at eye level. Repeat Steps 3 and 4. Do this three times.

11. Enter your data in Table 1.

• 12. Look at Table 1. How far away did the nearest square land when dropped from eye level?

• 13. How far away did the farthest square land?

14. Compare your results with those of your classmates.

• 15. From what height did the squares fall the farthest?

• 16. How can you explain this?

• 17. What affects how far away a square will fall?

B. TWIST AND TURN

Your teacher will give you two envelopes. Each contains a different kind of seed. Handle the seeds carefully.

18. Examine the seeds from the envelope marked "Apple."

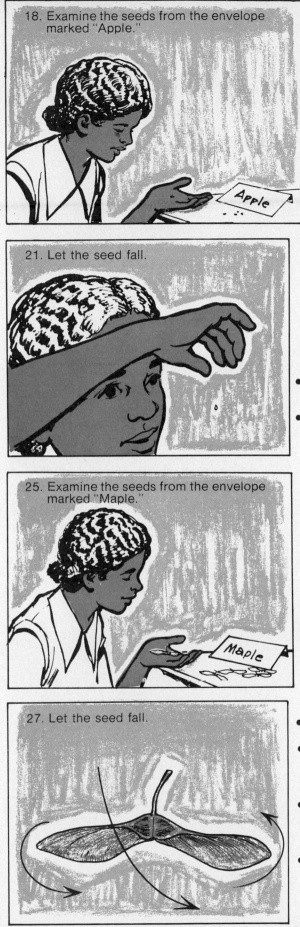

•19. What do these seeds look like?

20. Hold a seed at eye level.

21. Let the seed fall.

22. Repeat Steps 20 and 21 twice more.

•23. How does the seed move?

•24. How does the seed's shape help it move?

25. Examine the seeds from the envelope marked "Maple."

26. Hold a seed at eye level.

27. Let the seed fall.

•28. How does this seed move?

•29. How does the shape of the seed help it move?

•30. Which moved farther, the apple seed or the maple seed?

•31. How can you explain this?

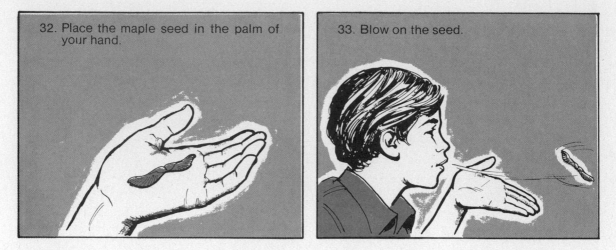

32. Place the maple seed in the palm of your hand.

33. Blow on the seed.

• 34. What happened to the seed?

• 35. Why do you think height is important for moving seeds?

• 36. How does wind help seeds move?

• 37. How does shape affect how a seed moves?

You have learned that seeds can move from one place to another. This is called *dispersal*.

• 38. From what you learned in Parts A and B, what affects a seed's dispersal?

C. SHARP STUFF

You will be given two more envelopes with seeds. Handle these carefully.

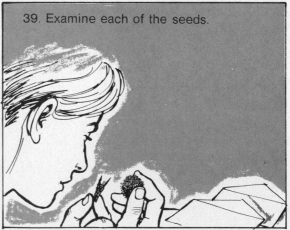

39. Examine each of the seeds.

• 40. What do you notice about the seeds?

• 41. How are these seeds different from the other seeds you studied?

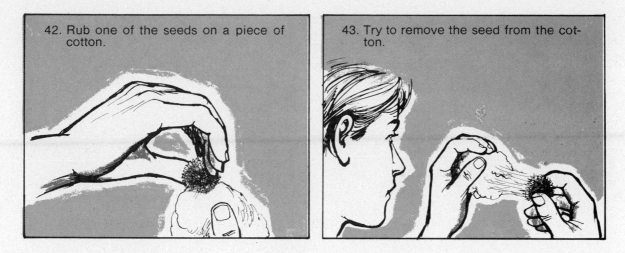

42. Rub one of the seeds on a piece of cotton.

43. Try to remove the seed from the cotton.

•44. Describe what happens.

•45. What do you think might happen if an animal brushed up against a plant having these seeds?

•46. How would this help dispersal of these seeds?

•47. What is another way seeds are dispersed?

D. KEEP IT MOVING

•48. How does dispersal take place among seeds?

•49. How does dispersal take place among animals? (*Hint*: See Investigation 3, pages 302 and 303.)

•50. Why is dispersal important to living things?

•51. What effect does dispersal have on organisms?

•52. What can you say about dispersal and where organisms live?

THE CONCEPT.

TWO CAN LIVE BETTER THAN ONE

You have learned many things about where organisms live. You have studied some organisms that live in water, in soil, and on land. The last Investigation helped you learn how they get there. The story is not finished yet.

Paul has something on his mind. David seems to be tuned in. Let's see if we can help Peter and Maria tune in and turn on.

A. A REAL LIVE TOOTHPICK

Compton's Encyclopedia

Here's a real teeth cleaning job. It may look like dinner time for the crocodile, but it's not. He's probably enjoying it. The crocodile bird cleans the teeth of the crocodile. It picks out small pieces of meat. In return for this service, the crocodile does not harm the bird. Everybody's happy! A free cleaning for the crocodile; a free meal for the bird. Both animals depend upon one another.

• 1. What does the crocodile bird get from the crocodile?

• 2. How does this help the crocodile?

• 3. Why do you think these animals are good neighbors?

Here are other happy neighbors. The tick bird and the rhinoceros. The tick bird picks insects out of the skin of the rhinoceros. Again, a free cleaning and a free meal.

• 4. What does the tick bird do for the rhinoceros?

• 5. How does this help the rhinoceros?

• 6. Why do you think these animals are good neighbors?

B. WHAT'S IT ALL ABOUT, ALGAE?

Plants may also live together as good neighbors. Each neighbor helps the other. Sometimes plants depend upon other plants. Sound strange? Let's see.

HOW COME PLANTS NEED HELP?

WHAT KIND OF HELP CAN THEY NEED?

I THOUGHT ALL PLANTS COULD MAKE THEIR OWN FOOD!

MAYBE NOT!

That's right, David! Not all plants can make food. Only green plants can. You remember, the ones that have chlorophyll. The simplest of all green plants are the *algae*. Almost all algae live in water. Many are microscopic.

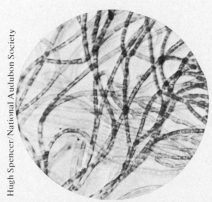

• 7. What are algae?

• 8. Where do algae live?

• 9. How do algae get food?

Idea 9/Investigation 5   311

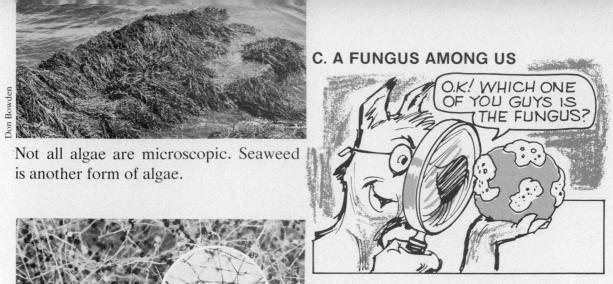

Not all algae are microscopic. Seaweed is another form of algae.

Don Bowden (left photo)

Walter Dawn / *Grant Heilman* (left photo)

C. A FUNGUS AMONG US

O.K! WHICH ONE OF YOU GUYS IS THE FUNGUS?

You have done several experiments with yeast. Yeast cells are non-green plants. They do not contain chlorophyll.

• 10. Where do yeast cells get their food?

Bread mold is another example of a non-green plant. It grows on bread.

• 11. Where do you think this plant gets its food?

Yeast and bread mold belong to a group of plants called *fungi*. Fungi do not contain chlorophyll. They cannot make their own food. They must get their food from what they grow on.

• 12. What do fungi depend upon for food?

• 13. Why must fungi live where they can get food?

D. HOW CLOSE CAN YOU GET?

Your teacher will give you a small piece of plant material.

Algae and fungi sometimes grow and live together. Each organism has an important job. Each helps the other.

John H. Gerard/National Audubon Society

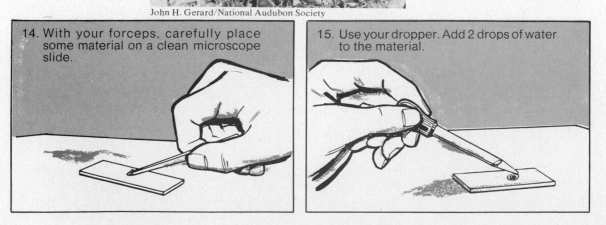

14. With your forceps, carefully place some material on a clean microscope slide.

15. Use your dropper. Add 2 drops of water to the material.

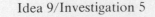

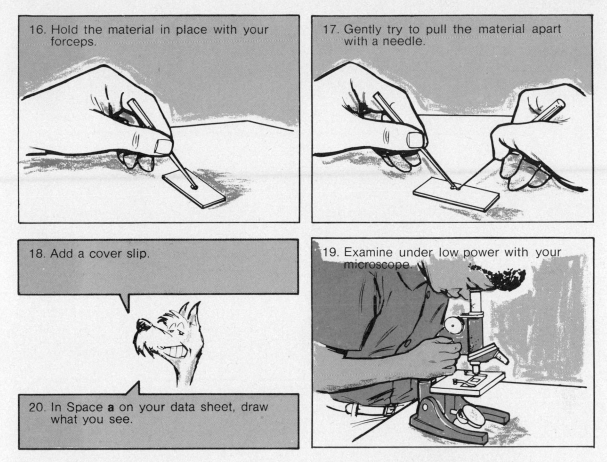

16. Hold the material in place with your forceps.

17. Gently try to pull the material apart with a needle.

18. Add a cover slip.

20. In Space **a** on your data sheet, draw what you see.

19. Examine under low power with your microscope.

•21. What part of the plant do you think is the algae?

•22. How can you tell?

•23. What part of the plant do you think is the fungi?

•24. How can you tell?

•25. What part of the plant makes food?

•26. How do you know?

•27. What does the fungi look like?

The plant you are studying is called a *lichen*. Lichens are made up of algae and fungi. The fungi take in water and hold the plant in place.

•28. How do the fungi depend upon the algae?

•29. How do the algae depend upon the fungi?

•30. How does one organism help the other?

•31. Why do some plants live together?

•32. Why do some animals live together?

•33. What can you say about why some organisms live where they do?

Re-read your answers to questions 31-33. Write the concept.

THE CONCEPT.

IT'S NOT HARD TO FIND

WHAT YOU SEE IS WHAT YOU GET!

In Idea 5, you learned that living things need energy. Green plants get their energy from the sun. They use this energy to make food. Animals get their energy from the foods they eat.

Thus far, in this Idea, you have learned where animals live. You have also learned how they get there.

ONCE THEY GET THERE, WHY DO THEY STAY?

IT'S ONE THING TO GET SOME-PLACE!

IT'S ANOTHER THING TO STAY ALIVE!

WHAT ARE YOU GUYS GETTING AT?

ENERGY PHIDEAU! THEY NEED ENERGY!

A. PREPARE THE BEAST

I WONDER WHO I'LL HAVE FOR DINNER TONIGHT!

You know how our friend gets his energy. You also know that all living things do not eat the same foods. You have seen that sugar is food for yeast. Sugar supplies yeast cells with energy. Let's see if we can find out how important energy is for the yeast cells.

1. Get 2 large test tubes. Label one "Control." Label the other "Experiment."

2. Fill both tubes 1/2-full with a yeast mixture.

3. Weigh out 1 gram of sugar.

4. Add the sugar to the tube marked "Experiment."

B. IT'S EASY NOW

5. Use the tube marked "Experiment." Place a drop of the mixture on a microscope slide.

6. Add a cover slip.

7. Focus under high power with the microscope.

8. Count the number of yeast cells you can see in your field.

Idea 9/Investigation 6   **315**

• 9. How many yeast cells did you count?

•10. How does the experimental tube differ from the control tube?

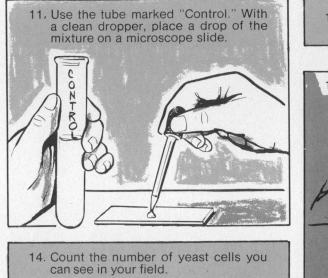

11. Use the tube marked "Control." With a clean dropper, place a drop of the mixture on a microscope slide.

12. Add a cover slip.

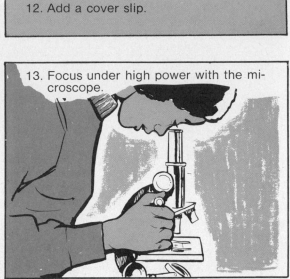

13. Focus under high power with the microscope.

14. Count the number of yeast cells you can see in your field.

•15. How many yeast cells did you count?

•16. How does the control tube differ from the experimental tube?

•17. How is the number of yeast cells different on the two slides?

•18. How are the control and experimental tubes different?

•19. How are they the same?

20. Store your experiment in a warm place for 1 day. Do not disturb.

APRIL 19

DO NOT DISTURB UNTIL APRIL 20

C. BACK TO THE COUNT

When the Count isn't getting his energy, he rests. Let's see if this is true of our yeast.

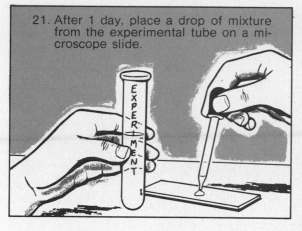

21. After 1 day, place a drop of mixture from the experimental tube on a microscope slide.

22. Add a cover slip.

23. Focus under high power. Count the number of yeast cells you can see in your field.

•24. How many yeast cells did you count?

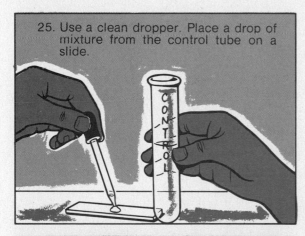

25. Use a clean dropper. Place a drop of mixture from the control tube on a slide.

26. Add a cover slip.

27. Focus under high power. Count the number of yeast cells you can see in your field.

•28. How many yeast cells did you count?

•29. How is the number of yeast cells different on the two slides?

•30. Why do you suppose this is true?

•31. Which of the tubes is more cloudy?

•32. Why do you suppose this is true?

•33. Which yeast cells are more active?

•34. Why do you suppose this is true?

●35. Where did these yeast cells get their energy?

●36. In what kind of environment do yeast cells live best?

D. LET'S TAKE A GIANT STEP

ENERGY IS THE KEY TO IT ALL !

In this Investigation, you learned how important energy is. In the last Investigation, you learned about some friendly neighbors. Energy really is the key to it all.

The crocodile bird is happy where he lives.

●37. What does the crocodile bird get from his environment?

●38. How do lichens get their energy?

●39. Why can lichens live almost anywhere?

●40. What happens when organisms are not able to get energy?

●41. What must the environment of an organism supply?

●42. Why must organisms live where they can get energy?

●43. Where must organisms live?

Re-read your answers to questions 41 and 43. Write the concept.

THE CONCEPT.

Boss! You've completed another Idea. This Idea had to do with where organisms live. It also had to do with why they live there. Where do organisms live? What kind of environment do they need? Why is where they live so important?

You have been studying the homes of many organisms. You learned that:

    (a) Many organisms live in water.
    (b) Many organisms live in the soil.
    (c) Vertebrates live in many habitats.
    (d) Organisms live where they do because of dispersal.
    (e) Where an organism lives depends upon other organisms.
    (f) Organisms live where they can get energy.

•44. What must the environment of an organism supply?

•45. Why must organisms live where they can get energy?

All organisms cannot live in the same environment. Many organisms live in water. Many organisms live in the soil. Many organisms live on land. Some groups of organisms make their home almost anywhere. But they all have a home. They all find a place to live.

•46. What do all organisms find in their environment?

Re-read your answer to question 46. Summarize the Idea.

THE IDEA.

THINGS CHANGE

In Idea 8, you studied the environment. You learned that the environment can be living or non-living. Plants and animals make up the living environment. Heat, light, and water are parts of the non-living environment.

The environment is always changing. Sometimes these changes are slow. They may take millions of years.

Sometimes they are fast.   Some changes last for long periods of time.

Bill Males/National Severe Storms Laboratory, NOAA

Davis/DPI

Other changes may last for only a short time.

That's right, David. Many organisms can make changes.
Organisms must be able to sense changes in the environment.
They must also be able to respond to these changes. As a matter of fact, life may depend upon it.

A. CAN SHRIMP REALLY DANCE?

Your teacher will give you a covered bottle. The bottle contains shrimp. Do not uncover your bottle until you are ready to begin your experiment. You are going to study how these animals behave in dim and in bright light. To do this, you must begin your experiment with the room as dark as possible.

1. Light your candle. It will help you observe the shrimp.

2. Place the candle about 60 cm from the bottle.

3. Uncover the bottle of shrimp.

4. Slowly move the candle closer to the bottle. Stop when there is enough light for you to see the shrimp.

5. Study the movements of the shrimp.

• 6. What are the shrimp doing?

• 7. In which direction are the shrimp moving?

• 8. Move your hand up and down between the bottle and the candle. What happens?

9. Carefully move your candle to the other side of the bottle. Do not move the candle closer to the bottle.

•10. What are the shrimp doing?

•11. In which direction are the shrimp moving?

•12. Did the shrimp respond quickly? Why?

13. Cover your bottle.

14. Store your shrimp in a dark place. Do not disturb.

B. WATCH THIS STEP

DIG!

GROOVY!

The room will be made dark again.

15. Uncover your bottle of shrimp.

16. Turn on the flashlight. Place it against one side of the bottle.

17. Study the movements of the shrimp in the beam of light.

• 18. In which direction are the shrimp moving?

• 19. After awhile, where are most of the shrimp?

• 20. Why do you think this happens?

21. Turn off the flashlight for about 3 minutes.

• 22. What are most of the shrimp doing now?

• 23. Why do you think this happens?

24. Shine your flashlight into the bottle from the top.

• 25. How do the shrimp respond?

• 26. Why do you think this happens?

27. Compare your results with those of your classmates.

• 28. What change in the environment of the shrimp did you make?

• 29. How do you know that the shrimp noticed this change?

• 30. How did the shrimp respond?

• 31. Did the shrimp respond quickly or slowly to the change?

C. SHRIMP AREN'T THE ONLY ONES

Shrimp are only one example of organisms that can respond quickly to changes in the environment. Most organisms can. You can too.

In Idea 2, you learned that the eye responds to changes in the environment.

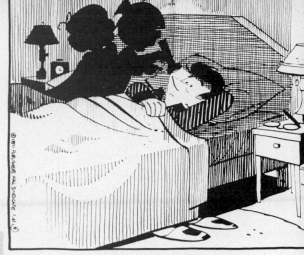

"THAT BLACK THING IN THE MIDDLE OF YOUR EYE GOT REAL TINY ALL OF A SUDDEN."

- •32. What happened to the iris?

- •33. What change in the environment caused this response?

- •34. How long did it take the eye to respond?

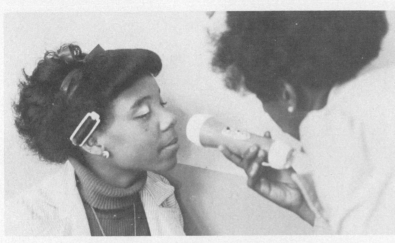

D. A CHANGE FOR THE BETTER

- •35. What is always happening to the environment?

- •36. What can shrimp do when their environment changes?

- •37. If you touch a hot bulb, what do you do?

YEE-YOW! SOME LIKE IT HOT. I DON'T!

- •38. If you touch a hot iron, how long does it take you to respond?

- •39. What can people do when their environment changes?

- •40. What can organisms do when their environment changes?

THE CONCEPT.

Investigation 2

STAY COOL, BROTHER

In the last Investigation, you learned that organisms can respond to changes in the environment. You have seen how quickly the eye responds to light. You have seen how quickly shrimp respond to light. These responses to changes in the environment are important. They work to protect the organism.

That's a good question, Paul. But scientists have an answer. They can measure responses that cannot be easily seen.

You often respond to nervous, jumpy people. Another way of telling them to relax is to tell them to "be cool."

That's a good word to use, Phideau. It means a lot to living things. How? Let's find out.

A. WHAT'S YOUR TEMPERATURE?

Pro Pix/Monkmeyer

UNICEF

What happens to your body temperature when the weather is cold?

What happens to your body temperature when the weather is hot?

Does your body respond to temperature changes in the environment? Does your body temperature change when the temperature of the environment changes?

Work in teams for this experiment. You will use two different kinds of thermometers. Your teacher will review how to use each.

One student will be the subject. Another student will take the body and water temperatures.

• 1. Which thermometer will you use to measure body temperature?

• 2. Which thermometer will you use to measure water temperature?

3. Fill a large container with cold water. Add ice. The colder the better.

4. Take the body temperature of the subject. Enter your data in Table 1 on your data sheet.

5. Take the temperature of the ice water. Record this in Table 1.

B. LET'S TAKE A DIP

6. The subject should place as much of one hand and arm as possible into the water.

7. Place the small thermometer in the subject's mouth.

•8. What time is it now?

•9. What time will it be 4 minutes from now?

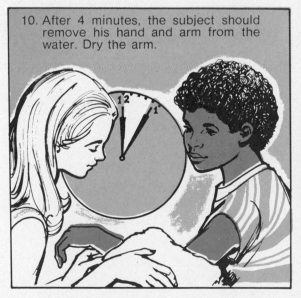

10. After 4 minutes, the subject should remove his hand and arm from the water. Dry the arm.

•11. Feel the arm. How does it feel?

12. Read the subject's body temperature. Record the temperature in Table 1.

13. Take the temperature of the water. Record this in Table 1.

C. THAT'S WHAT I CALL STEADY!

- 14. What was the subject's body temperature at the start of the experiment?

- 15. What was the subject's body temperature at the end of the experiment?

- 16. How much did the body temperature change?

- 17. What was the temperature of the water?

- 18. What effect did this have on the subject's arm?

- 19. What effect did this have on the subject's body temperature?

- 20. What happens to the inside body temperature when the outside temperature changes?

- 21. Why is this important?

- 22. From this experiment, what do you predict *some* organisms do when the outside environment changes?

Re-read your answers to questions 20 and 22. Write the concept.

THE CONCEPT.

SEEING IS BELIEVING

In this Idea, you have learned that:

(a) Organisms can respond quickly to certain changes in the environment.

(b) *Some* organisms keep a steady inside environment when the outside environment changes.

Let's look at another kind of response to changes in the environment. Remember, life depends on response.

A. I CAN'T COUNT THAT FAST

Your teacher will give you a jar containing water and Daphnia. Daphnia are small water organisms. They belong to the same group of animals as shrimp and lobster. Daphnia are interesting little animals because you can see through them.

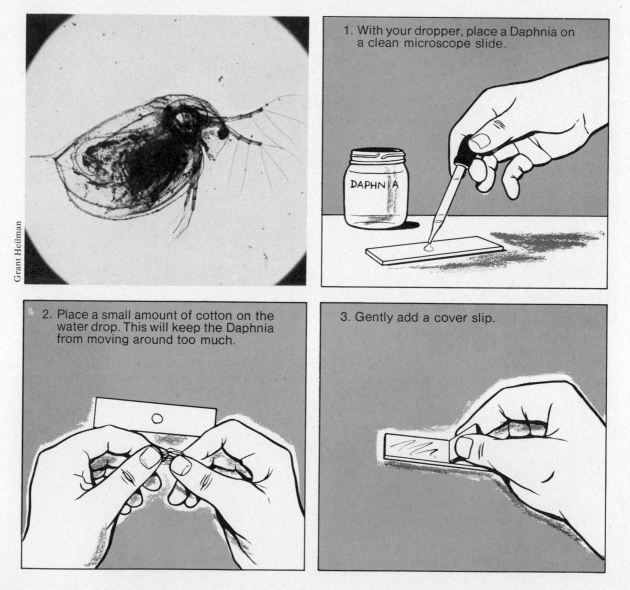

Grant Heilman

1. With your dropper, place a Daphnia on a clean microscope slide.

2. Place a small amount of cotton on the water drop. This will keep the Daphnia from moving around too much.

3. Gently add a cover slip.

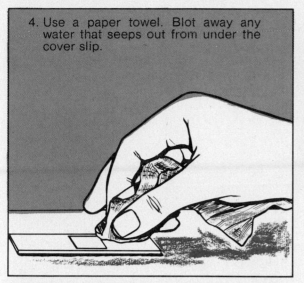

4. Use a paper towel. Blot away any water that seeps out from under the cover slip.

5. Focus under low power with your microscope.

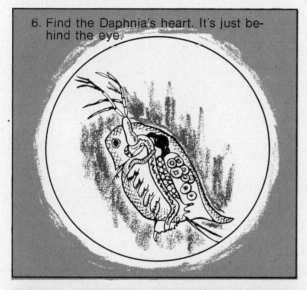

6. Find the Daphnia's heart. It's just behind the eye.

B. TAKE A DEEP BREATH

You are going to count the number of heartbeats of your Daphnia. You will need some practice doing this because the heart beats so fast.

You may want to cut down the amount of light on your slide. This will help you see better. It will also cut down the amount of heat.

You're doing a great job. If you need help, ask your teacher.

• 8. How many beats did you count?

7. Count the number of heartbeats in 15 seconds.

9. Multiply your answer by 4. This will give you the number of heartbeats in 1 minute.

70 x 4

• 10. How many beats are there in 1 minute?

11. Write this number in Table 1 on your data sheet.

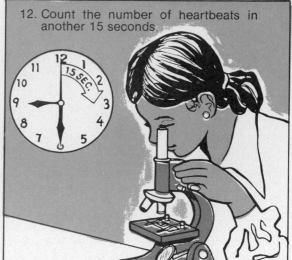

12. Count the number of heartbeats in another 15 seconds.

•13. How many beats did you count?

14. Multiply your answer by 4.

•15. How many beats are there in 1 minute?

16. Enter your data in Table 1.

Do you remember how to find averages?
You did it way back in Idea 1.

•17. What is the average number of heart-beats per minute for your Daphnia?

18. Enter this number in Table 1.

C. SLOW DOWN

Your teacher will give you a bottle containing a test liquid.

19. Use a clean dropper. Place a drop of test liquid at the edge of the cover slip.

Make sure that the liquid moves under the cover slip. Let it do its own thing.

20. Wait at least 20 seconds.

20 SECONDS

21. Count the number of heartbeats in 15 seconds.

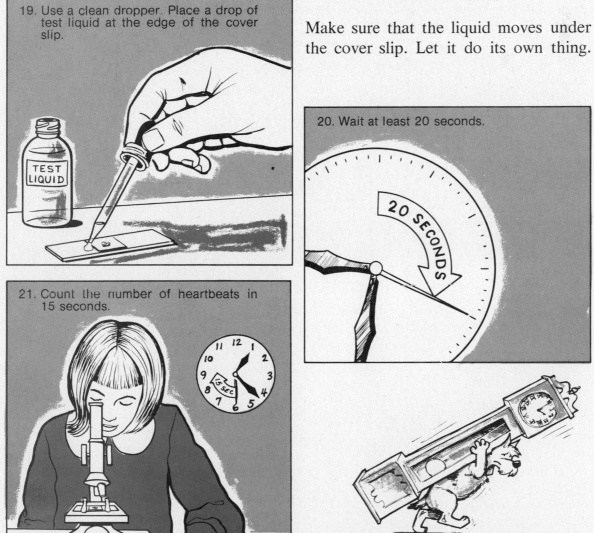

22. Multiply this number by 4.

•23. How many beats are there in 1 minute?

24. Enter this number in Table 1.

25. Count the number of heartbeats in another 15 seconds.

26. Multiply your answer by 4.

•27. How many beats are there in 1 minute?

28. Enter your data in Table 1.

•29. What is the average number of heartbeats per minute for your Daphnia?

30. Enter your data in Table 1.

D. WHAT DOES IT MEAN?

• 31. Look at Table 1. What was the average heartbeat of your Daphnia in water?

• 32. What was the average heartbeat after you added the test liquid?

• 33. What is the difference in average heartbeats?

• 34. What do you think caused this change?

• 35. What is the natural environment of Daphnia?

• 36. How did you change this environment?

• 37. How did your Daphnia respond?

• 38. What happened to the Daphnia's inside environment when the outside environment changed?

• 39. In this Investigation, what happened to the inside environment when the outside environment changed?

• 40. What might happen to the inside environment of *some* organisms when the outside environment changes?

Re-read your answers to questions 39 and 40. Write the concept.

THE CONCEPT.

IT CAME FROM OUTER THE SINK

Chances are you've never seen a bug like this. Chances are that you never will. Nobody knows for sure. Scientists do know that organisms change. They may change in many ways.

Thus far in this Idea, you have studied changes in organisms. You have learned that:

(a) Organisms respond to changes in the environment.
(b) *Some* organisms keep a steady inside environment when the outside environment changes.
(c) *Some* organisms change their inside environment when the outside environment changes.

How else do organisms change? How do we know that changes really take place? That will be the question for this Investigation.

A. IS IT FOSSIBLE?

Here's an animal that may be familiar to you. It lived millions of years ago. Have you ever seen a living one?

Here is another animal that lived millions of years ago. Have you ever seen one of these fly over? Was it ever really alive?

Your teacher will give you 2 Petri dishes and 2 pieces of meat.

1. Fill the dishes with water.

2. With your forceps, place a piece of meat in each dish.

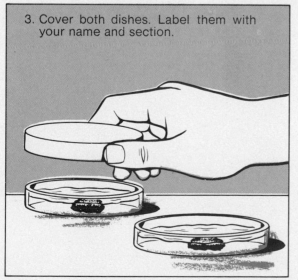

3. Cover both dishes. Label them with your name and section.

There will be 2 large trays set up in the room. One of the trays is marked "Freezer"; the other is marked "Room Temperature."

Idea 10/Investigation 4   **339**

4. Place one dish on the tray marked "Freezer."

5. Place the other dish on the tray marked "Room Temperature."

6. Do not disturb your experiment for 2 days.

7. After 2 days, examine the meat in both dishes.

• 8. What happened to the meat in the freezer?

• 9. What happened to the meat left at room temperature?

• 10. How did freezing affect the meat?

• 11. How did leaving the meat at room temperature affect it?

This huge animal was buried in ice. It lived thousands of years ago.

NOVOSTI/SOVFOTO

•12. What modern animal does it look like?

•13. How did freezing affect this animal?

•14. How does freezing affect animal tissue?

B. HAVE YOU EVER HEARD THE FOSSIL RECORD?

The fossils aren't a new "rock" group. In fact, they're one of the oldest groups known. In Part A, you studied one of the ways in which fossils are made. Animals that were buried in ice did not change. The tissues did not decay. They were *preserved*. Scientists call the preserved parts of plants and animals *fossils*.

Let's see another way in which fossils were formed.

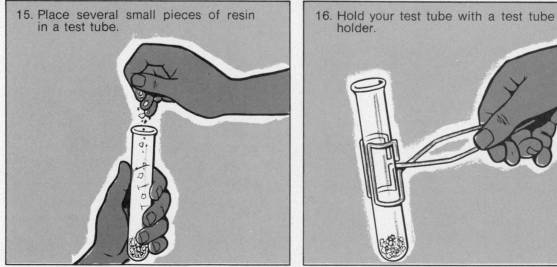

15. Place several small pieces of resin in a test tube.

16. Hold your test tube with a test tube holder.

17. Melt the resin over a low flame.

Your teacher will give you a small cardboard box and some model insects.

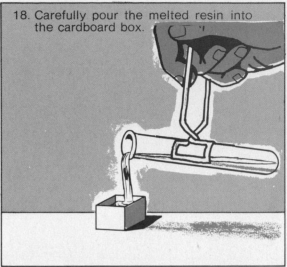

18. Carefully pour the melted resin into the cardboard box.

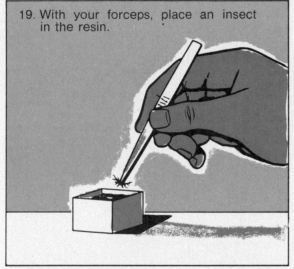

19. With your forceps, place an insect in the resin.

20. Let the resin cool at room temperature.

21. After the resin hardens, soak the box in water. Then peel off the paper.

Congratulations! You have made an insect fossil. Ants and flies were trapped in resin which dripped down the bark of trees. In this way, they were preserved for millions of years.

C. THE IMFOSSIBLE DREAM

Let's take a closer look at what Maria is asking about.

Scientists often find fossils of animals that lived millions of years ago.

By putting the bones of these animals together, scientists may learn what an animal looked like.

Moore/Black Star

Courtesy of the American Museum of Natural History

Look at the following:

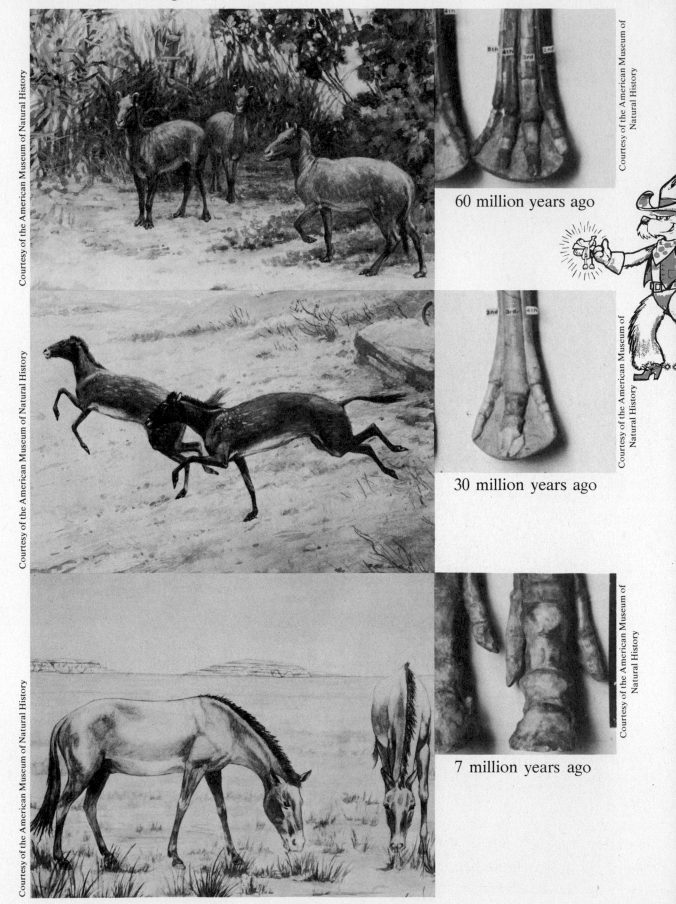

60 million years ago

30 million years ago

7 million years ago

Courtesy of the American Museum of Natural History

Courtesy of the American Museum of Natural History

1 million years ago
to the present

- 22. Which horse is the oldest?

- 23. How many toes does it have on each front foot?

- 24. Which horse is the modern horse?

- 25. How many toes does it have on each front foot?

- 26. Which horse is the smallest?

- 27. When did this horse live?

- 28. Which horse is the largest?

- 29. When did this horse live?

- 30. What happened to the number of toes over millions of years?

- 31. What happened to the appearance of the horse over millions of years?

- 32. What happened to the size of the horse over millions of years?

- 33. What has happened to the horse over millions of years?

- 34. What do you think can happen to living things over millions of years?

THE CONCEPT.

Idea 10 Investigation 5

MAKE IT OR FORGET IT

In the last Investigation, you studied fossils. Fossils tell us many things about organisms that were once alive. By studying fossils, we can learn what an organism looked like. We can also learn how an organism changed over millions of years. Change is the name of the game. As the environment changes, so must organisms, if they are to stay alive. We call this *adaptation*. To adapt means to change.

David and Peter are asking an important question. What happens to organisms that cannot adapt to changes in their environment? Let's see if we can find an answer.

A. CAN YOU WIGGLE YOUR EARS?

Do all rabbits have the same size ears? Have you ever seen a shorter-eared rabbit? Where are they? What happened to them?

Many animals that once lived are no longer alive. You saw this in the last Investigation. What happened to these animals? What happened to the dinosaurs? What happened to the giant bird? What happened to the shorter-eared rabbit? Scientists are still trying to answer these questions. Let's look at one possible answer.

At one time, all rabbits did not have the same size ears. Some rabbits had longer ears. Other rabbits had shorter ears.

The rabbit has many enemies. He is a favorite food for many animals. The rabbit depends upon his ears to warn him of danger.

• 1. Which ears do you think are better able to hear—longer or shorter?

• 2. Which rabbits are better able to hear—longer-eared or shorter-eared?

• 3. Which rabbits might be safer from their enemies—longer-eared or shorter-eared?

In time, shorter-eared rabbits became fewer. More of them were caught and eaten. Many of them never grew old enough to reproduce shorter-eared rabbits.

• 4. Which rabbits increased in number?

• 5. Which rabbits decreased in number?

• 6. Which rabbits were better able to stay alive—longer-eared or shorter-eared?

• 7. Which rabbits were better able to adapt to the environment?

• 8. What effect did this have on the type of rabbits that lived?

Since longer-eared rabbits were able to adapt, they were able to stay alive.

• 9. In time, what do you think happened to all the shorter-eared rabbits?

•10. In time, what do you think happened to the number of longer-eared rabbits?

•11. In one word, what did the longer-eared rabbits do that the shorter-eared rabbits could not do?

B. A CHANGE FOR THE BETTER

The fossil record shows that many organisms changed over millions of years. Some of these adaptations were successful. They helped the organisms stay alive. Other adaptations were not successful. Many of these organisms died.

Groups of organisms that once lived but are not alive today are *extinct*. They have disappeared from the earth.

•12. What happened to the dinosaur?

•13. What happened to the giant bird?

•14. What happened to the shorter-eared rabbit?

•15. What may happen to organisms that cannot adapt to their environment?

THE CONCEPT.

MAKE IT, OR DISAPPEAR

I THOUGHT ALL THESE GUYS WERE LONG GONE!

Zap! Another Idea completed. This Idea was about what may happen to organisms that cannot adapt to changes in the environment. What may happen to organisms that cannot adapt?

You have been studying how the environment of living things may change. You have learned how organisms may respond to these changes. These are the five concepts you have learned. Look at them.

(a) Organisms respond to changes in the environment.
(b) *Some* organisms keep a steady inside environment when the outside environment changes.
(c) *Some* organisms change their inside environment when the outside environment changes.
(d) Living things can change in size and appearance over millions of years.
(e) Organisms that cannot adapt may become extinct.

• 16. What do we call the surroundings of an organism?

• 17. What is always happening to the environment?

• 18. What must an organism do as the environment changes?

Re-read questions 16-18. Write the Idea Summary.

THE IDEA.

Idea 11 Investigation 1

STOP HASSLING ME

Every 10 years a *census* is taken. A census is a count of all the people in an area. What do they call the number of people living in an area?

A. COUNT ME IN

1. Turn to page D173 in your Data Book. Cut out all the squares.

2. Sort the squares.

3. Count the number of rats.

4. Count the number of dogs.

• 5. How did you sort the squares?

• 6. How many rats did you count?

When you count living things, you are counting their population.

• 7. What's the population of dogs you counted?

When you count a population, you must think about three things:

(a) What one kind of organism are you counting?
(b) How many are counted?
(c) Where are the organisms found?

8. Count the pigeons.

• 9. What one kind are you counting?

• 10. What is the pigeon population?

• 11. Where is your pigeon population?

• 12. What is a population?

• 13. What do you have to know to describe a population?

• 14. Describe one population in your classroom.

B. CAN YOU STAND INSIDE A SQUARE?

Imagine that your classroom is 10 meters by 12 meters. A diagram of this classroom is shown on page D169 of your Data Book. The classroom has been divided into 1-meter squares.

• 15. How many squares are in the diagram?

• 16. What is the student population of your classroom?

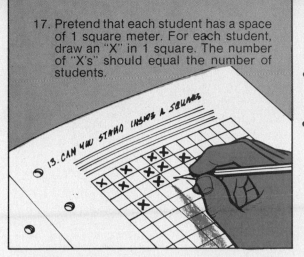

17. Pretend that each student has a space of 1 square meter. For each student, draw an "X" in 1 square. The number of "X's" should equal the number of students.

Imagine that the student population doubles in 1 year.

• 18. How many students would there be in 1 year?

• 19. How many more "X's" would you have to draw to equal the population?

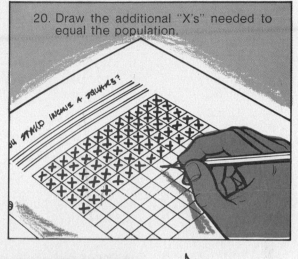

20. Draw the additional "X's" needed to equal the population.

Imagine that the student population doubles again in 1 year.

• 21. How many students would there be in 2 years?

• 22. How many more "X's" would you have to draw to equal the population?

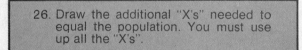

23. Draw the additional "X's" needed to equal the new population.

Imagine that the student population doubles again in 1 year.

• 24. How many students would there be in 3 years?

• 25. How many more "X's" would you have to draw to equal the population?

26. Draw the additional "X's" needed to equal the population. You must use up all the "X's".

• 27. If you run out of squarcs, what will you have to do with the extra "X's"?

• 28. What is a population?

• 29. What is overpopulation?

C. CAN YOU COUNT TO A BILLION?

Look at the clock and count the seconds. Do you know how long it would take you to count 1 billion seconds? 30 years. Yes, 30 years!

• 30. How long would it take to count 8 billion seconds?

The world population is expected to be 8 billion by 2010. But if you started counting *now*, you couldn't even count that many people! And the world's population is expected to double again 35 years later!

Today, 70 percent of the world's population lives on less than 4 percent of the land. Do you know how crowded that is?

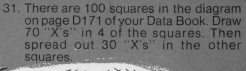

31. There are 100 squares in the diagram on page D171 of your Data Book. Draw 70 "X's" in 4 of the squares. Then spread out 30 "X's" in the other squares.

If you don't think the earth is crowded already, look at this.

Aoki/Rapho-Guillumette

In Manhattan, there are 78,000 people per square mile.

Lukas/Rapho-Guillumette

If we all lived like this, the entire United States population could live in one large city.

• 32. What is a population?

• 33. What is overpopulation?

D. COUNT IT ALL UP

Let's summarize this Investigation.

• 34. Every organism is part of a ?

• 35. What three things must you know about a population?

• 36. What is a population?

THE CONCEPT.

354   Idea 11/Investigation 1

Idea 11 Investigation 2

LIFE IN THE YELLOW PAGES

Together. That's the way it is in biology. You learned this in Idea 3.

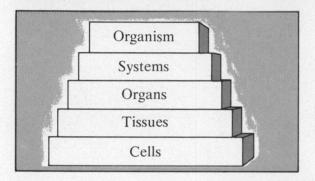

You are an organism. So is an ant, a rose bush, and a sea gull. All organisms are organized from cells, tissues, organs, and systems.

In the last Investigation, you learned that each organism is part of a population. A population tells you how many there are of something. A population also tells you where the organisms are found. For instance,

(a) There are 64,000 people in Altoona.
(b) I counted 40 frogs in the pond.
(c) I have 7 goldfish in my aquarium.

Putting it all together, this is how it's organized.

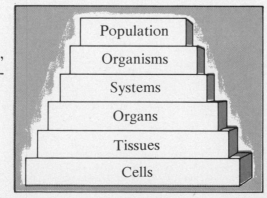

If a population is a group of organisms, what is a group of populations?

A. WHAT IF I CAN'T COUNT?

1. Observe the aquarium in your room.

2. Observe the different kinds of organisms in the aquarium. List each kind in Table 1 on your data sheet.

3. Count each population. Record your data in Table 1.

There are many organisms in your aquarium. There are several populations. The aquarium is a *community*.

UPI

Haines/Rapho-Guillumette

Laping/DPI

There are other kinds of communities.

• 4. What is in a community?

• 5. What do you call a group of populations living together?

B. NO ONE LIVES ALONE

Now you're going to make a population count of a community. You will have to find a community of your own. This will mean going outside. Why not? That's where it's all happening.

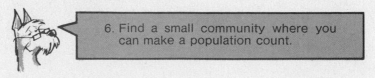

6. Find a small community where you can make a population count.

It isn't hard to find a community.

Lift up a rock.   Turn over a log.

Dr. Harold R. Hungerford

Heiniger/Rapho-Guillumette

Look over, under, and around the rocks at the seashore.

M. Woodbridge Williams

Study the cracks in the cement.   Observe the life around a city building.

Examine life in a drop of water.

Photo Researchers

Get down on your hands and knees. What do you find in a square meter of lawn?

M. Woodbridge Williams

Armstrong/Rapho-Guillumette

•8. How many kinds of organisms did you find?

• 9. Each kind of organism is a population. How many different populations did you find?

•10. Does each population live by itself? Explain.

•11. What do you call a group of populations living together in an area?

C. WE'RE IN IT TOGETHER

M.W.F. Tweedie/National Audubon Society

Van Campen/DPI

The community can tell you a lot about the environment. For instance, what is under a rock? You may find ants, sowbugs, and perhaps a beetle. They live there because they need a wet and dark environment.

•12. Where would you find a community with cactus in it?

Grant Heilman

•13. Look at this community. Where would you find it?

Let's see if you can describe a community without seeing it.

You can describe a community from the data given in its telephone book. To help you get started, plan ahead! Don't just thumb through the telephone book. Know what you are looking for. For instance, here are some questions and suggested places to look for the answers.

(a) Is it a city or rural community? (Look up "Farm Equipment.")

(b) Are there any Greek people living in the community? (Look up "Restaurants—Greek.")

(c) Is the community religious? (Count the number of churches and synagogues listed.)

(d) Is the community near water? (See if there are any "Boat Dealers.")

(e) Is the community rich or poor? (Count the number of doctors.)

• 15. On your data sheet, list some other questions you may want to ask.

16. Work in small groups. Write your findings on pages D177 and D178 of your Data Book and report to the class.

A community is more than a place on the map. A community is a happening.

The telephone book is just one way to tell what's happening in a community.

D. LET'S LUMP IT ALL TOGETHER

Let's put everything together from the last two Investigations.

• 17. What is a population?

• 18. "A community is a happening." What does this sentence mean?

• 19. What is a community?

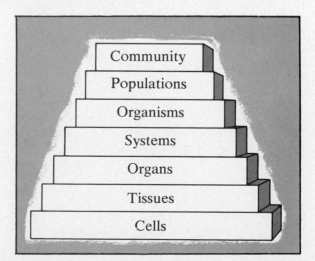

Community
Populations
Organisms
Systems
Organs
Tissues
Cells

THE CONCEPT.

Idea 11 Investigation 3

HAWKS DON'T EAT ZUCCHINIS

You are doing very well. You have just learned that:

(a) The number of one kind of organism in an area is the population.

(b) A group of populations living in an area is a community.

Yes, what's the action? Why are the organisms in a community? In the next four Investigations, you will try to answer one question: What is the function of a community?

A. HE DOESN'T CHEW HIS FOOD

Carolina Biological Supply Co.

It looks like a monster, but it isn't. This animal is called a Hydra. It spends its life under lily pads in a pond. You have to look hard to find it. It is about 8 mm long and almost clear.

1. Your teacher will give you a Hydra in a test tube.

•2. Do not shake the tube or disturb the Hydra. Observe it for 3 minutes. Describe everything you see.

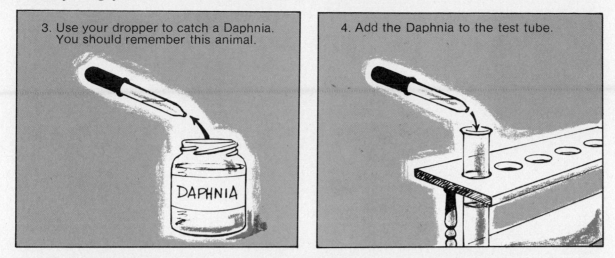

3. Use your dropper to catch a Daphnia. You should remember this animal.

DAPHNIA

4. Add the Daphnia to the test tube.

•5. Do not disturb the Hydra. Be very patient. Observe for 5 or more minutes. Describe everything you see happen between the Hydra and the Daphnia.

•6. In a community, what may one organism do to another?

An animal that catches, kills, and eats other animals is a *predator*. The animal that is caught and eaten is the *prey*.

•7. Is the Hydra or the Daphnia the predator?

•8. Which one is the prey?

•9. Which is the predator and which is the prey?

Treat Davidson/National Audubon Society

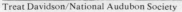

•10. Which is the predator and which is the prey?

•11. Give another example of a predator-prey relationship.

•12. What is a predator?

•13. What is a prey?

B. LET'S PLAY PRETEND

Keep one question in mind. What is the function of a community? To help you answer this question, you will play a game.

Leonard Lee Rue III/National Audubon Society

Pretend that you are looking at an area with two populations. They are the hawk and fieldmouse populations. The hawk is the predator and the fieldmouse is the prey. Your teacher will give you hawk cards and fieldmouse cards.

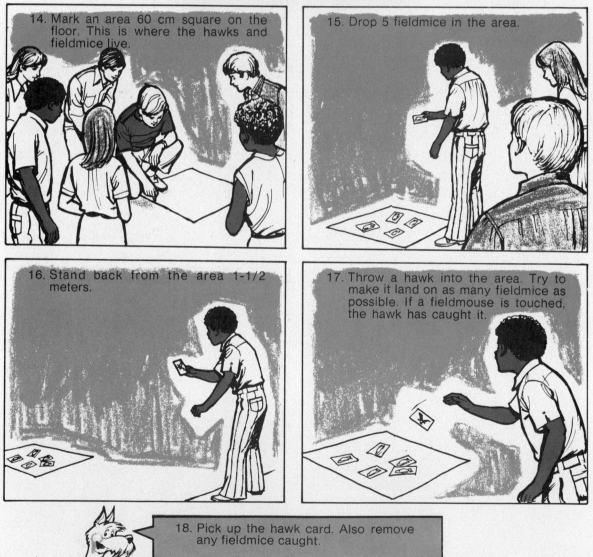

14. Mark an area 60 cm square on the floor. This is where the hawks and fieldmice live.

15. Drop 5 fieldmice in the area.

16. Stand back from the area 1-1/2 meters.

17. Throw a hawk into the area. Try to make it land on as many fieldmice as possible. If a fieldmouse is touched, the hawk has caught it.

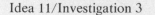

18. Pick up the hawk card. Also remove any fieldmice caught.

Before you learn how to keep score, you will have to learn a new word. The new word is *generation*.

When parents have babies, the babies are the next generation.
A generation is the next group of babies.

Parents

Generation 1

Generation 2

You will play this game for 20 generations. Keep a record of each new generation in Table 1 on your data sheet. Follow these rules:

   (a) The fieldmice left will double each generation. If you have 3 fieldmice left after Generation 1, throw in 3 more fieldmice. You will then have 6 fieldmice for Generation 2.

   (b) In order to live, a hawk has to land on 4 fieldmice. For each 4 fieldmice caught, the hawk will reproduce another hawk. If your hawk catches 4 to 7 fieldmice, add another hawk for the next generation. If it catches 8 fieldmice, add 2 more hawks.

   (c) If a hawk does not catch 4 fieldmice, it dies from lack of food. Do not let the hawk population drop below 1. Pretend that a new one flies into the area looking for food. Start with 1 again in the next generation.

   (d) Do not rush this game. Ask your teacher to help you keep score.

• 19. Which population reaches higher numbers? Why is this?

• 20. As the fieldmouse population gets bigger, what happens to the population of hawks?

• 21. Notice that as the hawk population rises, the fieldmouse population falls. Why?

• 22. Why do populations rise and fall?

• 23. What do predators do to the size of a population?

C. YOU CAN'T KEEP ME DOWN

Let's see what you've learned, especially from the game.

• 24. What is a predator?

• 25. What is a prey?

• 26. What is a predator-prey relationship?

THE CONCEPT.

IT'S FINGER-LICKIN' GOOD

Lettuce, carrots, celery, corn, and green food pellets. They are all the same. They are all plants. Plants are eaten by fieldmice. Thus,

$$\text{Plants} \xrightarrow{\substack{\text{eaten} \\ \text{by}}} \text{Fieldmice} \xrightarrow{\substack{\text{eaten} \\ \text{by}}} \text{Hawk}$$

A. THE COLONEL IS COMING

We all eat because we need energy. Food gives us energy. Hawks eat fieldmice because fieldmice mean energy. Fieldmice eat plants because plants mean energy.

• 1. Where do plants get their energy?

• 2. Complete the diagram on your data sheet.

In the last Investigation, you learned about predators and prey. A predator is an animal that eats another animal. Some animals eat plants. Some animals eat other animals that have eaten plants. Thus, food passes from plants to animals to other animals. This food relationship is like a chain. By itself, each link is not useful. Put the links together and you have a chain.

Living things cannot live alone. They are related to each other by what they eat. We call this relationship a *food chain*.

Here are some examples of food chains:

(a) Algae ⟶ Daphnia ⟶ Hydra
(b) Grass ⟶ Cow ⟶ Man ⟶ Mosquito
(c) Grass ⟶ Mouse ⟶ Snake ⟶ Hawk
(d) Seeds ⟶ Rat ⟶ Cat ⟶ Flea
(e) Corn ⟶ Chicken ⟶ Man

Look at the food chains carefully. They all have one thing in common.

• 3. They all start with ___?___

• 4. Where do the plants get their energy?

• 5. Food passes from one animal to another in a food chain. What else passes along a food chain?

• 6. Start with the sun. What passes along a food chain?

• 7. Therefore, what is a food chain?

B. DON'T PASS ME THE FRIES; PASS ME THE ENERGY

Can you find the food chains in these pictures?

• 8. On your data sheet, complete the food chain.

• 9. On your data sheet, complete the food chain.

•10. On your data sheet, complete the food chain.

• 11. Suppose you had some bread for lunch. Trace the energy back to the sun.

• 12. What is the source of all energy?

• 13. Why do plants need the sun?

• 14. Why do animals need plants?

• 15. Why do some animals need other animals?

• 16. What is passed in a food chain?

• 17. What is a food chain?

C. IT'S PILING UP ON YOU

Energy may not be the only thing passed in a food chain. You may have seen newspaper articles about mercury poisoning.

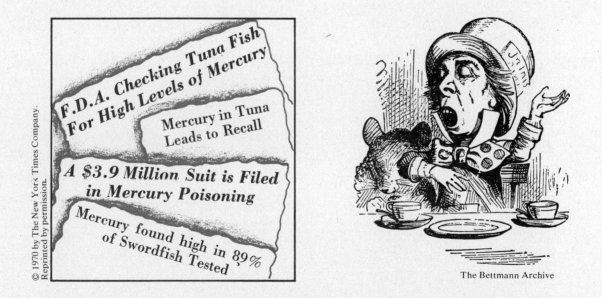

© 1970 by The New York Times Company. Reprinted by permission.

F.D.A. Checking Tuna Fish For High Levels of Mercury

Mercury in Tuna Leads to Recall

A $3.9 Million Suit is Filed in Mercury Poisoning

Mercury found high in 89% of Swordfish Tested

The Bettmann Archive

In the 19th century, mercury was used to make hats. Many hat makers had brain damage and went mad. In 1970, many Japanese died from eating fish containing mercury. At the present time, you can't fish in Lake St. Clair, which is near Detroit. The fish in this lake have 14 times the safe level of mercury.

How did the mercury get into tuna, swordfish, and other fishes?

There are now laws against using DDT. DDT is a poison used to kill insects. The trouble is that DDT does not break down and go away. Notice what happens to DDT in a food chain.

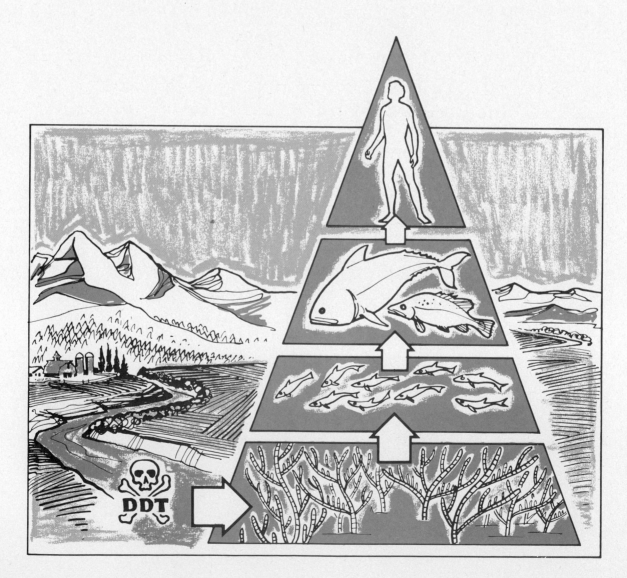

D. DON'T BREAK THE CHAIN

You have been doing very well. You have learned about food chains. You can even look at a community and find a food chain. Now, we are going to put together some food chains. This will be done with a card game.

Here are the rules of the game (for 2 to 4 players per deck):

To Start: Shuffle well and deal five cards to each player. Place the leftover cards face down on the table. Turn the first card over next to the pile. You now have a draw pile and a discard pile.

To Play: The play starts on the dealer's left and goes clockwise. Each player picks up the top card from the draw pile or the discard pile. Each player must then discard one card, except when he wins. The winner should yell, "Food Chain."

To Win: The winner is the first person to lay down six cards belonging to one food chain. The cards must be placed down in the correct order. There are five food chains in the deck:

Sun ➔ Algae ➔ Shrimp ➔ Small fish ➔ Tuna ➔ Man
Sun ➔ Grass ➔ Insect ➔ Frog ➔ Snake ➔ Hawk
Sun ➔ Seed ➔ Insect ➔ Turtle ➔ Raccoon ➔ Mountain lion
Sun ➔ Algae ➔ Daphnia ➔ Sunfish ➔ Man ➔ Mosquito
Sun ➔ Leaves ➔ Deer ➔ Wolf ➔ Vulture ➔ Mite

To Renew: If the draw pile runs out, keep the last discard face up. Shuffle the others and place face-down.

E. LET'S LINK IT ALL UP

Try to pull yourself away from the game. Let's see what you've learned.

• 18. What is passed in a food chain?

• 19. What is a food chain?

THE CONCEPT.

SPIN, SPIN YOUR TANGLED WEB

A cow eats grass. Man eats a steak. A mosquito bites man. That's a food chain.

Here is a food chain:

Grass ⟶ Mouse ⟶ Snake ⟶ Hawk

Here is another food chain:

Grass ⟶ Rabbit ⟶ Fox

Very smart! Food chains are really part of a bigger picture. This is what your picture would look like.

A. IT LOOKS LIKE A WEB

1. Turn to page D187 of your Data Book. Cut out the pictures of the worm, fish, and girl.

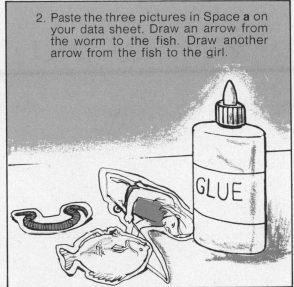

2. Paste the three pictures in Space **a** on your data sheet. Draw an arrow from the worm to the fish. Draw another arrow from the fish to the girl.

You have just put together a simple food chain.

3. Cut out the pictures of the rabbit, carrot, and cow.

4. Add these pictures to Space **a**. Draw all the new arrows needed.

Now, you do not have a chain. You are beginning to get a picture that looks like a net or web.

5. Cut out the pictures of the cat, grass, and horse.

6. Add these pictures to Space **a**. Draw all the new arrows needed.

You have been making a *food web*. The word "food" is used because it shows what eats what. And the arrows spread out and look like a web.

- 7. What is a food chain?

- 8. What do you call many food chains put together?

- 9. What does a food web show?

B. IT KEEPS A COMMUNITY GOING

Here is a picture of a pond community. Some of the living things in the community are:

(a) Bass (f) Minnows

(b) Frog (g) Plants

(c) Fly (h) Snail

(d) Man (i) Turtle

(e) Sunfish

10. Use words and arrows to draw a food web of these 9 organisms. Do this in Space **b** on your data sheet.

You have just drawn a food web of life in a pond. The pond is a community. Life continues as long as there is food.

• 11. What does a food web tell us about living things?

• 12. What does a food web tell us about a community?

• 13. What is a food web?

C. IT KEEPS US GOING

You have been doing very well. You have drawn two food webs. Let's see if you can make one up on your own.

This is a class activity. Your task is to create a food web. Your teacher may ask you to use the chalkboard, bulletin board, or a large sheet of paper.

14. Get a 3 x 5 card. Draw a picture and write the name of one living thing on the card.

15. Your teacher will begin by sticking "Sun" to the board.

16. If you have something that needs the sun, raise your hand. Attach your card to the board. Draw the arrows that are needed.

17. See if your organism will eat the new organism just posted. If it does, raise your hand. Attach your card to the board. Draw the arrows.

18. Draw new arrows as you see new relationships.

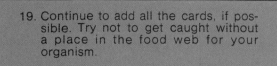

19. Continue to add all the cards, if possible. Try not to get caught without a place in the food web for your organism.

• 20. If an organism does not get posted, what will happen to it?

• 21. What does a food web tell us about life?

• 22. What is a food web?

D. WE'RE ALL PART OF A WEB

Energy is what it's all about. All living things need energy to live. Energy comes from food. Therefore, living things must live where they can get food.

• 23. What does a food chain tell you about food?

• 24. What is a community?

• 25. What is a food web?

• 26. How are a food web and a community related?

Re-read questions 25 and 26 before writing the concept.

THE CONCEPT.

Idea 11

Investigation 6

THIS IS MY WORLD

"This land is your land; this land is my land,
From California to the New York island,
From the redwood forest to the Gulf Stream waters;
This land was made for you and me."

Woody Guthrie

THIS LAND IS YOUR LAND
Words & Music by Woody Guthrie
TRO — © Copyright 1956 & 1958 LUDLOW MUSIC, INC.,
New York, N.Y.   Used by permission.

Which one of these two communities will be your land? The decision is up to you. No organism lives alone. All living things interact with each other to make a community.

Idea 11/Investigation 6   **375**

A. WE MUST ALL LIVE TOGETHER

All organisms must live together with the living and
non-living factors in a community. Everything in the
environment is related to
everything else. Change one
thing and something else
happens.

Jon Brenneis

Oil is an important natural resource. It is used to heat
homes. It is made into gasoline used in cars. Oil has
helped man's progress.

Vernon Merritt/Life Magazine © Time, Inc.

This surfer is covered with
oil. Ships sometimes dump
large amounts of oil into
the ocean. How will the oil
affect fish and plants? How
will it affect man? How do
other changes in the en-
vironment affect man?

Let's play a game to find out. This is another one of those let's pretend games. Your teacher will read the directions and help you play it.

B. WHAT DID IT ALL MEAN?

• 1. When man changes the environment, how does it affect the population?

• 2. What happens to some communities as changes are made?

• 3. How does life depend on communities?

• 4. What is a community?

• 5. How does a community stay alive?

• 6. Only man can decide to change the environment. Thus, what is man's responsibility to the environment?

Re-read questions 4 and 5.

THE CONCEPT.

IT'S LIKE TOGETHER, YOU KNOW

You've done it again! Another Idea finished. This Idea was about "getting along" with other living things. How do living things live together?

To find out how living things get along, you learned six concepts. They are:

(a) A population is the number of one kind of organism living in an area.
(b) A community is a group of populations living in an area.
(c) Living things may eat other living things in a predator-prey relationship.
(d) A food chain shows how living things are related to each other by what they eat.
(e) A food web shows the food relationships in a community.
(f) Living things must live together with other living things in a community.

Remember this picture? It is of a pond community. There are many different kinds of living things in the pond community.

- 7. What is a community?

- 8. Explain this statement: "No man lives alone."

- 9. In order to survive, who must living things get along with?

- 10. What must all living things interact with?

Re-read questions 9 and 10. Summarize the entire Idea.

THE IDEA:

Idea 12 Investigation 1

WE HAVE TO BE TOGETHER

Everyone is talking about pollution. You would think ecology is a new scene. It's not. The word "ecology" means the study of homes. The word is over a hundred years old. Even before the word appeared, people were concerned about ecology.

You learned a basic idea of ecology in the last Idea. All living and non-living things are related to each other. They depend on each other for survival.

A. IT'S TREES, OF COURSE

What is a forest?

A forest is not just trees alone. The forest may be swarming with different kinds of animals.

•1. On your data sheet, list all the kinds of animals you see in this picture of a forest.

No plant or animal can live alone. You learned this in the last Idea. There are some frogs in the picture.

- 2. What does the frog need to stay alive?

- 3. What will the frog eat?

- 4. What do you call the animal that does the eating?

- 5. What do you call the animal that is eaten?

- 6. What animal might eat the frog?

- 7. What do you call the relationship when one animal eats another?

- 8. What other animal might eat the frog?

- 9. A frog eats an insect. A snake eats the frog. What do you call this relationship?

- 10. What do living things get from this relationship?

- 11. What must all living things obtain to stay alive?

- 12. How are all the animals related to each other?

You might say: The animals do not only *live* in the forest. They are *part* of the forest!

B. YOU MEAN IT'S NOT TREES?

What is a forest?

A forest is not just trees and animals. Living in the shade of the trees may be other plants.

• 13. What kinds of plants do you see in the picture of the forest on page 380?

Each kind of organism plays a role in the forest. The role is part of a web. Change one part and you change another. You might even destroy the forest itself.

• 14. Look at the picture again. What things must the plants obtain to stay alive?

• 15. What things must the animals obtain to stay alive?

• 16. How are the plants and animals related to each other in a forest?

Yes, we do, David. Life is not just taking. Life is giving, too. In fact, giving is sometimes more important. Organisms take what they need from the environment. They also give back materials to the environment. You studied this in Ideas 5 and 11.

• 17. What things do the plants and animals give back to the environment?

Thus, the sun, air, water, soil, plants, and animals are all related. They are all together in a system. This system is called an *ecosystem*.

C. IT'S A CHANGING, SWINGING SYSTEM

The forest is a system. All the parts must work together. The forest is an ecological system or ecosystem.

• 18. What are the parts that must work together in an ecosystem?

You saw this diagram in the last Idea.

To this diagram, we can add "ecosystem."

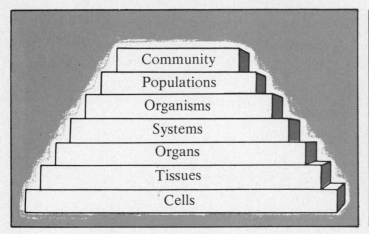

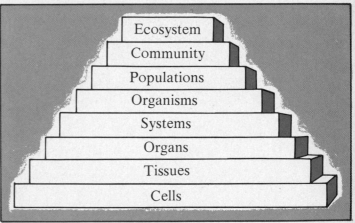

• 19. How do living things depend on each other for survival?

• 20. Plants and animals do not only live in the forest. They are the forest. What do these sentences mean?

• 21. Explain the title of the Investigation, "We have to be together."

> Cells, organisms, populations, and communities. Energy, food, air, and water. When we put it all together, we have an ecosystem.

• 22. What is an ecosystem?

THE CONCEPT.

THE GREATEST INVENTION SINCE THE WHEEL

The only thing constant in nature is change.

Everything changes. An ecologist is interested in the changes in an environment.

An ecosystem is very complex. There are all kinds of things going around in an ecosystem.

A. HOW DOES THE WATER GET OUT?

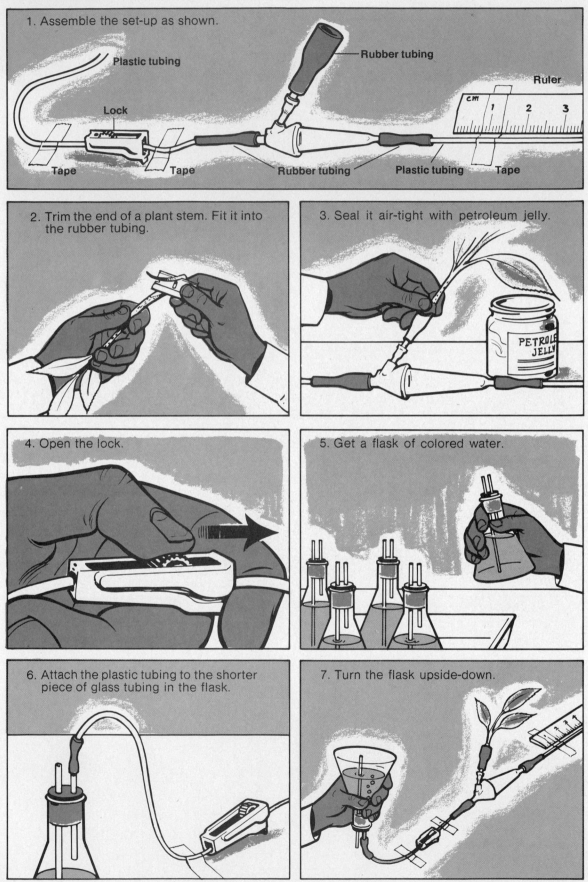

1. Assemble the set-up as shown.

Plastic tubing

Rubber tubing

Ruler

Lock

CM 1 2 3

Tape

Tape

Rubber tubing

Plastic tubing

Tape

2. Trim the end of a plant stem. Fit it into the rubber tubing.

3. Seal it air-tight with petroleum jelly.

PETROLE JELLY

4. Open the lock.

5. Get a flask of colored water.

6. Attach the plastic tubing to the shorter piece of glass tubing in the flask.

7. Turn the flask upside-down.

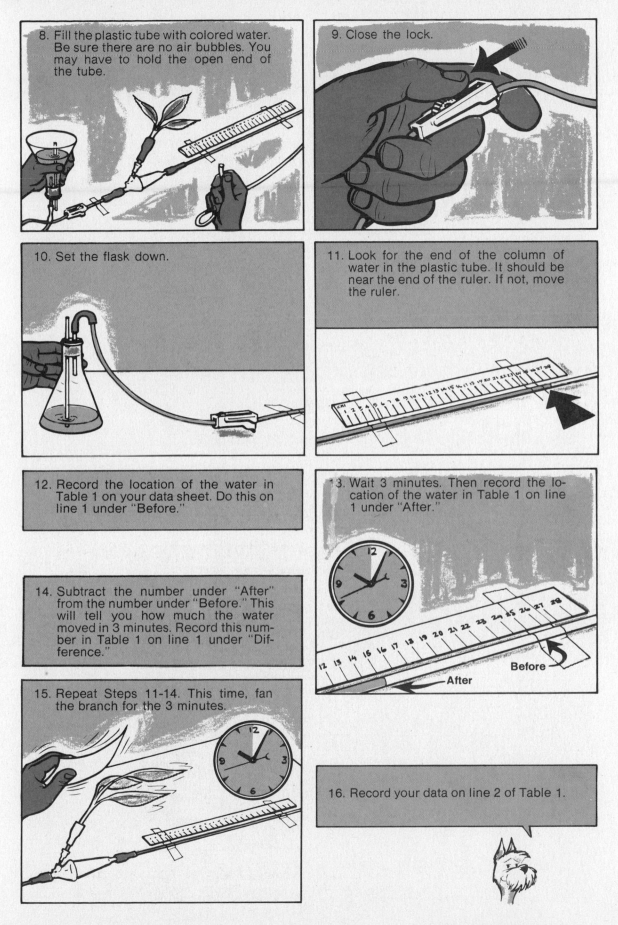

8. Fill the plastic tube with colored water. Be sure there are no air bubbles. You may have to hold the open end of the tube.

9. Close the lock.

10. Set the flask down.

11. Look for the end of the column of water in the plastic tube. It should be near the end of the ruler. If not, move the ruler.

12. Record the location of the water in Table 1 on your data sheet. Do this on line 1 under "Before."

13. Wait 3 minutes. Then record the location of the water in Table 1 on line 1 under "After."

14. Subtract the number under "After" from the number under "Before." This will tell you how much the water moved in 3 minutes. Record this number in Table 1 on line 1 under "Difference."

15. Repeat Steps 11-14. This time, fan the branch for the 3 minutes.

16. Record your data on line 2 of Table 1.

17. Repeat Steps 11-14. This time, hold a light bulb near the branch for the 3 minutes.

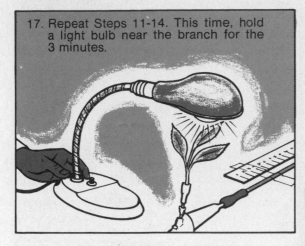

18. Record your data on line 3 of Table 1.

In Idea 4, you looked at some leaves under the microscope. You found stomates, or tiny holes, in the leaves. Air and water can move in and out of these holes.

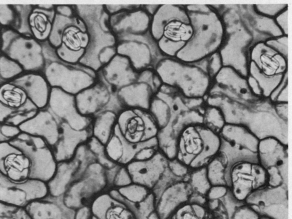

Grant Heilman

• 19. What do you think caused the water to move in the plastic tube?

• 20. Look at three differences in Table 1. When did the water move the most?

• 21. Why do you think this happened?

• 22. Where do you think the water was going?

• 23. How would you design an experiment to test your answer to question 22?

B. UP, UP, AND AWAY

Thanks for your help, Maria. The word is *evaporation*.

24. Your teacher will show you 3 jars.
  (a) Jar **A** is in a cool place.
  (b) Jar **B** is in sunlight.
  (c) Jar **C** is under a 150-watt lamp.

25. Do not touch the jars. Look inside each jar. Write your observations in Table 2 on your data sheet.

Water which evaporates cools. The vapor changes as it cools. It becomes water again. This is called *condensation*.

• 26. In which jar did the water evaporate the most? How do you know?

• 27. In which jar did the water evaporate the least? How do you know?

• 28. Which jar was heated the most?

• 29. Which jar was heated the least?

• 30. How does temperature affect evaporation?

Look at Table 1 and question 21.

• 31. Why did the water in the tube move in Part A?

C. WHAT GOES UP, MUST COME DOWN

32. Turn off the lamp over jar **C**. Rub an ice cube across the top of the jar.

33. Carefully observe the sides of the jar.

• 34. What happened on the inside of the jar?

• 35. What happens to water in the air as it cools?

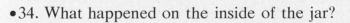

• 36. When water evaporates, where does it go?

• 37. When water in the air cools, where does it go?

• 38. Put it together and you have a *water cycle*. What is a water cycle?

D. PLEASE KEEP RAINING

The water goes around and around. There is a water cycle. The water is used again and again.

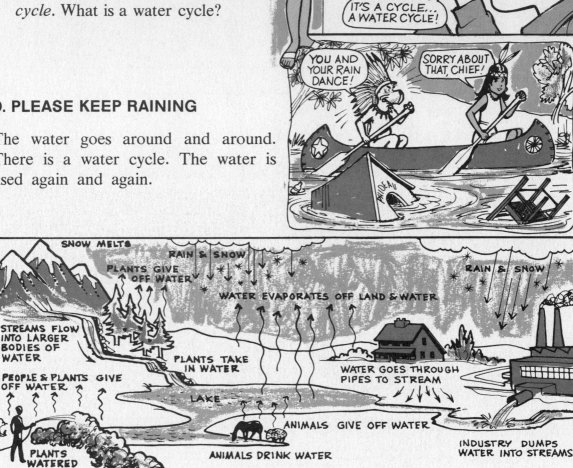

Study the picture above. Discuss it in class.

• 39. List on your data sheet all the ways water is evaporating.

• 40. List all the ways water returns to earth.

All the earth's water is in a narrow band at the surface. It's all we have. If the cycle doesn't keep going around and around, we're in trouble.

• 41. What is the water cycle?

THE CONCEPT.

WE'RE STILL GOING AROUND AND AROUND

Everyone's recycling today. We're using up lots of paper, aluminum, and glass. But we're trying to put them all back into the system, too.

Crow/Monkmeyer

You have learned about one cycle.

The water cycle: Water goes around in a cycle and is used over and over again.

What is another cycle needed to keep the ecosystem in balance?

A. BLUE CHEESE, PLEASE

The average person produces 5 pounds of garbage each day. Toilets are flushed many times each day. Leaves fall by the millions. Plants and animals die. What happens to all of these waste products?

1. Label half of a Petri dish with your name and section.

2. Spread some blue cheese onto a piece of bread.

3. Put the bread in the dish. Do not cover.

4. Store in a warm, dark place for several days.

5. Observe the bread each day. Record your observations in Table 1.

DO YOU WANT ONIONS OR BACTERIA ON YOUR SALAD?

There are millions of different kinds of bacteria. Only a few are harmful. Most are helpful. For example, bacteria are used to make cheese. One kind is used to make blue cheese.

• 6. What happened to the bread?

• 7. What do you think caused the bread to decay?

Lopez/N.Y.C. Department of Water Resources

You are looking at part of a sewage plant. The round tanks contain waste materials. Bacteria are added to the tanks to speed up decay. The decayed materials make good fertilizer. This is one way plant and animal wastes are put back into a *nutrient cycle*.

B. I'M GOING TO DONATE MY BODY TO BACTERIA

Study the drawing carefully.

- 8. When plants or parts of plants die, what happens to them?

- 9. What happens to animals that die?

- 10. What happens to animal droppings?

- 11. What causes materials to decay?

- 12. What living things use the nutrients in the decayed materials?

- 13. Who eats the plants?

- 14. What is going around in this cycle?

C. KEEP THE FOOD A-COMIN'

Animals and plants are part of the nutrient cycle. Nutrients are foods, minerals, and other materials needed by plants and animals to stay alive. Nutrients move in a cycle. They move from plants and animals to the soil. Then, they move back to the plants again. From the plants they move to the animals once more.

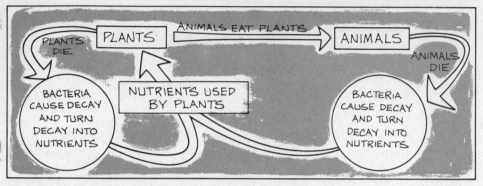

• 15. What causes plants and animals to decay?

• 16. The decayed materials are changed into nutrients and dissolved in water. What takes in the dissolved nutrients?

• 17. What must an animal do to take in nutrients?

• 18. How do animals put nutrients back into the cycle?

• 19. How do plants put nutrients back into the cycle?

• 20. How do living things put nutrients back into the cycle?

• 21. What is the nutrient cycle?

THE CONCEPT.

DON'T GET ALL TAPPED OUT

Suppose you lay one hair on the surface of a globe. The hair represents the thin layer of air around the earth. This layer is about 7 miles thick. It's all the air we have. It's our atmosphere. If we leave our atmosphere, we need to take a supply of air with us.

A. SNAIL ONE TO CONTROL MODULE

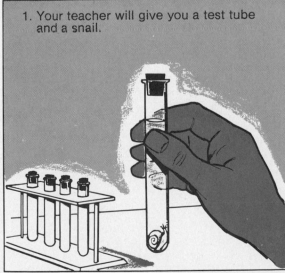

1. Your teacher will give you a test tube and a snail.

Here's your problem. Pretend that you are going to send the snail to someone. You would have to seal the tube. How would you keep the snail alive for at least a week?

Good show, Phideau. Ask questions. Just like a scientist. Here are some questions you should ask.

- •2. In Idea 9, you learned that organisms live in a certain place. Where does a snail live?

- •3. In Idea 8, you learned that the environment is made of many factors. What factors are needed by a snail?

- •4. In Idea 5, you learned that organisms need energy. This means the snail may need some food and certain gases. What does a snail need for energy?

- •5. In Idea 11, you learned that organisms must interact with other organisms. What other organisms will you seal in with your snail?

- •6. In Idea 4, you learned that plants interact with animals. What gases do they exchange?

Let's see what you've learned.

7. Complete Table 1 on your data sheet.

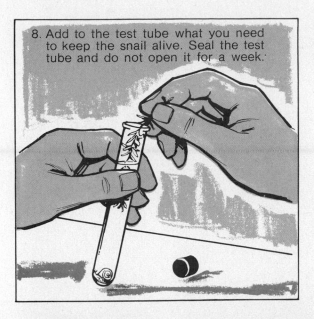

8. Add to the test tube what you need to keep the snail alive. Seal the test tube and do not open it for a week.

You now have an ecosystem. If you have designed a good ecosystem, everything should stay in balance.

B. KEEP THOSE CYCLES SPINNING

When an ecosystem is in balance, the cycles keep going. You have learned about the water cycle and the nutrient cycle. Here is another cycle.

- 9. Study the picture. What gas is Phideau breathing in?

- 10. What gas is Phideau breathing out?

- 11. What gas are the green plants taking in?

- 12. What gas are the green plants giving off?

- 13. Look at the cars and chimneys in the picture. What gas are they giving off?

- 14. What two gases are going around and around in this cycle?

C. ARE YOUR VIBES TOGETHER?

In 1771, Joseph Priestley did an experiment.

- 15. A plant sealed in a jar died. What gas was missing?

- 16. A mouse sealed in another jar died. What gas was missing?

- 17. But when Priestley put a mouse and plant together, they both lived. What gas was the mouse breathing out?

- 18. What gas was the mouse breathing in?

- 19. What gas was the plant taking in?

- 20. What gas was the plant giving off?

- 21. What two gases were going around and around in a cycle?

Look again at your sealed test tube. A snail and a plant are inside. They are interacting with each other.

- 22. What gas is the snail breathing out?

- 23. What gas is the snail breathing in?

- 24. What gas is the plant taking in?

- 25. What gas is the plant giving off?

- 26. What gases are the snail and plant exchanging?

- 27. What cycle has this Investigation been about?

THE CONCEPT.

Idea 12
Investigation 5

LIVE DANGEROUSLY—TAKE A DEEP BREATH

Yes, take a deep breath. It has no shape, no taste, no color. But we all know it's there.

Kites fly on it.

Tafoya/Detroit Free Press

Rubber rafts float because of it.

Mannheim/DPI

Schulke/Black Star

Living things thrive on it.

What are we talking about? *Air*, of course.

The air we breathe is mostly nitrogen and oxygen. It also contains carbon dioxide. These gases are part of earth's resource cycles. You learned about one of these cycles in the last Investigation.

You learned that life depends on these cycles staying in balance. They are part of an ecosystem. An ecosystem includes all the living and non-living factors. These factors must interact with each other to keep the system in balance. What happens if the resource runs out? What happens if the balance is upset?

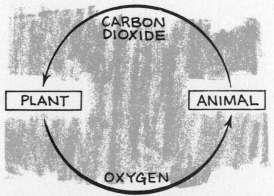

The Oxygen-Carbon Dioxide Cycle

A. HELP, I'M TRAPPED IN JELLY

Do you know that you breathe about 4000 gallons of air each day? You need the air because of the oxygen. Your body uses oxygen to get energy from foods.

What else is in air besides oxygen and other gases?

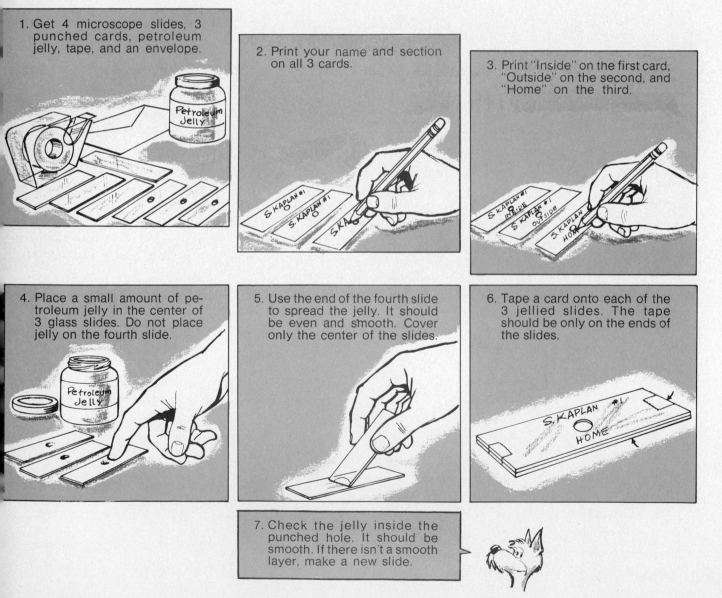

1. Get 4 microscope slides, 3 punched cards, petroleum jelly, tape, and an envelope.

2. Print your name and section on all 3 cards.

3. Print "Inside" on the first card, "Outside" on the second, and "Home" on the third.

4. Place a small amount of petroleum jelly in the center of 3 glass slides. Do not place jelly on the fourth slide.

5. Use the end of the fourth slide to spread the jelly. It should be even and smooth. Cover only the center of the slides.

6. Tape a card onto each of the 3 jellied slides. The tape should be only on the ends of the slides.

7. Check the jelly inside the punched hole. It should be smooth. If there isn't a smooth layer, make a new slide.

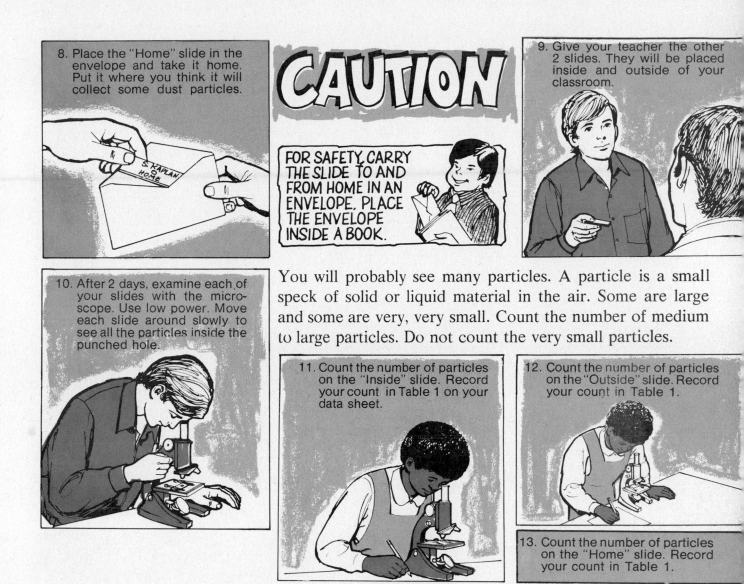

8. Place the "Home" slide in the envelope and take it home. Put it where you think it will collect some dust particles.

CAUTION

FOR SAFETY, CARRY THE SLIDE TO AND FROM HOME IN AN ENVELOPE. PLACE THE ENVELOPE INSIDE A BOOK.

9. Give your teacher the other 2 slides. They will be placed inside and outside of your classroom.

10. After 2 days, examine each of your slides with the microscope. Use low power. Move each slide around slowly to see all the particles inside the punched hole.

You will probably see many particles. A particle is a small speck of solid or liquid material in the air. Some are large and some are very, very small. Count the number of medium to large particles. Do not count the very small particles.

11. Count the number of particles on the "Inside" slide. Record your count in Table 1 on your data sheet.

12. Count the number of particles on the "Outside" slide. Record your count in Table 1.

13. Count the number of particles on the "Home" slide. Record your count in Table 1.

• 14. Which of your 3 slides had the most particles?

• 15. Where was this slide placed?

• 16. Which of your 3 slides had the fewest particles?

• 17. Where was this slide placed?

• 18. Compare results with your classmates. Find out who had the slide with the highest particle count. Where was it placed?

• 19. Find out who had the slide with the lowest particle count. Where was it placed?

• 20. Besides gases, what else is in the air you breathe?

Idea 12/Investigation 5   **399**

B. THE LAST GASP

Anything in the air that may be harmful to living things is a *pollutant*. The particles you saw under the microscope may make up air pollution.

Sometimes you can see air pollutants, such as soot and smoke. We call it smog. Most pollutants are too small to see except with a microscope. Some are poisonous gases; you can't see these at all. But they add up.

How dangerous is polluted air? Here are some examples.

"ON A CLEAR DAY YOU CAN SEE THE SMOG IN THREE STATES."

Richard Nairin/National Audubon Society

Air Pollution Control District County of Los Angeles

•21. What do you think is causing this plant life to die?

Polluted air can kill plants. Nearly 200,000 acres of pine trees in Southern California are dying.

Pollution like this had killed people in Donora, Pennsylvania, and London, England.

•22. How can air pollution affect humans?

•23. What is air pollution?

•24. Why do you think these children in Tokyo wear masks on smoggy days?

•25. Why do you think children in Los Angeles are excused from physical education on smoggy days?

•26. What do living things need?

Wide World Photos

C. LET'S KEEP IT CLEAN

Air is a resource. There is a limited supply. Factories, automobiles, and cigarettes all add pollutants to the air.

•27. Who builds factories?

•28. Who drives automobiles?

•29. Who smokes cigarettes?

•30. Who pollutes the air?

THE CONCEPT.

I WISH WE HAD SOME FRESH AIR!

WELL, WE CERTAINLY WON'T FIND IT HERE!

Idea 12 Investigation 6

ALL IT NEEDS IS A LITTLE LOVE

This book has been presented in two parts. The first part asked two questions:

(a) What is a living thing?
(b) What is man?

You learned that a living thing has certain characteristics.

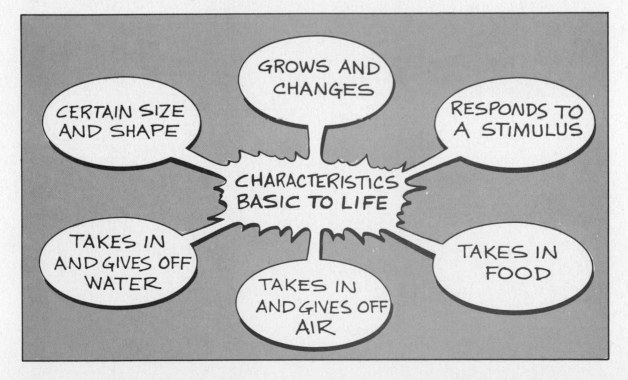

A living thing is composed of cells.

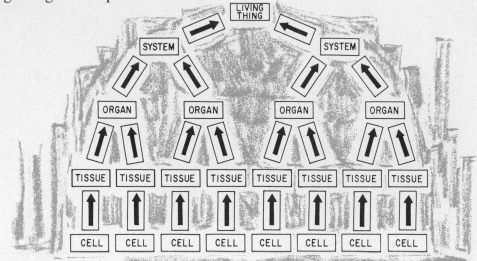

A living thing must get energy.

A living thing must use energy.

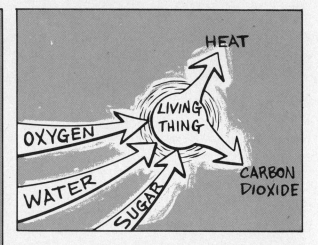

All living things have common life activities.

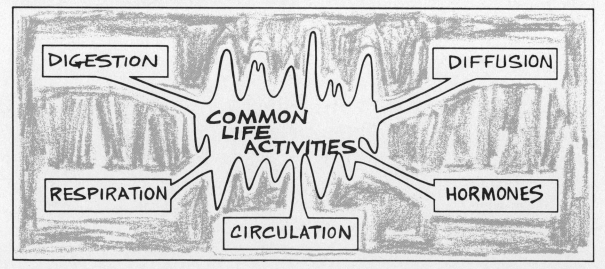

All living things must reproduce.

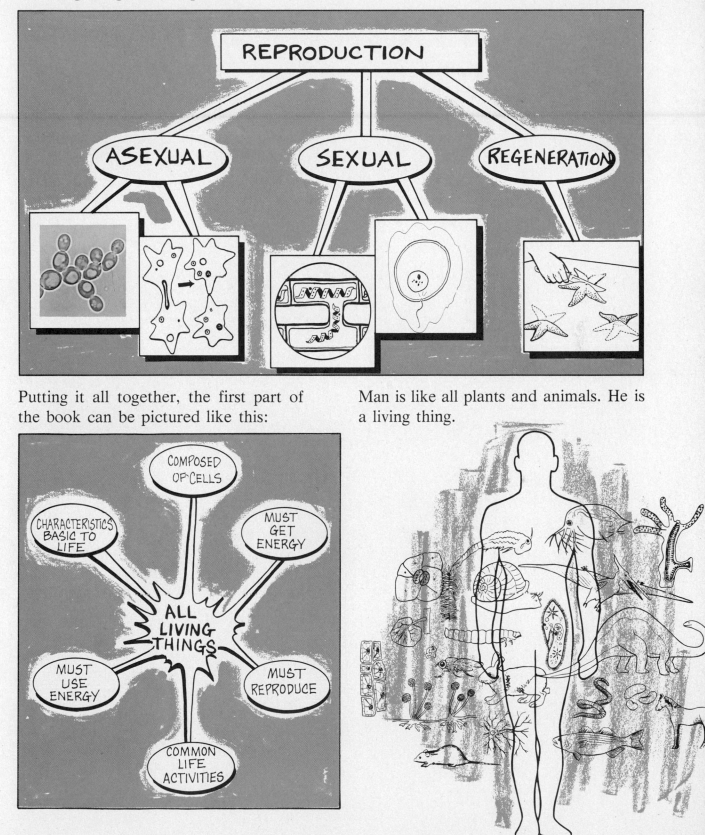

Putting it all together, the first part of the book can be pictured like this:

Man is like all plants and animals. He is a living thing.

A. THEY GO TOGETHER

The second part of this book had to do with the environment. You learned that the environment is made of many factors.

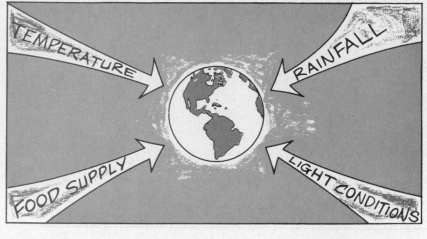

There are different kinds of environments. Each kind of environment is called a habitat.

A living thing must adjust to each kind of environment.

Living things adjust by interacting with each other.

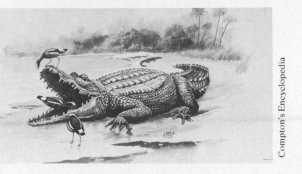

But you can't separate the two parts. Man and his environment are tied together.

And in this last Idea, you have learned that living things must live in balance with their environment.

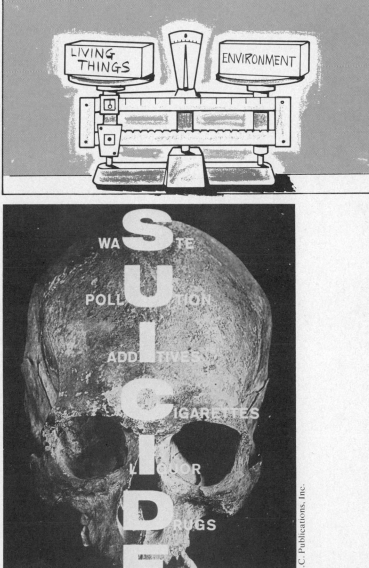

B. WHY DOES MAN WANT?

Trouble begins when man and the environment are not together.

The resources on the earth are all we have.

"America the Beautiful?"

OH (COUGH) BEAUTIFUL (SNIFFLE)
FOR (COUGH) SPACIOUS SKIES (HAK)...

THIS WATER MAY BE INJURIOUS TO YOUR HEALTH

But, there is a greater resource.

THE GREATEST RESOURCE IS MAN HIMSELF

There is only one man in the world
    and his name is All Men.
There is only one woman in the world
    and her name is All Women.
There is only one child in the world
    and the child's name is All Children.

Carl Sandburg

From the Prologue by Carl Sandburg in *The Family of Man,* created by Edward Steichen. Copyright © The Museum of Modern Art, New York, and reprinted by permission of the publisher.

Man is real.

Man knows sadness.

Man knows hate.

Man knows what he has done.

But, man knows what he can do.

Man is love.

Love is real.

C. ALL BEINGS AND ALL THINGS ARE RELATED

A student in Kansas wrote:

Apathy

It never fed a hungry child
    nor housed an outcast.
It never cured disease
    nor ended war.
Instead it helped pollute our skies,
    separate brothers.
It drove some to seek answers from drugs,
    lesser numbers turn to God
Conquer it .... your life depends on it.

            Vicki Brooks, student

In your Data Book, answer the following questions in any way that is meaningful to you. Do your own thing.

- 1. What is man?
- 2. What has man done?
- 3. What can man do?
- 4. What must man do?
- 5. What will you do?

With all beings and all things we shall be as relatives.
            Sioux Indian

- 6. What is man's greatest resource?

THE CONCEPT.

LET'S KEEP IN BALANCE

Super! You've learned the whole thing! And you should be proud of your achievement. This Idea was about staying in balance with the environment. How do living things stay in balance?

To find out how living things stay in balance with their environment, you learned six concepts. They are:

  (a) All living and non-living things interact with each other in an ecosystem.
  (b) Water on the earth goes around in a cycle.
  (c) Nutrients go around in a cycle.
  (d) Oxygen and carbon dioxide go around in a cycle.
  (e) Man can pollute the air.
  (f) Man's greatest resource is man himself.

•7. What three cycles are pictured?

- 8. If any part of a cycle stops, what will happen to the whole cycle?

- 9. Living things take from different cycles. They also put back into the cycles. Each cycle must be kept in __?__

- 10. When is a community in balance?

- 11. Who must help keep the community in balance?

- 12. In order to survive, what must living things stay in balance with?

Re-read question 12. Summarize the entire Idea.

THE IDEA.